ORGANIZATIONS
CASES, ISSUES, CONCEPTS

ORGANIZATIONS
CASES, ISSUES, CONCEPTS

SECOND EDITION

Edited by

ROSALIND ARMSON AND ROB PATON

WITH THE ASSISTANCE OF

Suzanne Brown, Susan Carr, Jake Chapman, Mike Floyd, John Hamwee, John Martin, Roger Spear, Jennie Moffatt and Tony Walsh

AT

THE OPEN UNIVERSITY

Published in association with
The Open University

P·C·P
Paul Chapman
Publishing Ltd

Paul Chapman Publishing Ltd
144 Liverpool Road
London
N1 1LA

British Library Cataloguing in Publication Data

Organizations: Cases, Issues, Concepts. –
2 Rev.ed
I. Armson, Rosalind II. Paton, Rob
658

ISBN 1–85396–280–5

Typeset by Dorwyn Ltd, Rowlands Castle, Hants
Printed and bound by Athenaeum Press, Gateshead, Tyne & Wear

B C D E F G H 9 8 7 6 5

This Reader is one part of an Open University integrated teaching system and the selection is therefore related to other material available to students. It is designed to evoke the critical understanding of students. Opinions expressed in it are not necessarily those of the course team or of the University.

Contents

PREFACE TO FIRST EDITION

In preparing this Reader I was closely assisted throughout by colleagues in The Open University Systems Group. Since the term 'systems' has many connotations it may be worth saying that the Systems Group is not a collection of Operations Researchers, or computer analysts, or O & M practitioners, or general systems theorists; it is a multi-disciplinary group, located in the Faculty of Technology, whose members share a common interest in the development of appropriate methods for action and policy-oriented studies. Those of us who produced this Reader were working as a team to produce the course entitled 'Managing in Organizations'. It was a team in far more than the formal sense.

Suzanne Brown's enormous contribution deserves special mention: it ranged from suggesting and commenting on innumerable articles through to the really formidable task of preparing 'clean copies' for our publishers. Although not a member of the Course Team, John Hughes gave us considerable assistance. In the face of absurdly overdue manuscripts, June McGowan, Sue Snelling and other secretaries saved us from the wrath of the University's publishers.

Finally the publishers have also earned our appreciation. They were prepared to back our belief that the sort of material we were gathering for our course would constitute a viable Reader making some useful material easily accessible to other teachers and students.

ROB PATON
Walton Hall, September 1983

PREFACE TO SECOND EDITION

In editing the second edition of this Reader I find myself very much in debt to the editors of the first. This new edition builds on the foundations of the previous edition and includes new case studies and articles which reflect the changing experience of organizational life.

These new articles could not have been assembled without Susan Carr, John Martin, Roger Spear, Jennie Moffatt and Tony Walsh. I am also indebted to Tony Netherclift without whom the final assembly would have been even more fraught.

ROSALIND ARMSON
Walton Hall, June 1994

Acknowledgements

We thank those listed below for permission to reproduce the following copyrighted material:

CASE 1 is copyright © 1980 The Open University; Chapters 12 and 16 are copyright © The Open University 1983; Cases 2, 3, and 4 are copyright © The Open University 1994; all are reprinted by permission of The Open University.

CASE 5: Doctors Making Ends Meet, by Nicholas Timmins, first published in *The Independent*, 2 November 1988, reprinted by permission of Newspaper Publishing plc.

Hospital may opt out, *Daily Mail*, 5 January 1989, copyright © *Daily Mail/Solo*.

The Guardian for: More choice means little voice for patients, 8 February 1989; Opt-out questions anger Guy's staff, by David Brundle, 24 March 1990; Guy's budget under the knife, by David Brundle, 26 April 1991; Guy's goes into profit, by David Brundle, 21 October 1992; Hospital trust trailblazer loses job in merger, by David Brundle, 2 March 1993; Guy's falls victim to changes, by David Brundle, 11 February 1994; Stitch-up undone, by Martin Wollacott, 17 May 1989.

Setback for NHS Reform as Guy's man quits, by Jill Sherman *The Times* 27 June 1989, © Times Newspapers Ltd 1989; and St Thomas's closure recommended in leaked report, by Alison Roberts *The Times* 28 July 1992; © Times Newspapers Ltd 1992.

People who look glum may lose their jobs, *Daily Telegraph* 22 June 1991, and Guy's staff poll rejects hospital independence, *Daily Telegraph* 9 February 1990, © The Telegraph plc, London, 1990, 1991.

Guy's expects to balance budget, *Financial Times* 14 November 1991, reprinted by permission of the Financial Times.

CHAPTER 6: Reprinted from Studs Terkel, *Working*, (1972, 1974) Pantheon Books, New York.

CHAPTER 7: Engineers and the Work that People Do. H H Rosenbrock, © 1981 IEEE. Reprinted, with permission of the publishers and the author, from IEEE *Control Systems Magazine*, Vol 1 no 3, pp 4–8, September 1981.

CHAPTER 8: Reprinted from C. Eden, S. Jones and D. Sims (1983) *Messing About with Problems*, Pergamon Press, Oxford, pp 1–5, 8, 13–17.

CHAPTER 9A AND 9B from R. Richard Ritti *The Ropes to Skip and the Ropes to Know* 4/e New York, John Wiley & Sons Inc. Copyright © 1994 by John Wiley & Sons Inc. Reprinted by permission of John Wiley & Sons Inc.

CHAPTER 10: Managing Technological Change, by K D Eason, *Behaviour & Information Technology*, Vol 1 no 2 (1982), reprinted by permission of Taylor & Francis.

CHAPTER 11A: The evolution of planning approaches, from B Taylor and D Hussey (1982) *The Realities of Planning*, Oxford, Pergamon; reprinted by permission of the authors.

CHAPTER 11B: Reprinted by permission of R M Hogarth and S Makridakis, Forecasting and Planning: an evaluation (1981) *Management Science*, Vol 27 no 2. Copyright © 1981 The Institute of Management Sciences, 290 Westminster Street, Providence, RI 02903.

CHAPTER 11C: Reprinted by permission of *Harvard Business Review*, The Tactics of Strategic opportunism, Daniel J Isenberg, March/April 1987. Copyright © 1987 by the President and Fellows of Harvard College; all rights reserved.

CHAPTER 13A: Charles Perrow, The Analysis of Goals in Complex Organizations, *American Sociological Review*, Vol 26, December 1961 pp 854–6.

CHAPTER 13B: A O Hirschman and C E Lindblom, Lindblom on Policy Making, *Behavioural Science* Vol 7, 1962. Reprinted by permission of *Behavioural Science*.

CHAPTER 13C: James G March, (1982) Theories of Choice and Making Decisions, *Society*, Vol 20 no 1 Copyright © 1982 by Transaction Inc.

CHAPTER 14: from D S Pugh, D J Hickson and C R Hinings *Writers on Organizations* (1971, third edition 1983), Penguin Books, copyright © D S Pugh, D J Hickson and C R Hinings, 1964, 1971, 1983. pp. 147–50.

CHAPTER 15: Reprinted by permission of J R Galbraith, Organization Design: An Information Processing View, (1974) *Interfaces* Vol 4 no 3 pp 28–36. Copyright © 1974 The Operations Research Society of America and the Institute of Management Sciences, 290 Westminster Street, Providence, RI 02903.

CHAPTERS 17A, 17B AND 18 are reprinted from: Gareth Morgan, *Images of Organization* (1986) pp. 88–105, 121–123 and 125–126. Copyright © 1986 by Gareth Morgan. Reprinted by permission of Sage Publications, Inc.

CHAPTER 17C: Tao Te Ching, The Way of Subtle Influence, translated by R L Wing; reprinted by permission of Aquarian/Thorsons, imprints of HarperCollins Publishers Limited.

CHAPTER 17D, from Charles Handy, *The Age of Unreason* (1991) Century, London, pp. 105–108. Reprinted by permission of the publisher.

CHAPTER 17E: Excerpts (edited) from pp. 276–83, from *Truth or Dare*, by Starhawk. Copyright © 1987 by Miriam Simos. Reprinted by permission of HarperCollins Publishers, Inc.

CHAPTER 19: P Bate (1984) The Impact of Organizational Culture on Approaches to Organizational Problem Solving, *Organization Studies*, Vol 5 no 2 pp 43–66. Reprinted by permission of the author.

CHAPTER 20: Walter W Powell, Neither Market nor Hierarchy; network forms of organization, *Research in Organizational Behaviour*, Vol 12 (1990) pp 295–336. Reprinted by permission of JAI Press Inc., Greenwich, Conn.

Introduction

This collection of readings was designed as a resource for courses on organizations. It will support courses in management education, broadly conceived – including not just administration but any practically oriented concern for organizations and their problems – rather than social scientific courses. It embodies the view that there is considerably more to managing in organizations than some popular notions of management suggest. The material is intended to promote an understanding of organizations and the things that go on in them, and explores issues that face managers, employees and specialist staff in the organization and conduct of their work.

The readings are intended for introductory or basic courses on organizations at degree level. So the material was selected to be appropriate for first or second-year students (or equivalent on non-degree courses) in business studies and for those whose principal subject of study would lie elsewhere – in computing, engineering, accounting, operations research, or wherever.

Although this is certainly not the sort of Reader that aims at a comprehensive treatment of the subject, the readings were selected to provide a rudimentary coverage. So in Part 1 the cases cover large and small, public and private, organizations; and in Part 3 the concepts range from interpersonal to interorganizational levels of analysis. In Part 2, by contrast, our aim was much more to present some topics that concern people in organizations in a stimulating form. Taken together, the need for basic coverage and the attempt to maintain a fairly consistent level of treatment meant that, on occasions, we had to fall back on providing material ourselves, and on other occasions we had to edit articles heavily. The argument that it is good for students to learn to tackle 'real' academic writing in this field is only sound if they are going to need that ability; otherwise, it's much more important that they learn the content. On this basis, our choice of articles was often swayed by the prose style.

The central difficulty in teaching about organizations and their problems is to provide ideas that have the generality to be useful in a myriad of different circumstances and then to ensure that students can bridge the gap from somewhat unfamiliar and abstract terms to their own particular experience. Unless the ideas are applied to realistic contexts and students gradually find they can make them work, the teaching remains, literally, an academic exercise. The catch is that, often, the more general and potentially valuable the ideas, the wider the gap becomes. The division of the Reader into three parts (Cases, Issues, Concepts) reflects a strategy for addressing this basic teaching dilemma. The three sections represent progressively higher levels of abstraction and generalization and the essential point is to draw the connections between the material in the three sections – and from that material to the student's own experiences (in which respect most of our Open University students, combining work and study, are at an enormous advantage compared to full-time students).

In brief, the issues provide middle-level generalizations about particular problem areas; they can be fairly easily related to students' own experiences, and further discussed and analysed using the concepts. The cases can provide illustrations of particular issues, and also provide examples of, or practice at, the application of concepts. The concepts represent more theoretical ideas selected for their contribution to a practical understanding of issues and particular cases (as opposed to their value in research). Teachers (and indeed students) should be able to see the scope for numerous connections between the sections of the Reader, and this was another consideration in selecting pieces.

PART 1

CASES

Case studies are a step towards the real world, a substitute for it that can be readily shared, a way of learning from other people's *experience. They demonstrate the richness of organizational life and the inadequacy of simple formulae. In many ways, stories of failure, of things going awfully wrong, make good material: disasters are not just interesting but demand explanations in a way that success or normal competence do not. The first and third of these case studies are of that sort, but they should be read sympathetically: would you or I really have been able to foresee and avoid the problems? Organizations are easy to knock, particularly with hindsight, and difficult to change. But success and (most common of all) outcomes which are neither one nor the other, can also be interesting and instructive, as the three other studies show. The cases were chosen because they 'ring true', they have the 'richness' of real events – in particular, they all display something of the variety of points of view that existed in the events recounted. And that variety of viewpoints is, ultimately, what makes organizational work difficult.*

CHAPTER 1

Changing Complex Information Systems: Medical Records at Anersley Hospital

J. BERRIDGE

While computer systems handle many patient-related functions in hospitals, paper records remain an important part of the hospital records system. Letters between GPs and consultants, test reports and X-ray records continue to be retained as hard copy. Anersley Hospital and the entire case study are fictional, while based on real-life problems that may be met in hospital or other administrations. The case was written as the basis for study and discussion rather than to illustrate effective or ineffective handling of an administrative situation.

THE BACKGROUND

Anersley Hospital is a long-stay psychiatric and geriatric hospital of some 600 beds which sprawls across an extensive site in a suburb of a large town. Its many piecemeal additions over the past seventy years have no architectural distinction. Many of them are wooden and metal huts and buildings erected during the 1939–45 war. During the last three years, the hospital has become a centre for psychiatric treatment for the town and surrounding area, as small peripheral hospitals and wards are closed down in a rationalization drive. In numbers of beds, the hospital has declined as more patients are treated on an out-patient basis, and the concept of community care spreads. So out-patient clinics have conversely become a more major part of Anersley's activities, and new facilities have been built to cater for the greatly increased number of out-patients.

THE CHANGING ROLE OF MEDICAL RECORDS IN THE HOSPITAL

The rather unplanned and erratic nature of Anersley's expansion over a period of years was reflected in the haphazard siting of facilities and departments. Perhaps medical records illustrated this type of growth particularly clearly. The medical records filing section was at the end of a long corridor on the extremity of the hospital, and was accommodated in a wooden hut – one of a series of large huts leading off the corridor, and now

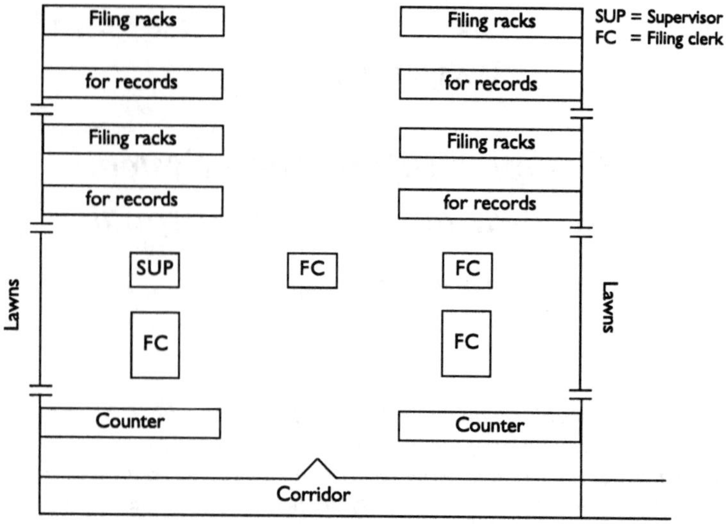

Figure 1.1 Physical layout of original medical records filing section

mainly used as stores. The hut was dilapidated on the outside, but inside it had been made cheerful by colourful posters and cartoons that the staff had pinned on the walls, and other touches of homeliness and individuality. An example of this was the hand-painted sign on the door, above the official name-plate of 'Medical Records Department'; it simply read 'The Shack'. The desks and equipment of the medical records filing section were worn and out of date, and the actual racks and shelves for the storage of patients' records were a selection of miscellaneous designs and various ages that had just accumulated over the years. The physical layout is shown in Figure 1.1.

The function of medical records has changed greatly in Anersley Hospital over the past years. For a long period it had been little more than a storage activity to aid the medical and nursing staff, who made manuscript notes on fairly straightforward forms. These were then filed in manilla folders and in box files on long shelves, subsequently to be located through a set of dog-eared index cards. While the record still remains traditionally the responsibility of the consultant, for any one patient it is now a much more complex set of documents, containing, in addition to clinical information, a variety of observations from other practitioners such as midwives, health visitors, social workers, physiotherapists, radiographers and laboratory staff. At the same time, the functions of medical records departments have become more complex. They include medical secretarial activities, as well as clerks and receptionists on wards and clinics. They receive a range of demands for information, not only from within the hospital, but also much more widely for uses as diverse as national statistics for central government, or for specialized research into clinical and social aspects of health care.

Working methods in the filing section at Anersley Hospital had evolved over time, and there were few rigid procedures or methods. Patients' records were collected and returned quite informally by a variety of staff – nurses, orderlies, clerks, porters. The only security seemed to be whether they were known to the staff of the medical records department. Sometimes clerks or porters who came regularly for records and knew the methods of filing would ask permission to look out records themselves, if the records clerks were particularly busy. Appointments clerks from out-patient clinics would often come down casually to the department two or three days before a clinic and, jointly with the records clerk, search out the records needed, having a pleasant talk at the same time. Reciprocally, it was not unknown for a records clerk to make a private arrangement with an appointments clerk to assist with the running of a clinic, if things were busy at that end of the hospital. The surprising thing to a stranger was that the records department worked markedly well. The success rate in finding records was very high – even those old, odd, elusive ones. The degree of cooperation with medical and nursing staff was also high. There was never any quibbling about demands for records at awkward times or at the last minute when extra patients attended a clinic. Undoubtedly the department worked on good memories and easy personal relationships, but it *did* work!

For the past ten years Mrs Price has been in charge of the filing section of the medical records department, as senior medical records clerk; in all she has spent nearly thirty years in this department of the hospital. Hence she has seen medical records expand from little more than a filing activity employing a small handful of people to the present complex function involving more than thirty staff, including medical secretaries, receptionists, appointment clerks, clerical and statistical staff. Particularly over the last ten years, these newer sections of the medical records department have grown much faster in numbers of personnel than the original filing section, which has almost remained static in staff numbers. The new sections, as they evolved, had supervisors appointed, and they reported directly to the Hospital Secretary, as did Mrs Price. With an administrative reorganization of the National Health Service, the Hospital Secretary was redesignated as Unit Administrator, but Mrs Price and the other section heads continued to report to him as before. Everybody in the hospital seems to know Mrs Price, and she is liked for her equable temperament and pleasant disposition. Four filing clerks report to her in turn, and they perform the filing activities.

Although Mrs Price was in charge of the section, in practice she and her four assistants all used to do the same work, allocating it among themselves approximately equally by mutual agreement. There never seemed to be any problem of keeping up with the constant stream of filing and requests, even as the volume of work built up as out-patient clinics became more numerous. In a busy period, people would work through tea-breaks, and in slack spells they would liaise (that is, gossip) with their counterparts in other departments. At tea-time, mornings and afternoons, one of the clerks would slip down the road to the local bakery, and bring back cream doughnuts for all of the staff, plus any visitors who happened to be there. Not surprisingly, visitors were frequent! The doughnuts were financed through a peculiar custom. In the corner of the working space was a large waste-paper basket, into which the staff would throw from time to time crumpled balls of scrap paper from their desks; if they missed the waste-paper basket, they had to pay a fine of one halfpenny into the doughnut fund. Other clerical workers in the hospital regarded the medical records clerks with some envy as having a nice job.

THE MOVE

About a year ago, with the decision to centralize many of the psychiatric and geriatric out-patient clinics for the catchment area of Anersley Hospital, and with the drive to reduce the number of in-patient beds, a greatly increased load of out-patient clinic work resulted. To cope with these new demands, new clinic facilities were built or rebuilt, new equipment was purchased, and new staff appointed, often from large integrated hospitals of the District General Hospital type. Such staff seemed to the old staff to show a tendency to be less friendly, more impatient for results, and less inclined to build up easy working methods through the slow process of first creating bonds of friendship and trust. Medical records staff in 'The Shack' sensed some of this slight strain, isolated as they were on the edge of the hospital; but with increasing workloads, they cooperated and worked even more closely together, and counted themselves fortunate to be part of a small but good team, and to have still the goodwill of their old colleagues in wards, clinics and departments.

Medical records functions were also included in the reorganization. A study by the Regional Management Services Department's Organization and Methods (O & M) team had confirmed suspicions about the inefficiency of the old scattered medical records department. The filing section had been at one end of the hospital, while the out-patient clinics and the appointment clerks had been at the other end of the hospital, where they were much under the influence of nursing staff. The medical secretaries had been located in various offices around the hospital, for instance, in small rooms attached to wards where they could be at hand for medical staff. Often they were underoccupied, due to lack of work in their particular area. The O & M team's report had indicated the administrative advantages to be gained by the centralization of many of the medical records activities, on the lines of similar exercises carried out by the team in other hospitals of the region. A standard form for an integrated medical records department therefore already existed, and the team was able to suggest its adoption at Anersley, with certain minor modifications to meet local conditions.

Thus the three main functions of the medical records department (records filing, appointments and secretarial) were gathered together into an integrated department for reasons of economy and convenience in obtaining and processing records. A fourth section was created in the medical records department; this was the records administrative office, to handle the many requests for statistical data arising from patients' records. A spare pavilion was found (recently vacated by long-stay patients) and the two large wards were comprehensively converted, one into an extra out-patient facility and the other into the new integrated medical records department.

As is customary, the planning and design work was carried out at the Regional Health Authority headquarters, in liaison with administrative staff of the Health District in which Anersley Hospital was situated. The pavilion was completely rebuilt internally, tastefully decorated, carpeted, air-conditioned and equipped with modern furniture, office equipment, and records storage methods. The old storage racks from 'The Shack' were completely replaced with new equipment designed by a well-known firm specializing in records' storage. Patients' information would still be held in folders using the standard forms, but the old tiers of shelves were replaced by a modern space-saving system involving purpose-built metal staging exactly fitting the size of the folder and running on tracks so that one rack could easily be slid back by hand to reveal a second rack behind, holding less frequently requested files. The capital cost of the new equipment for the department was high, but the O & M team's main criterion for its adoption was whether it could cope with all demands for the foreseeable future.

Shortly before these alterations were completed, and with the increasing complexity of the medical records function, a new post of hospital Medical Records Officer (MRO) was created. The MRO was to be in charge of the new integrated department, with the various section heads reporting to him. A major responsibility for him was to supervise the change-over of records to the new building and to organize the start-up of the new procedures. The person appointed was Mr Fraser, who had held various posts in medical records in different parts of the country; he was in his early forties, and was well informed about the technicalities of medical records and keen to set up a new service to good standards. Before coming to Anersley Hospital, his job was as a Deputy MRO in a large hospital where he had gained a good reputation. Mr Fraser impressed the interviewing panel at his appointment as having drive, being keen to be in charge of his own medical records department, and wanting to show his capabilities, possibly as a basis for a future promotion to a coordinating post in medical records at District level. Mr Fraser reported to the Unit Administrator at Anersley Hospital, Mr Littlewood, who could be regarded as middle management.

Since Mr Fraser's arrival at Anersley was some two years after the planning period, the decisions had all been taken regarding the physical facilities and equipment for the new medical records department. Nevertheless, he reviewed the future needs for the reorganized hospital, using the O & M team's data bases and research studies in other hospitals which had undergone similar changes of function to that proposed for Anersley. When he studied the records filing section in 'The Shack', he found that (after making allowances for their out-dated equipment and unrationalized working methods) the section was unlikely to be able to cope with the projected increasing volume of records since it was already working at some 110 per cent of normal expected output. Although Mr Fraser took care not to give the members of the section this information, it did enable him to assure them that the change to the new building would mean less hard work for them, as a result of the new layout and improved equipment. He was a little disappointed to find that this news did not produce any marked enthusiasm among the staff of the section.

In the early days after his arrival at Anersley, Mr Fraser spent a considerable amount of time with the O & M team and the Architect's Department at regional headquarters, so that he appreciated their proposals and recommendations and could use the equipment to the full. He was particularly impressed with the elegance and logic of the plans, which would improve access to records for key users, and provide a much faster processing of information on a reliable basis. Subsequently he worked out master plans for the transfer of equipment, records and personnel to the new office, and for the detailed operation of the new department and Records Library, as he renamed the filing section, in line with current practice. He then converted these plans into working instructions for each member of staff to follow after the transfer, and he issued these instructions some ten days in advance of the move via supervisors and section heads to each person. Like others in charge of groups of staff, Mrs Price received a substantial sheaf of instructions from Mr Fraser, and, after a short briefing, he entrusted her with the task of instructing her staff. The group of five in 'The Shack' worked meticulously through the detail and did their best to understand the new procedures. A few days before the actual moving day Mr Fraser checked with the staff in order to ensure a smooth change-over; neither Mrs Price nor her staff had any questions in advance and they acknowledged that the instructions certainly were thorough. Mr Fraser was a little disappointed at this passive response to his new instructions; he had put a great deal of painstaking work into them, and had hoped that staff would react with more recognition. He put the lack of involvement down to Mrs Price's limitations as a supervisor in leading her staff, and to their lack of concern for and knowledge of proper standards of good practice in medical records.

The actual movement of the records to the new department was Mr Fraser's masterpiece of planning, to such an extent that the Unit Administrator congratulated Mr Fraser on the continuation of the records service, scarcely with any disruption. Friday clinics were cancelled that week, and the records staff cleared up all outstanding documents on Friday morning – and then were given the Friday afternoon off as a holiday. At 1 p.m. a veritable army of porters and helpers descended on 'The Shack' to perform the heavy task of moving every document right across the hospital to the new office. With Mr Fraser and another administrator in charge and following the master plan, everything was correctly filed by 4 p.m. on the Sunday afternoon. At all times Mr Fraser was at hand to check the removal team's instructions and to give supplementary orders. On the Monday morning, the new medical records department started up, almost as if the change had never occurred, and disruption was minimized.

THE NEW INTEGRATED DEPARTMENT

Although filing procedures were not very different in the new department, the overall mode of operation of the department was considerably streamlined and more efficient in concept. Mr Fraser felt that his concern before the move in getting people trained in advance had helped them to get used

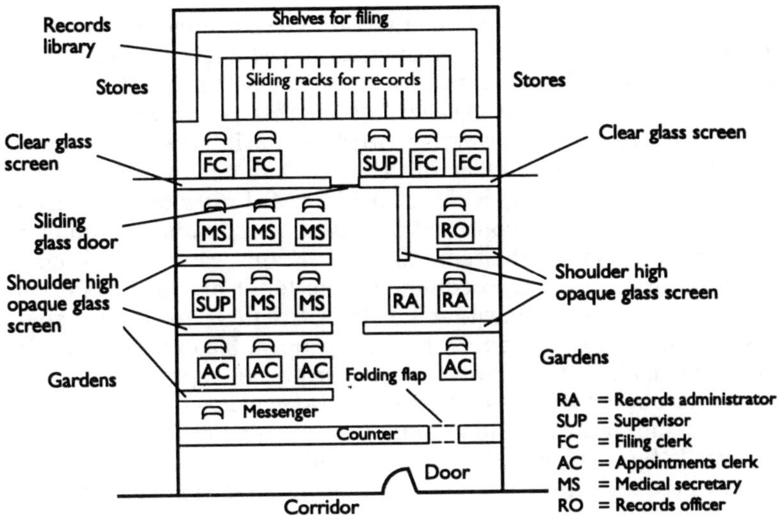

Figure 1.2 Physical layout of new integrated medical records office

quickly to the changed physical layout and conditions, and to the new standards which he hoped to inculcate. A diagram of the new department is shown in Figure 1.2.

So that a real measure of security could be retained over records, a floor-to-ceiling glass screen had been erected at the end of the Records Library. All the staff in that section had desks behind the screen and behind them were the filing racks, shiny and new. The only entrance to the Records Library was through the one sliding door next to Mrs Price's desk, and she had instructions only to admit persons designated on a list which Mr Fraser had drawn up. The Records Library staff were expected in their turn to leave the office only at specified times, unless in special circumstances. A messenger was appointed for the department, and his duties included collecting and receiving clinic lists and requests for records, transmitting them to Mrs Price, subsequently collecting records from her and conveying them to wards and clinics. Anyone outside the department making a single request for records would pass the details via the messenger or sometimes directly to Mrs Price, and she would either find the file herself or allocate the work to one of her staff. The Records Library staff queried the need for these procedures when Mr Fraser was explaining methods at a post-move training session. He explained its logic with two reasons: first, it would prevent excessive interruption of their work by a constant flow of requests; secondly, it helped introduce a suitably professional standard of security with records – and he cited the unfortunate case that had befallen him some years earlier when a drunken porter had recited some rather explicit case notes to an enthralled audience in the 'spit and sawdust' bar of a local pub!

In many ways, the new methods introduced by Mr Fraser began, as he put it, to 'get a grip' on the Records Library. Gone were the piles of unfiled records that sometimes used to lie on desks overnight at times of rush; all work had to be cleared before the night records clerk/telephonist came on duty. The use of tracer cards was made mandatory whenever records were removed, even for use within the medical records department. The master index was no longer treated in a 'cavalier fashion' that had prevailed before – Mr Fraser's expression for everyone working on it; it was made the responsibility of one member alone of the staff. An attempt to paste pictures on the glass screen was quickly checked by Mr Fraser on grounds of unsightliness. Tea-break now consisted of a fixed period of fifteen minutes in the staff dining-room. At the same time, Mr Fraser was able to keep a general supervisory eye on proceedings, and he felt it his duty to squash some rather irresponsible behaviour involving attempts to throw paper balls through the sliding glass door when it was open. He explained to Mr Littlewood that, in all, he was slowly instilling professional pride and standards into the staff of the Records Library. He also made a point of building up Mrs Price's supervisory position, and he gave her the opportunity to show such skills by making certain that changes and instructions always reached her as requests, for her to pass on as instructions to her staff.

PROBLEMS ENCOUNTERED

During the six months that followed the move the service provided by the Records Library deteriorated. Records were obtained far less reliably than previously; there were frequent delays and sudden requests at the last minute were often the subject of argument. Filing of records began to get behind, and so Mr Fraser instituted a rule that any records unfiled at the end of the day should be returned to Mrs Price for safe-keeping. The stock of such records grew alarmingly. Mrs Price attempted to file them the following day, in addition to her normal work, but never seemed to catch up. It became assumed that once records had been passed over to Mrs Price, they ceased to be the responsibility of the clerk to whom they had originally been assigned. The old habit of team effort in helping to find apparently missing records seemed to disappear, and problems were experienced with deficiencies in the master index.

Faced with such issues, Mrs Price requested Mr Fraser to let her staff work half an hour's overtime each evening for a week to clear the back-log. Mr Fraser refused, with the words 'If the staff spent less time chatting and got on with the job they're paid to do, there'd be no problem – the O & M team didn't recommend any overtime'. Although her staff several times again mentioned this solution to her, Mrs Price was never willing to raise the matter again.

Staff in clinics which were experiencing difficulties in getting patients' records in good time complained eventually through consultants to Mr Littlewood, the Unit Administrator. His wide range of responsibilities meant that he had little time to exercise day-to-day control over medical records – or any other section. He believed in delegation, and thus his contact with departments occurred mainly when problems or changes arose. As a result of the complaint, Mr Fraser made a ruling that records must be passed over to clinics even earlier, to allow for errors and omissions to be corrected. Even the easy relationship within the department between records clerks and medical secretaries began to suffer with the increasing work load and pressure for a faster turnround of work. All the staff felt real concern that their service was deteriorating, and tried hard to retrieve the position, even to the extent of working through tea-breaks. Mr Fraser perhaps did not see all the problems, as he was often out of the office at meetings, or in outlying hospitals in the District, preparing for their integration into a comprehensive scheme for medical records.

Within the Records Library work became slower due to missing or misplaced records, and the back-log became larger than ever. In an attempt to speed up the pace of work the clerks began to omit the tracer cards when records were removed – on the grounds that they had always managed well enough without them in 'The Shack'. When he discovered this habit, Mr Fraser used to carry out periodic checks; there were hard feelings on both sides when (inevitably) he discovered missing cards, and the staff used to refer to him as 'the bloodhound'.

Certain vague reports that all was not well in medical records reached Mr Littlewood again. Still believing that Mr Fraser should have a full chance to sort out teething troubles without interference from above, he did not intervene. Mr Fraser, in his view, was showing energy and determination, implementing a major change in the hospital's procedures, and, in any case, it might well not be prudent to involve the hard-pressed O & M team again in sorting out matters at Anersley, before every effort had been made within the hospital to resolve the problems.

THE CRISIS

Matters came to a head one evening at about 11.30 p.m., when Mr Littlewood was called from bed to the telephone by an icily-polite consultant who wished to inform him that he had been waiting for exactly three hours for the records of a patient who had just been admitted under a section of the Mental Health Act 1959. It was known that the man had been both an in-patient and an out-patient of the hospital before, but three hours' search by the night records clerk/telephonist had failed to reveal any notes or reference at all. Mr Littlewood rang Mr Fraser and tersely asked him to come to the hospital at once to meet him.

It took Mr Fraser about twenty-five minutes to find the patient's records, which were wrongly filed, and, in addition, apparently incomplete to some extent. Mr Littlewood searched also, and was dismayed with what he found. There were piles of case notes stuffed in desks, bundles of reports from departments lying, weeks old, in the innermost racks, there were missing or incomplete tracer cards and the master index seemed very inefficient. Beside Mrs Price's desk was a new addition – a small wooden rack from 'The Shack', with three shelves marked 'Pending' (all full) and one for 'Unaccountable' (part-full). As Mr Littlewood searched, the consultant stood beside him and related a series of carefully documented and heartfelt incidents about the shortcomings and failures of the new medical records department.

The consultant departed to the ward, bearing the records. Mr Littlewood regarded Mr Fraser sourly. 'We will meet at nine o'clock today in my office to find out why this has occurred, and what we are going to do about it. Goodnight'.

THE AFTERMATH

The meeting in Mr Littlewood's office was quite brief and, for Mr Fraser, relatively undistressing – perhaps reflecting the health service's tradition of civilized administration. It was agreed between the two men that 'serious teething troubles' still existed, that Mr Fraser would spend much more time in the hospital medical records office sorting out problems, and that, finally, he would report back formally to Mr Littlewood in three months' time.

Once back in the department (which was 'buzzing' with speculation and comment over the news of the previous night's events), Mr Fraser sat down to make his plans to get the service running more smoothly. After a couple of days' reflection, he set about energetically putting them into practice.

First he concentrated on technical difficulties with the records storage equipment and in the identification and tracing of individual patients' records. Then he reviewed all routines adopted by clinics, wards and departments for requesting and returning records, reconsidering the deadlines, the internal movement of records between sections in the medical records department and instituting a procedure for emergencies. Thirdly, he endeavoured to involve Mrs Price more in the exercise of her supervisory role, through playing a greater part in the allocation and control of work, through insisting on strict observance of the deadlines for requests, and through trying to get her to take a more consistent approach to dividing the 'trouble-shooting' activity between herself and her staff. Finally, he tried to ensure that each of the medical records filing clerks knew the procedures and routines exactly and adhered to them, especially in respect of handling problems of missing, incomplete or unidentifiable records. As a result of all these activities, Mr Fraser felt that an additional full-time appointment was necessary to the Records Library on the grounds of the increasing volume of work; a school leaver with clerical training was duly recruited.

On balance, Mr Fraser felt that from these measures he could detect an improvement of service in many respects, especially in the response time for records, in the night service and in the level of complaints from users of records. The department seemed to be settling into a routine of operation and was developing smoother relationships with other departments – as he was able to report to Mr Littlewood. Yet Mr Fraser could detect other matters which concerned him a little. Staff turnover had risen from the previous extremely low level, and staff seemed to work without any conspicuous enthusiasm. Mrs Price continued in her post, but never made any original contribution to improving standards or solving problems. It was generally accepted among staff that she would seek retirement at the earliest permissible point, in a year's time, and that her replacement would be a much younger person, with professional training in medical records and a career orientation towards middle or senior management in the health services.

Mr Fraser reflected one day on the direction of the change, on the manner in which it had been conducted, on the present standard of service, and on the present capacity of his department to respond to future demands – and he wondered whether he was as confident still in his own knowledge and abilities as he had been on appointment! He began to think about taking advice . . .

CHAPTER 2

Banks of the Wear

L. A. WALSH AND R. ARMSON

The Banks of the Wear Housing Cooperative was set up in response to housing needs in the city of Sunderland. It had enormous success in enabling people to take control of their own housing projects and in conducting its own affairs in a non-hierarchical way. Changes in the political environment of housing and emerging internal difficulties required painful changes if the organization was to survive.

HOUSING IN SUNDERLAND

The economy of the city of Sunderland was built on heavy industry, shipbuilding and coal-mining. Until the late 1980s, public-sector council housing dominated housing provision within the city but there were also traditional single-storey, terraced, two-bedroomed 'cottages' and Victorian terraces. These cottages and terraced houses were owned mainly by individual landlords or by employers, such as the National Coal Board. They were characterized by their lack of amenities.

During the 1970s, the council sought either to demolish the cottages and terraces or to improve them by designating Housing Action Areas (HAAs). Grants were available from central government to deal with the housing and environmental problems within HAAs. In 1976, some local residents and local community activists, together with the council, recognized the opportunities for major improvements in the local housing stock and formed a cooperative known as Banks of the Wear. This housing cooperative was concerned primarily with the Mowbray Road Housing Action Area in the Hendon area of the city.

THE EARLY DAYS OF BANKS OF THE WEAR

The vision of the Banks of the Wear Cooperative (BOW) was simple: to help and encourage tenants and residents to improve their homes. The cooperative's mission was to facilitate people working together to articulate and achieve their aims. Its culture was firmly entrenched in tenant participation, which enabled residents to have control over their homes and the improvements made to them. It would not itself act as a builder or architect to carry out improvements. Its role would be to

- help tenants form action groups and to register those action groups as cooperatives;
- provide them with information and help with accessing improvement grants;
- facilitate their decisions about the type and extent of the improvements they wanted;
- offer guidance and advice about engaging contractors to do the improvement work; and
- help them to set up their own systems for managing the improved housing.

The housing cooperative concept was in vogue and there was very little political opposition to the project, although some councillors worried that BOW might undermine the council's traditional role in providing social housing. The aim was that, as housing improvement schemes came into being, the action committees would themselves evolve into cooperatives. These would become 'primary housing cooperatives'. BOW would move away from direct tenant action and become a 'secondary cooperative' providing support and services to the new primary cooperatives.

BOW worked first in Hendon. Hendon epitomized many of the problems of inner-city life: poor housing, poverty and high rates of unemployment. Yet Hendon had benefited from a traditional sense of community. For all these reasons the area needed substantial investment in housing improvements and so it became a HAA.

BOW started with the appointment of three workers. Their first job was to go from door to door making people aware of the housing improvement opportunities and setting up action meetings to get the local ball rolling. Their office was an old butcher's shop in the centre of Hendon where tenants and residents of the area were encouraged to meet to develop ideas for change. The 'shop' was a community action centre providing advice on employment and benefits. It later became an important meeting place from which other cooperative ventures developed.

The original workers, though keeping to the broad aim of facilitating the development of local housing cooperatives, also helped to develop other initiatives to improve the area and provide employment. There were improvements to the area's environment: allotments were developed and play schemes were provided for children. Some of these schemes were funded by the Manpower Services Commission (a government agency concerned with alleviating unemployment) and they employed people from the area. There was great excitement as residents began to have a direct impact on Hendon.

To control BOW and to develop policy, a management committee was formed. Members were local residents who had become involved in the primary cooperatives. They were elected at the annual general meeting attended by all local cooperative members and residents. Workers and committee members worked together to introduce radical new forms of housing management. They were passionate about developing the concept of tenant-driven cooperative housing and about challenging traditional housing practices and norms. They were determined that tenants should make the decisions about their own housing.

Decision-making processes were informal. The management committee met whenever it was important to discuss something. The management committee was intimately involved in day-to-day activities and people got on with the task in hand. It was very much hands-on work for both committee members and workers. There was little formal structure to the organization and the workers did whatever was needed for the project – which might be knocking on doors to persuade residents of the area to become involved with the project, boarding up vacant property or helping residents to move into revitalized property. It was a time of action and of celebrating successes.

Both workers and committee members were missionaries. Some committee members became very active in promoting tenants' cooperatives and shaping the strategy of BOW. They all took an active part in persuading organizations and residents, wedded to traditional housing approaches, to accept and finance alternative housing structures. They were continually spreading the word to tenant groups and encouraging the formation of new cooperatives throughout the north east. Throughout, BOW representatives encouraged and helped people to establish their own cooperatives to deal with their own housing needs. At times, BOW had to guide tenants through administrative traps and negotiations with obdurate landlords and bureaucracies.

The work had a high profile. The Bishop of Durham said of BOW: 'Cooperatives give people a real opportunity to overcome their sense of powerlessness and despair, as well as helping to rebuild the urban area in which they live.' BOW sought to develop its committee structure so that client housing cooperatives would be represented. The late 1980s were a period in the development of BOW when the committee had to spend time in understanding and developing housing cooperative practice and the concepts of cooperative decision-making. Arguments over policy and direction were inevitable, but the style was one that encouraged debate, new ideas and tenant control. It was not unusual for meetings to last six hours. Meetings were not controlled by a rigid agenda. Most issues were discussed, including strategies, day-to-day issues and the feelings of workers and tenants. It had been decided that there would be no specialist advisers or cooptees on the committee although some members began to develop expertise and experience in particular areas. The meetings also had a social context. With the development of more primary cooperatives, the number of committee members increased. People enjoyed going to committee meetings. They provided an important social context for tenants to meet and discuss issues of common concern. This enjoyment helped maintain enthusiasm and commitment. The workers, present at committee meetings as advisers, helped tenants to feel in touch with wider issues.

In the early years of BOW it was not easy to see who made the decisions and whether it was workers or committee members who formed policy. The boundaries between workers and committee members blurred as people got things done. At times coordination was difficult. Not only were there no clearly defined committee procedures but workers also had no formal hierarchy. With the growth in workload during the 1980s there was inevitably conflict within BOW. BOW tried to make decisions by consensus. There was no traditional management imposing its views since all were equal. It was often hard to deal with differences of opinion. If consensus could not be reached then there was a majority vote. People in the minority would then find themselves at odds with the organization and sometimes felt that leaving BOW was their only option. Other workers left quite amicably to develop their own projects.

SUCCESS AND GROWTH

By 1986, BOW employed 14 workers. Two of the original workers had left to develop other cooperative and housing initiatives. By this time, BOW provided a range of services for cooperatives throughout the north east and had offices in Sunderland, Middlesborough and Newcastle. The workers promoted the housing cooperative concept and provided assistance to tenants and others wishing to form coops. They supplied education and training, administrative support, and architectural and housing management services.

In its first ten years, BOW had

- helped develop 30 primary cooperatives throughout the north east, assisting them in producing over 700 new or improved housing units;
- survived and grown from three to 14 workers;
- maintained the principle of 'management by tenants' and a non-hierarchical organizational structure;
- survived growth and retained the commitment of staff and committee members; and
- become self-financing from fees, allowances and consultancy services.

BOW was thought of with affection by its associated primary cooperatives and by other housing coops, housing associations and local authorities for whom it provided consultancy services. It was respected throughout the north east as a supplier of specialized services. It had contacts with the Housing Corporation (the main government agency for housing matters) and local authorities and it had a reputation for professionalism.

It was also providing specialist architectural services to tenants' groups. This supported the aims of shifting control of housing improvement projects to tenants and away from 'professionals' and experts. The architectural staff came to understand the issues of working with tenants, a client group that few architects work with regularly. The services were cheaper than equivalent services available elsewhere in the commercial market and generated additional income for BOW.

THE NON-HIERARCHICAL ORGANIZATION

BOW achieved these successes with a non-hierarchical approach to management. There was no director or coordinator: each coop worker was a specialist in his or her own field and an equal-pay structure had been introduced. The *Ten Years of Achievement* report, published in 1986, described BOW's unconventional style:

> An organization with fourteen employees and an annual cash budget of around £2 million would normally operate along well-known traditional lines. The Director would be paid three times the salary of one of the typists, and only the highest paid three or four officers would be involved in policy formulation.
>
> The traditional approach can have serious draw backs; there can be too many chiefs and not enough indians; those employees on the bottom tier have no involvement at all in policy formulation and the broader aspects of running the organization.
>
> The non-hierarchical approach used at Banks of the Wear represents a quite deliberate attempt to avoid these sorts of problems.

The report went on to say: 'Policy-making within the workforce is a job for everyone, not just those with the most experience or the most eloquent tongues. Fortnightly workers' meetings, which last around three hours, bring everyone together on a regular basis, not to rubber-stamp decisions, but to help make them.' In an attempt to bring structure to the non-hierarchical framework, three team coordinator posts were created. The team coordinators had little hierarchical status within the organization but spoke for each of the three teams within BOW: housing management, tenant participation, and finance and administration.

The benefits of this non-hierarchical task-based structure were that each worker contributed to developing and maintaining both the cooperative and the work of their own team. The equal-salaries pay system was thought to be a fair and proper method for staff who worked within the cooperative philosophy, and that it would encourage all staff to develop equally.

By 1988 the success of BOW was widely recognized. It had maintained its ethos and had grown sufficiently to provide a range of services for primary cooperatives, many of which it had helped to initiate.

INTERNAL FACTORS LEADING TO CHANGE

Some problems of this style of management emerged when some staff, who did not agree with the majority decision, were forced out of the organization by a 'war of attrition'. Others left because they felt at odds with the direction BOW was taking. The majority-vote method of cooperative decision-making was leading to tensions within the organization. An example was the vote for the equal-salaries policy. Each worker had one vote. Some of the more experienced and qualified workers did not consider that this reward mechanism was fair, and some then left BOW.

The process of trying to reach consensus on decisions did not encourage BOW to face unpleasant issues or to develop strategic plans. For example, in the early part of 1988 it became clear that the architectural services were operating at a loss. The search for consensus made it impossible to close the section and force redundancies until 1993. By this time some people were working at much less than their 'market' salary while, conversely, others earnt far more than their market salary. In an uncertain climate such discrepancies created further tensions and some people left for career and financial reasons. By the late 1980s there had been significant staff turnover. There was a feeling that some of those who remained had inflated salaries when compared with market rates. These people were effectively trapped in the organization with only smaller salaries available to them elsewhere.

As early as 1988 it was clear to the workers that effective communication was a problem. Because of the difficulties of interpreting the wishes of the management committee, each of the three team coordinators handled information in a different way. The dispersed office locations made this worse and team members often received contradictory messages. Staff meetings became difficult forums for strategic decision-making.

In 1989, BOW faced a financial crisis. Expenditure had exceeded income. The main cost was staffing. Time allocation sheets were introduced to monitor expenditure. It became evident that certain services were not financially sound and there was a planned reduction in the number of staff. Architectural staff who left the organization were not replaced. BOW abandoned the system of equal pay and equal status and introduced a six-grade staffing structure. As part of the grading procedure, all staff now had job descriptions. Staff were allocated specific responsibilities and this signalled the start of new and hierarchical ways of working. The grading structure went some way to clarify responsibility but it was not until 1992 that a director was appointed and strategic and business issues were dealt with effectively.

By 1989, the management committee was already aware that change would be needed for survival and consultants had advised on the options available to BOW within the new housing market. The consultants laid the foundations for a more focused approach to the management of the business. They highlighted the need for strategic and business analysis and clarification of the purposes of BOW.

By 1990, a significant number of the skilled and specialist staff had left, including the last of the original workers. The organization faced making major changes in order to survive in the new housing environment.

EXTERNAL FACTORS LEADING TO CHANGE

In the end it was not just the internal issues that changed the ethos of the organization: external factors forced change. The late 1980s proved to be a challenging time for cooperatives. The Housing Act 1988 introduced market-led housing philosophies and changed the rules and the environment for social housing. There was increased emphasis on financial viability. Competition between housing associations for developmental work was encouraged and it became necessary to raise project money from the private sector. Government policy was to reduce public expenditure, to reduce the level of grants to housing associations and to promote a policy of economic rents. This threatened social housing provision. The Housing Corporation saw housing associations as the main providers of social housing and not housing cooperatives or local authorities.

There were also indications that, by 1992, the Housing Corporation would only fund a limited number of housing associations. This would include only those classified as financially secure. BOW was outside the set criteria and its survival was under threat. The new legislative environment forced organizational and financial changes on BOW. To meet the challenge of the new legislative and administrative framework, BOW had to transform itself into a housing association. To persuade the Housing Corporation to provide financial support for its projects, it needed sufficient assets and adequate financial and management procedures.

In October 1990, the BOW Cooperative ceased to exist. Its assets and staff were transferred to the BOW Community Housing Association Ltd (BOW Housing Association). The new organization appointed management consultants to assist in developing a business strategy. The consultants took the view that the lack of a developed staff structure was a weakness and that workers had '. . . suffered from a lack of clear internal career structure and vocational training'. They also considered that the workers had so many external clients to serve that they frequently overworked to a stand-still.

Although the BOW *Cooperative* had faced a number of threats, the new environment provided opportunities for the BOW Community Housing *Association*. Some local authorities were divesting themselves of their traditionally paternalistic housing role and were looking at new models of decentralized housing provision. This provided an opportunity for work in developing schemes for tenant participation. The Department of the Environment was encouraging and financing schemes that encouraged tenant-centred management. BOW Housing Association had valuable expertise in this field and, by 1992, consultancy work on tenant participation provided BOW Housing Association with 60 per cent of its income.

BOW HOUSING ASSOCIATION AND ITS CLIENTS

The changes in the financial arrangements created some tension between BOW Housing Association and its primary cooperatives over payment for services. Previously, the Housing Corporation allocated block grants to cover service costs but, in the 1990s, grant arrangements changed to encourage the operation of market forces in housing. Cooperatives were encouraged to accept the cheapest tender for services and BOW Housing Association found itself undercut. The original work of encouraging and assisting tenants to organize coops had been very time consuming and the development costs had formed part of the total service costs for each project. With financial restrictions, BOW Housing Association's client coops could now sometimes obtain services at lower cost elsewhere. Representatives from these client cooperatives were also members of BOW Housing Association and they expressed their concerns over the costs of BOW Housing Association services. This created tension within the organization as some coops sought other organizations to provide house-management and architectural services.

The economic and political environment discouraged the development of new cooperatives. Increasing poverty and social stress in communities, as their heavy-industry employment base declined, had a depressing effect on people's willingness to become involved in setting up new coops.

The 1990s brought a near halt to the development of new cooperatives. Instead, BOW Housing Association moved into new roles in providing housing for rent as a housing association and in providing consultancy on tenant participation. Because of its community links and reputation, it was able to develop housing schemes for the Chinese community in Newcastle and the Bangladeshi community in Sunderland.

FORMAL STRUCTURES: FORMAL MANAGEMENT

In 1991, an audit report by the Housing Corporation criticized the performance of BOW Housing Association. This prompted the cooption of three people with specialist housing and management skills on to the management committee to provide professional support for the newly formed BOW Housing Association. A subcommittee was appointed to deal with personnel and finance issues. The emphasis of the committees changed. They no longer discussed the philosophy and issues of a cooperative. Instead they became concerned with strategy and day-to-day management of the organization. Decision-making responsibility gradually shifted from the committee members (mostly representatives from the client cooperatives) to people whose primary interest was the BOW Housing Association itself.

The early 1992, BOW Housing Association appointed consultants to help plan for the future. They advised that a director be appointed, a clearly hierarchical structure be introduced, a business analysis be carried out and that merging with a stronger housing association be considered. The director and the three team coordinators would now form a 'management executive' team. The director was appointed in October of that year and a corporate review was undertaken by the management executive assisted by a steering group comprising staff and committee representatives. The business analysis showed BOW Housing Association as the region's leading body in tenant participation, housing association developments for black and other ethnic-minority communities and, to a lesser extent, agency services for existing housing cooperatives.

Committee meetings were now more formal. Clear agenda items were supported by background papers and financial and managerial reports. There were also procedures allowing the director delegated authority for dealing with urgent matters and items approved by the committee. Financial and administrative procedures formed an important aspect of the new management style.

Previously the committee had been worn out and frustrated by the former system of collective management. The tension between the search for consensus and the need for quick decisions, and between collective ideas and efficient communication, had taken its toll. The management committee gave its full support to the director in his difficult role. Some of the staff welcomed the appointment of a director as they, too, sought clear leadership and relief from the strains of collective working in times of rapid change. All the staff in one way or another recognized that change had to come. But change was very painful.

In 1993 analysis showed that BOW Housing Association faced another financial crisis following further changes in funding arrangements. There were three options:

- Merge with another large housing association.
- Change the focus of service provision and reduce staff costs.
- Stop trading.

Although the merger option was still being investigated, in 1993 the committee had to reduce expenditure, which was exceeding income by 30 per cent. Six people were made redundant. One commented that it had been obvious that he should have been redundant in 1989 but that it was not his responsibility to make recommendations that would eliminate his own job. The redundancies signalled changes in management style and the need to take hard decisions for the long-term benefit of BOW Housing Association. Staff were persuaded to take a collective pay-cut. New staff were appointed on temporary contracts. The organization was restructured and staff had to compete for the remaining jobs. Staff who were unsuccessful in obtaining the job of their choice left the organization. Staff were transferred from the Newcastle office to the central office in Sunderland and the office facilities and space at Newcastle were reduced.

The period 1992–3 saw many people leaving BOW. By early 1994, staff morale was low. Staff were fearful of future reorganizations and changes. Much of the staff unhappiness focused on the director, who was blamed for the changes that have been made. Aware of the tensions, the director tried to improve matters by better staff communications and improved relations with the staff trade union.

The problems of transforming the organization were acute. Many staff had been committed to the cooperative ideals of BOW and there was deep regret for the lost ideals of non-hierarchical working. Some experienced this as a painful personal loss. The director and the new management executive walked an uncomfortable road between the ideals of staff and the pressures of a restructured housing market. However, he now had clear objectives specified by the management committee.

The culture was very different from the non-hierarchical and informal style of the earlier days when idealists and activists achieved so much. Success, growth and a changed and somewhat hostile environment had seen the adoption of a business culture. Changes had to be made for the organization to survive. Once BOW had been an innovative and fun place to work with a great deal of success measured in terms of community development. Workers could see the improvements to houses and the infrastructure of the area and now they grieved for the loss of the old camaraderie.

THE TRADE UNION

The Manufacturing, Science and Finance Trade Union now represented staff interests. It was formally recognized by BOW Housing Association and the two shop stewards had facilities and time off from work for union duties. With the changes made by management, the union's role had become more proactive. Previously, trade unionism had been relatively low key as workers made the decisions. Not all staff were members of the trade union. Prior to restructuring, staff had direct access to the management committee. Although this was no longer so, staff were encouraged to inform the management committee of their views through the trade union. The shop stewards received copies of all management committee working papers and the two stewards became observers at the personnel subcommittee where they might be asked for comments.

There were still meetings that involved all the staff. These meetings produced prepared comments for the management committee prior to its monthly meeting. The union representatives saw the new staff meeting as issue-raising rather than decision-taking. The director was present at these meetings. There was concern that this gave him the opportunity to take control, leaving little time for the staff or union representatives to discuss issues and prepare strategies.

'THE FUN HAS GONE OUT OF WORK'

Fifteen years of decline in funding for social housing, together with the more recent internal changes, had reduced the social elements of work at BOW. Previously the done thing was to meet in the pub to discuss projects with colleagues and committee members. Informality was the style of management. Now the informal pub meetings were few. There were still informal celebrations of success for team projects but few for the whole organization.

Some people did not, and could not, agree with the changes in the organizational culture of BOW. They longed to return to participative management. They were suspicious of the new managers running the organization.

They felt that the ideology espoused in the *Ten Years of Achievement* report had been turned on its head. The director *did* earn three times the typists' salaries, and only the highest-paid three or four officers were involved in policy formulation. BOW Housing Association had adopted traditional approaches to management and was no longer a cooperative non-hierarchical workplace. But it had survived in turbulent times and had maintained the main original objectives of BOW in its new goals and aims.

At the beginning of 1994, BOW found itself moving into a new phase. The intense pressure of the competitive environment in which BOW operated brought the managers and senior staff together. They began to plot new marketing strategies and to develop new interteam approaches to the work. As the impact of the major changes of 1992 and 1993 was absorbed, a new, more trusting and more cooperative climate began to emerge within the organization. One long-serving staff member observed, '. . . there are glowing embers – we just need to blow on them in the right way'. Whether a new phase of 'structured cooperation' will bring successes for BOW like those seen in the 1970s and early 1980s remains to be seen.

CHAPTER 3

Information Systems Strategy: Royal Holdings responds to change

S. WALNOTT

This case study is fictional but based on real-life situations that may be met in large organizations. It is written as a basis for discussion of how decisions are made.

BACKGROUND

The company, Royal Holdings, is a wholly owned subsidiary of Royal International (RI), a large international financial organization whose main market is in Europe. Royal Holdings by itself is, by many standards, a large company in its own right. It has some 4,000 staff, all based in the UK where its single financial product has a dominant share of a stable market. There are two main competitors, each supplying a product almost identical to that of Royal Holdings. Over the last ten years the market share of each of the competitors has been stable with no serious market shift between them. Throughout the 1980s, Royal Holdings' profits were excellent and it was a highly valued subsidiary of RI. It was treated very much as a cash cow generating finance for developing other parts of RI. Very little was reinvested to develop Royal Holdings itself. The position of managing director of Royal Holdings was seen by the RI board as a relaxing two-year stint to be given as a reward for service elsewhere in RI.

AGENTS OF CHANGE

In the last few years, several external factors have come together to exert pressure for change on this happy contented company. First, the general financial climate changed in the UK as the country began to encounter economic problems. This halted the growth of what had previously been a continually increasing market for Royal Holdings' single product. In fact, the market began to decline, substantially reducing profits. Royal Holdings was no longer the reliable source of cash for RI it had previously been. Secondly, the government, in its intent to move towards a free market economy, deregulated the financial sector, opening up financial markets to much greater competition. The cosy world of the previous cartel was broken and other companies began to enter the market. Deregulation also meant that the product itself was under attack.

The product consisted of a prepaid card which customers could present at shops in return for goods. Previously each company had processed both its own cards and the associated paperwork returned from shops. Now other organizations were able to compete for processing paperwork returned by the shops even if they were not themselves card issuers. Soon competitors were entering the market to deal with the card purchasers while others entered the market to process the merchant paperwork. This was possible since all customer and merchant dealings were finally processed through a national clearing house which matched up each customer transaction with the relevant merchant one.

BROAD CHANGES

RI decided that the situation could not be allowed to continue. Royal Holdings' market was in decline, competition had increased substantially and there was every indication that the effects of these changes would continue to increase. Action was needed. The old management was retired early and new management from RI was installed with a brief to return Royal Holdings to its previously highly profitable situation.

Within Royal Holdings the accounting systems were unable to provide information on which functions were profitable and which were not, and which functions were efficient and which not. It was decided, because competition was on two specific fronts, that Royal Holdings' structure would reflect this and so two separate organizations were set up, Royal Customer and Royal Merchant. In the spirit of the times all processes within these two groups were to be costed out and charged for. Each manager was to be an entrepreneur and was given performance targets.

Unfortunately, the financial systems required substantial development and could provide little information of any accuracy. However, it soon became apparent that Royal Merchant, handling paperwork from the shops, was barely profitable and a programme of review and redundancies was initiated. Royal Customer, on the other hand, appeared to be profitable and to have less serious competition. Two distinct attitudes began to develop in the different companies: Royal Customer became expansive and had finance to invest but Royal Merchant developed a defensive stance and was short of investment finance.

THE PROBLEM

Although both companies were now managed as separate organizations under the Royal Holdings' umbrella, they both used Royal Holdings' single computer system for the operational processing. This was the same system that had been used for the previous dozen or so years.

The computer system had grown up with the company and had been designed on a monolithic basis to satisfy all Royal Holdings' processing requirements. There was a team of some twenty or so analyst programmers permanently employed on developing and maintaining the system. Their work schedule was planned 18 months in advance. The two companies now had both differing and common information requirements and, in the changed commercial world, each required both faster change and greater control over that change. An information-processing system that had served the organization well in the past was unable to cope. Change was needed and the decision was made to look for an alternative system.

THE PROCESS OF CHANGE

A steering committee was set up by Royal Holdings to review the options. This committee consisted of the managing director of Royal Holdings, Gordon Stebbing; the managing director of Royal Customer, Pippa Wells; the managing director of Royal Merchant, Peter Everest; and the information technology director from Royal Holdings, who had overall responsibility for IT within Royal Holdings. A senior manager, Joe Parsons, was appointed to identify alternative options and to make recommendations on the future development of the IT system.

Various alternatives were quickly identified:

1. Restructure the central database and purchase packages where possible to carry out modular processing functions.
2. Completely rewrite the system using internal staff.
3. Purchase a package currently being developed by some systems consultants, Scott Turner McBride, for a smaller purchase-card company in America.
4. Enter into a joint development with another company, ShopCard Belgium, where development was planned but not yet under way.
5. Do nothing.

Parsons made his choice; he had only a few years until retirement and, after a disappointing career, he saw this as his last chance to make his name. He was convinced that the package being developed by the consultants was the answer. The consultants, Scott Turner McBride (STM), were well regarded internationally. They had carried out previous assignments for Royal Holdings. They were, however, somewhat expensive and there had been some comments about missing functionality from their systems but they had generally implemented projects on time. The senior UK partner of STM was a long-standing business contact of Gordon Stebbing.

A joint presentation was made to the steering group by Parsons and the STM partner, Rosalie Harker. The various options were discussed. The company had to respond to commercial pressure, so doing nothing was not a real option. Purchasing modular packages was not an immediate option as packages were said not to be available. Writing a system internally was a major task and would use all IT resources for several years, casting a lengthy systems blight over the company. Joint development with Shop-

Card Belgium was not attractive because is would take too long and ShopCard's requirements would be different from Royal Holdings'. This only left purchasing the package currently under development for American Shopper by STM in America. This was strongly supported by STM who, because of their long successful association with Royal Holdings, would be able to offer certain financial discounts.

Since no other option was available the purchase of a total package was the obvious solution. The only doubts at this stage were expressed by Peter Everest, the managing director of Royal Merchant, and these were about the cost of the package. But then Royal Merchant always queried the cost of everything. The others were all in favour, particularly Pippa Wells who had previously been Royal Holdings' IT director. She had no confidence in the current IT department producing anything other than a shambles. She was more than happy for consultants to be involved. So Parsons was given the task of setting up a team to produce a first-phase evaluation of the package within three months.

THE FIRST-PHASE EVALUATION

Parson's first action was to find a project manager. Royal Holdings had a floating group of some dozen project managers who were outside the normal career structure and who simply managed project after project. Each project was, in effect, a short-term contract. If the project targets were met the manager was paid a bonus, and was also likely to get a bigger project next with the consequent possibility of a bigger bonus. If a project did not meet its targets then the project manager could expect the next project to be smaller. If a particular project manager was responsible for too many failures then it was back to a line management role. This was a powerful incentive to most project managers who saw themselves as high-flying agents of change, not boring day-to-day line managers. Project managers were therefore highly motivated and results orientated. The best project manager available at the time was John Barker, a highly experienced manager pleased to have been given what could turn out to be one of the biggest projects ever undertaken in Royal Holdings; certainly a project on which recognition and promotion would be given if successful. Fortunately, another large project had just finished and sufficient experienced project workers were free to join the project team. STM staff were also seconded to the team.

The first indication of likely problems began to surface. Although both Parsons and Barker were strongly motivated to make the evaluation successful, their motivations were different and their personalities clashed. Parsons was convinced there was no alternative to the STM package and that the evaluation should look at the benefits the package offered. Barker was convinced that the way to carry out the evaluation was to define what the business wanted and then see if the package could provide it. Barker refused to accept the terms of reference for the evaluation, which in essence formed his contract. Both Parsons and Barker presented their views to the project team, Parsons instructing the team in the tasks to be carried out, Barker discussing his views and explaining his reasoning. The project team sided with Barker and refused to carry out any work until the terms of reference were agreed. Although Barker was some way below Parsons in grade and salary, this left Parsons in a quandary. He had been instructed to produce an evaluation report yet he could only achieve this on Barker's terms. He was in danger of losing control of the project yet he could not remove Barker, commonly acknowledged to be the best project manager available and appointed by the steering committee.

A rapprochement was needed, quickly. Parsons agreed that Barker should run the project his way, and the terms of reference were amended and agreed. Parsons would be responsible for the final report and progress reports to the steering committee. The deal was done and the evaluation was under way. Tasks were allocated, and users were contacted to determine their requirements and anticipated benefits. The project staff interviewed all directors, heads of department and senior managers to determine how they saw the business and how they wished it to develop in the future. Each interviewee defined how work could be carried out more efficiently in their area and the likely cash- or staff-saving benefits.

These functional requirements were then checked against the already partly written STM system to see if they were there already or whether they could be incorporated into the final package. If they could be, then the associated benefit was claimed for the implementation of the American STM package. If they could not be incorporated, they were listed for development in subsequent phases of the package. The results of this evaluation rather depended upon who interpreted the requirements. Nevertheless, STM put benefits and staff savings into a computer model they had used on previous surveys to calculate financial benefits. All interfacing to the software team in America was carried out by STM, who clarified any of Royal Holdings' functional requirements to the software team and reported back on whether the functionality was already in the system or not. The process was recognized as superficial but the aim was to go as deep as possible within three months.

While investigation and costing of facilities were under way, some members of the project team were busy on other tasks, producing papers on methods, costs of conversion, adherence to main company standards for computing, risk assessment and overall culture change. These papers were widely circulated and discussed in the project team and generally consensus was reached on the views expressed in each paper. But the team began to polarize. The STM members believed the cost case to be overwhelmingly in favour of proceeding. Royal Holdings' staff were beginning to feel that the only plausible conversion scenario was a 'big bang' but that the risks of this approach were so great that there was a real danger of bringing the company down. Although Parsons could and did report progress to the steering committee, the two camps polarized further as the evaluation progressed. The committee was not informed of this. Minutes of the steering committee's report meetings were not circulated to the project team. In fact, the only members of the team to see them were the STM staff who were shown copies by Rosalie Harker.

Barker organized a straw poll of the twenty or so project staff. The Royal Holdings' faction unanimously recommended that the project should not proceed beyond this evaluation stage. The STM group, who now occupied one half of the project office while Royal Holdings' staff occupied the other, demurred from this view. A meeting was held among Parsons, Barker, senior project staff and senior STM staff to try to achieve a consensus view. The meeting was abrupt, entrenched positions were held, discussion was minimal and the meeting ended in acrimony.

It was by now clear to all parties that no compromise would be achieved and lobbying began in earnest. Barker and the rest of the Royal Holdings' staff on the team aired their views with users at every possible opportunity and generally decried the package at all possible occasions. Parsons assured the steering committee that all was well and the recommendation would be clear and effective and made on time.

The one member of the committee to know of the split within the team was Rosalie Harker, who was kept informed by STM project staff. The initial antagonism between Parsons and Barker increased. Parsons believed the best solution for the company was to install the modified American package as soon as possible. Barker believed that the initial question about Royal Holdings' real needs had not yet been asked, let alone answered, and the installation of an undeveloped package with its attendant risk was certainly not the way forward. There was no meeting of minds despite the approaching deadline.

Parsons collected the relevant papers and stayed at home for a week writing the final report. Odd queries were raised with members of the project team but little direct work was required from them. The final evaluation report was hand delivered to members of the steering committee prior to a presentation from Parsons supported by Rosalie Harker. The report recommended adoption of the package and the creation of a team headed by Parsons for its development and implementation. It also showed substantial operational and marketing benefits which outweighed the STM charges of £25 million for the package.

THE FIRST DECISION

The steering committee deliberated for three months. The omens were good; a clear recommendation had been received. The evaluation had been completed on time. Parsons was enthusiastic, as was the STM partner. STM reported that development of the system in America was proceeding on target, and that a couple of minor functions had had to be excluded to meet tight deadlines, but these were insignificant. The latest profit figures indicated further decline in Royal Merchant's profits, and Peter Everest again raised the question of cost as he always did – everyone expected him to. Pippa Wells checked that the requirements of Royal Customer's marketing department were included, and would show significant savings and improved market penetration, permitting the easy introduction of new products. Marketing benefits alone, albeit only assessed at a superficial level, would pay for the new system. The IT director was relieved; here was a sound proposal which would be implemented by the consultants following a steering committee decision.

Gordon Stebbing was pleased; despite cost quibbles from Peter Everest, the package showed a clear profit overall. Both parts of the organization would use the system to pass marketing and other information back and forth, but this would not be a constraint. Benefits to Royal Customer outweighed any possible costs to Royal Merchant, unlikely as these were. It was a pity that he would not see the final implementation through. His tour of duty in this subsidiary would finish in a year or so but he could still set it on the right path.

Soundings were taken with the board of RI and, although £25 million was a substantial sum in hard times, they recognized that something needed to be done. The STM chairman had assured them that none of their competitors had anything as advanced as this package. It would give them a lead of ten years over the competition. Conversely, if they did not take it, it could give their competitors ten years advantage over Royal Holdings. Being cautious, the board agreed to Royal Holdings issuing a letter of commitment to purchase the package subject to a further six-month in-depth evaluation confirming the costs and benefits.

THE SECOND EVALUATION

The steering committee was pleased and a budget of £1.5 million was set aside to pay for STM staff resources on the project team. Even at discounted rates they were somewhat expensive, but quality is always worth paying for. A new project team was set up to review the costs and benefits in more depth. The steering committee had heard from Rosalie Harker that the STM staff thought that Parsons had not been a particularly strong project director and was perhaps not the man to drive this second phase through. He went back into a line management position a disappointed man. A new project director was found. Jill Gilchrist was the obvious candidate, one of the main company's high flyers. Highly rated by everyone, she was one of the senior managers of the future. She was given the task for drawing up terms of reference, appointing a project manager, and producing the results in six months' time.

Jill Gilchrist quickly talked to all the project teams, potential system users and STM. Following this, she asked Barker to remain as project manager for, although she knew Barker disagreed with the report, he had delivered it on time and was regarded by the project team as one of the best project managers within Royal Holdings. Barker declined and, having made his views known about the decision-making process, he left the organization altogether. Several of the senior project members in the first evaluation were also identified by STM (again via Rosalie Harker) as being negative and were excluded from the second phase.

One of the floating project managers, Steve Jepson, was offered the job of managing the second phase. Aware, via the project managers' network, of the history of the previous evaluation project, he determined to decline the offer. However, a promotion stayed his hand and he accepted the job. Promotion for other selected members of the project team ensured a happy start.

The evaluation got under way. The aim was to repeat the work of the first team but at a greater depth: looking at requirements and facilities at a lower level to ensure that requirements would be met in detail and that the claimed benefits were accurate. It was also intended to review the development of the package in more detail and get Royal Holdings' requirements into the system.

Gilchrist and Jepson worked well together, the team was well motivated and the project progressed well. Problems soon became apparent. When users were asked to substantiate the financial benefits they estimated in the first survey, they were in some difficulty, and when they were asked to sign acceptance to the claimed benefits, they tended to provide estimates that were smaller than before. The benefits case began to look thin. Software development in America was still on schedule although STM admitted that some marginal functionality had been deferred into a second phase. The computing requirements for the developed parts of the system were much higher than expected but this was being worked on. STM had confidence that they would be reduced, although they advised that it would be sensible to budget cautiously and to include higher processing costs in the cost-benefit case. The higher development costs should also be included.

Jill Gilchrist's progress reports to the steering committee were beginning to cause concern. They had also become aware that not everyone in the organization believed that this package was the best approach for the future of the business. In particular, the risk of a big-bang implementation was worrying for a lot of line managers.

As the package was assessed in more detail it seemed that costs were continually escalating and functionality continually declining. The longer a decision was delayed the longer the systems-development blight would continue. In fact, all major development had ceased, and it was impossible to produce a positive cost-benefit case for any major changes because the changes could not realize any benefit before being overtaken by the implementation of the package.

Jepson's last progress report had indicated a likely cost of £40 million, a two-year development period with its consequent system blight and the increasingly doubtful nature of the claimed benefits. STM were still optimistic. Pippa Wells was worried about declining benefits; Peter Everest, as usual, was worried about costs. The IT director said that business decline was inevitable because of the lack of previous investment in IT. He remained convinced that STM's package was the way forward and STM had always delivered in the past. Gordon Stebbing commented that they had not always delivered full functionality. He was worried about how he would tell the RI main board that the project cost was now £40 million and nearly double previous estimates. He appeared to be presiding over a directionless, declining organization whose only idea of a way forward was to throw money into an ever-growing black hole.

THE SECOND DECISION

Jill Gilchrist proposed that the evaluation process continue, and she also offered an alternative: to review one of the original options, that of replacing only the core database at this stage, allowing other areas to be dealt with separately. These areas could then be dealt with internally or by purchase of specialized packages already on the market. This would reduce both the immediate cost and allow development in other areas without waiting for a big-bang approach. This proposal was accepted, despite disagreement from the IT director and Rosalie Harker. The final report recommended that a modular approach be adopted with the STM system at its core, for both Royal Customer and Royal Merchant at a cost of around £30 million. This proposal was put to the RI board for sanction to spend the £30 million.

Meanwhile, changes in the economic climate had hit RI and many investment projects had been halted. All projects, including this one, had to be evaluated together with those from other subsidiaries. After six months, investment money for the project was declined by the RI board.

The Royal Holdings' project team was disbanded after 18 months. A £1.5 million payment was made to STM for consultancy. Substantial opportunities had been missed. Royal Holdings' computer system was still inadequate for their needs. The package project was terminated. No competitor expressed any interest in adopting it. Its original development in America continued but operational performance was poor, system functions were limited and American Shopper, for whom it was originally developed, went into the American equivalent of receivership. Jill Gilchrist went to a directorship in another RI subsidiary. Jepson remains as a floating project manager.

The system finally adopted is a redevelopment of the original core system by internal staff and Royal Holdings' purchase modular packages to carry out various processing tasks as needed. Each package is chosen on its own merits and its own cost-benefit case. The system suffers more or less permanent low-level system blight.

Gordon Stebbing reflected on the whole débâcle. He decided to set up a project to review Royal Holdings' decision-making process. A project director and a project manager were appointed. They started to discuss the draft terms of reference. There were some disagreements to sort out.

CHAPTER 4

IDAF: The International Defence and Aid Fund

COMPILED BY JOHN N. T. MARTIN

The question 'What is an organization?' is not easy to answer but looking at a very unusual organization may help in understanding of more 'normal' ones. IDAF must be one of the most unusual organizations ever devised. It was a charitable organization, run by people of goodwill and yet it adopted the methods of a secret-service organization. It was highly organized and very effective and yet it lacked most of the characteristics associated with an organization. There was little information flow, almost nobody knew who their colleagues were or who directed their activities. There was no reward, status or sense of belonging from the organization itself – its network of helpers had only their own sense of 'doing something' to motivate them. Organizational arrangements are generally a reflection of the environment the organization has to operate in. A need for secrecy and protection against infiltration creates one kind of organization. A need for visible public accountability would create another.

IDAF was an organization set up by Canon John Collins, of St Paul's Cathedral in London, to provide financial aid to South African anti-apartheid activists. It started off in the 1950s as a public charity with a pacifist orientation, providing financial support for families and dependants of South African activists, where the bread-winner had been imprisoned or executed for anti-apartheid activities, leaving the families with no source of income. In 1956, when South Africa launched the first of its treason trials, this goal was extended to the payment of legal fees so that activists brought to trial had a proper defence. That in turn led to a general commitment to keeping the conscience of the world community alive to what was happening in South Africa. In 1965 it went international, with branches in the UK, New Zealand, Scandinavia, Holland and India. In 1966, IDAF was banned in South Africa under its Suppression of Communism Act, remaining as such until unbanned in 1990. Collins himself died in 1983, but IDAF continued under Archbishop Trevor Huddleston. It was wound up in 1993 with the ending of apartheid. The first multiracial elections in South Africa took place in May 1994.

Though IDAF had started out as a conventional charity, its banning in 1966 had the implication that anyone in South Africa found to be receiving money from it could be brought to trial, risking very long prison sentences or even death. IDAF responded by moving its money distribution system 'underground'. Some of its funds came from private donors but most came from national contributions: some 15 countries contributed via the United Nations and another 10–15 contributed directly. Sweden, Norway and Holland contributed most and even India contributed regularly; very little came from the UK or the USA. The scale of its support was staggering, with nearly £100 million distributed over the 40 years of its existence, with up to £10 million a year during the peak of its activity. For instance, IDAF supported 16,551 legal matters between 1985 and 1991. In some years, IDAF legal support was more than twice the amount South Africa paid in legal aid for criminal cases, and affected 20–30,000 South Africans in a year. Many rural law firms became heavily dependent on IDAF income, and though very few realized where the money came from, it had more than 150 attorneys and 80 advocates on its books. IDAF became such a major factor in the South African legal arena that it was able to impose fixed scales of pay for lawyers working on its cases, and to audit accounts and get overcharging scaled down so that misappropriation of funds seems to have been minimal. On the welfare side, some 45,000 people have benefited over the years, with hundreds of thousands of payments being made to individuals, and even whole communities, support often being sustained over decades from families of those who had been killed or given long prison sentences. BOSS, the South African security services, are reported to have regarded it as one of the very few external organizations of its type that had a significant impact on South Africa's internal affairs and it was one of the very few anti-apartheid organizations that BOSS was unable to infiltrate even though it was fully aware of its existence, had a fairly good idea of the scale of support being given and understood the basic principles of the way it worked, since BOSS itself and other secret services used much the same principles to conceal their own money flows.

At the London end, IDAF had a public and visible existence. It had a headquarters building, Canon Collins House, in Islington; public fund-raising activities; liaison activities with other anti-apartheid organizations and programmes to maintain public awareness about South Africa; and figures such as Canon Collins himself, who were very much in the public eye on various fronts (he was also very active in the Campaign for Nuclear Disarmament).

At the South African end, the payments themselves also had to be, in principle, 'public'. Most were simply sent through the post (which was surprisingly immune from theft and interception), and they had to appear to be legal and above-board such that, if the recipients were challenged, they could answer with complete honesty that they were not aware of any connection with IDAF. Lawyers called on to defend activists would often take on the case only if there were a guarantee that the funding did not come from IDAF since, otherwise, both they and the case would have been at serious risk.

It was the link between these two public modes that had to be covert. There were three major components of this. First, Collins set up a series of trusts headed by well-known establishment figures, including Lord Snow and Lord Campbell of Eskan, two Labour peers, a couple of well-known authors and a senior academic. In legal terms, the trusts were completely independent charitable funds, with titles such as 'Freedom from Fear International Charitable Foundation' set up with all the correct legal formalities, with no visible connection to IDAF and with wealthy sponsors who were prepared to claim that they provided the money and to deny any IDAF links if challenged (as once or twice they were). Since these trusts were not banned organizations, payments from them to people in South Africa were legal.

Secondly, there was a complex and indirect route for getting money to pay South African trial lawyers. For instance, an attorney in a remote part of the country who needed defence funds might hear through the grapevine that there was another lawyer in one of the big Cape Town law firms who had access to sources of funds. This lawyer would in turn contact a UK law firm that he or she was in touch with; there were in fact several UK firms with contacts in South Africa of this sort (and originally firms in half a dozen other countries as well) and money would be sent, apparently from one of the trusts described above. Alternatively, one of these law firms would write to a South African law firm who were mounting a defence, saying: 'We have read in the newspapers about the trial and have been asked by a British client to offer financial support.' Pretoria would not have seen any connection between these apparently unconnected donations from very different sources and these law firms, and the trusts they apparently had access to in fact became quite famous in South African revolutionary trials. However, all these apparently unconnected law firms outside South Africa were coordinated by one particular London firm, but agreed to treat their link to it as highly confidential, believing that the reason for sensitivity was that the London firm also acted for the major South African firm, Consolidated Goldfields, and didn't wish its role in the trust disbursements to cause Consolidated Goldfields any embarrassment. The London firm kept its own connections with IDAF and Canon Collins an even more closely guarded secret and, within IDAF, only Collins and the IDAF general secretary, Phyllis Altman, knew of the connection with the London firm. Communications between IDAF and the main law firm, and between the main law firm and the others, used all the spy-story paraphernalia of go-betweens, coded messages, secret meetings and so on. Money received for IDAF (e.g. from Sweden) was handled by the main law firm who concealed it by feeding it into the trust accounts via a Swiss bank account and other intermediaries.

The third major element, used for welfare payments to families, involved a team of some 600 letter-writers in several European countries. Letter-writers had no connection with IDAF or with South Africa and so were above suspicion. Each would keep contact with perhaps a dozen families and would keep this activity secret. They would introduce themselves to the family simply as a concerned person who had heard of the family's plight and whose friends would like to help by sending money periodically. There was a fixed scale of payments – £140 every two months per family plus a scale of extra payments for various eventualities. Every two months each letter-writer would receive a registered envelope of money from a

'Rev. Williams' (or similar) for conversion into postal orders and distribution, with directions about what to say to each family; most of these letter-writers had no idea that the money had come from IDAF. It was quite difficult for BOSS to intercept mail from the South African post because of the legal framework surrounding it, so most did in fact get through; but even if it were intercepted, there would be nothing in the letters to suggest anything other than a compassionate friend sending money, and close personal friendships often built up over the many exchanges of letters. Latterly, the registered envelopes were replaced by transfers to Barclays Bank, with which the letter-writers opened an account – a problem for some because at the time Barclays was much disliked by anti-apartheid activists because of its extensive South African connections – which was, of course, precisely why it was a suitable bank for IDAF to use.

The recipients would reply to their letter-writer confirming that the money had arrived and sometimes indicating if they had any special needs. This created the next hazard for IDAF, because it needed to see these replies to check that the money had got through and to adjust grants to meet special requirements. But if the letters had been forwarded direct to IDAF, BOSS would soon have been able to trace the links back from the letter-writers to IDAF. Therefore all letters were in fact forwarded to various neutral 'dead-letter' addresses which were changed periodically, and from which they were collected at irregular intervals by a variety of inconspicuous IDAF workers.

Within IDAF headquarters, the covert activities were restricted to the top floor of the building, and people involved in the ordinary public activities in the lower floors had no idea what was going on. 'Programme 1' (the legal support side) had a staff of six and 'Programme 2' had a staff of ten. They operated in total secrecy. For instance, the husband of one of these (who would himself have been utterly reliable) believed that his wife simply had a job as a filing clerk. The stress of having to deal with so many harrowing letters with no chance of talking about them was considerable.

The need for top security was very real, not just to protect the recipients but also to protect the operation itself. For instance, one BOSS undercover agent successfully worked himself into the position of liaison officer in one of the other major anti-apartheid organizations and successfully wrecked it by leaking information back to South Africa. He had contact with IDAF in his liaison role and tried to trick key IDAF staff into giving away key information. However, due to tip-offs and the integrity, astuteness and care of the staff involved, security was never breached, though this itself caused other problems, as when staff who wanted information about IDAF activities to support the publicizing and fund-raising campaigns on which IDAF depended found themselves unable to get it!

When IDAF was unbanned and it was possible to reveal the common source of all these funds, even those like Nelson Mandela who knew something of (and had benefited from) IDAF's activities are said to have been amazed at the scale of its operation. One Cape Town lawyer is quoted as saying: 'Nobody knew where the money came from. Nobody got the kudos. This was the key to its success.'

CHAPTER 5

Changes at Guy's Hospital

COMPILED BY L. A. WALSH

The late 1980s saw the start of major changes for the hospitals of the National Health Service. This case study charts the changes this period brought to Guy's Hospital, one of London's major health-care providers and a provider of specialist services to patients from outside the capital. Its purpose is not that the reader should understand the politics of health care, even less to form a judgement about the pros and cons of 'opting out'. Its purpose is to reflect the effects that the rapidly changing external environment had on the hospital, and the responses the hospital made.

CHRONOLOGY

This section has been prepared to give an outline of the main sequence of events covered by this case study.

During the 1980s, hospitals were forced to become cost-conscious and this led Guy's to its 1985 'Revolution' (*The Independent*, 2 February 1988; *Guardian*, 17 May 1989). By the late 1980s, Guy's was in buoyant mood and looked a likely candidate for 'opting out' of local health-authority control when the opportunity came. Opting out was politically controversial both among staff and the local community (*Daily Mail*, 5 May 1989; *Guardian*, 8 February 1989; *Guardian*, 17 May 1989). Meanwhile, Guy's was about to embark on the 'Phase 3' building programme (Philip Harris House).

In 1989, consultants were balloted on their attitude to opting out. Staff morale was not good (*Guardian*, 19 March 1989). The consultants opposed opting out and the recently appointed chief executive quit (*The Times*, 27 June 1989). In early 1990, several more ballots were organized (*The Daily Telegraph*, 9 February 1990; *Guardian*, 24 March 1990). Later that year, the Secretary of State announced that 56 hospitals, including Guy's, would be 'opting out' in April 1991. Within a month of opting out, and with Peter Griffiths back in charge, measures were taken to cut the hospital's budget deficit (*Guardian*, 26 April 1991; *The Daily Telegraph*, 22 June 1991). By late 1991, the budget was back on target and pay increases for staff were planned.

In 1992, the Tomlinson Inquiry was examining the future provision of health care in London (*The Times*, 28 July 1992). Guy's financial problems seemed to be solved (*Guardian*, 21 October 1992) and its high media profile suggested its future was secure. Tomlinson recommended a merger with St Thomas' Hospital and Peter Griffiths lost his job in favour of his opposite number at St Thomas' (*Guardian*, 2 March 1993). In February 1994, the Secretary of State announced that clinical services would be concentrated at St Thomas' (*Guardian*, 11 February 1994).

Doctors making ends meet

Nicholas Timmins on the success story at Guy's hospital

'WHEN I came to Guy's five years ago I couldn't believe it,' says Elaine Murphy, Professor of Psychogeriatrics at the London teaching hospital. 'It was anarchy. Consultants were sounding off to the newspapers, there was internecine warfare between one group of consultants and another, and an absolute slanging match between doctors and administrators. It was like walking into the middle of a war.

'There was a sense of hopelessness, that the place was going down and no one could do anything about it. A lot of that has changed. There is now a sense of purpose.'

What has changed at Guy's in numerical terms is awesome. Since 1983, the unit which includes Guy's Hospital has closed 28 per cent of its beds. It has cut its expenditure by 15 per cent, and its staff by 17 per cent. Yet, on the figures the hospital produces it may, just may, treat more patients this year than its previous record in 1982.

It has been done, at least in part, by getting doctors to take a central role in running the hospital. And whatever else comes out of the Government's NHS review, a key part of the package will require doctors and nurses to take more responsibility for the resources they use – a bigger role, if you like, in managing the health service.

What hit Guy's in the early to mid-1980s was the same downward spiral that affected every London teaching hospital. Money was pulled out of London to develop services elsewhere. In 1983 planned spending on the NHS was cut by 1 per cent, and the inexorable process of the Government underfunding pay awards and demanding efficiency savings had started.

The result at Guy's was mayhem. Cyril Chantler, Professor of Paediatric Nephrology, says: 'Every year we overspent. We'd discover that in June, pass July and August thinking about cuts, and September and October introducing them – usually by emergency ward closures which is a hopeless way of cutting spending. In 1984 we closed over 100 beds and in the next two months treated more patients than in the same period the year before. We thus had the dubious distinction of being the first London hospital to spend more by closing beds. It just couldn't go on.'

What the Guy's consultants did was agree to take responsibility themselves. In place of the old management system, 14 'clinical directorates', mini-hospitals within the hospital, were set up. Each consists of a consultant – one each for medicine, surgery, radiology, paediatrics, etc. – backed by a nurse and a business manager who run each directorate as a triumvirate.

The directorates are given a budget and report to a board which monitors how the hospital is doing month by month. Within their budgets, the doctors and nurses have considerable freedom to do what they like – so long as they stay within it.

While the hospital debated the idea in 1984, the financial situation went from bad to worse. In early 1985, Guy's yet again hit the headlines. Alan Yates, the hospital's cardio-thoracic surgeon, faced with patients literally dying on the waiting list, was told he would have to stop operating for six weeks because the money had run out. 'They told me I'd overspent my budget,' he says. 'But they couldn't actually tell me what my budget was. It was crazy.'

In April 1985, when the new management board took over, the hospital had a debt of £1.2m that threatened to reach £5m by the year's end.

Staff account for 70 per cent of NHS

(continued over)

spending. Guy's bit the bullet and cut – 10 per cent of staff, including doctors, went. New Cross Hospital, the other part of the Guy's unit, was closed. Nurses were given their own budgets. Records and other staff were decentralised to the directorates, which, wherever they could, started earning money by charging other NHS districts for specialised services. And the doctors began to look at just how they spent the cash.

As the savings were made, the doctors decided where to put them.

Alan Yates, director for the heart unit, says on balance the changes have been good: 'It's made us look at what we spend.' There is a plastic skin surgeons use to place over the chest incision. 'It costs £15 a time. When you are doing 750 patients a year, that's quite a lot of money. Before I had no idea what it cost, and if an administrator had told me to stop using it I'd have told him to get lost; what did he know about it? But having our own budget, we looked into it and found it doesn't in fact do anything to reduce wound infections. So we stopped using it. That's a fairly typical example, but only doctors can take those decisions.'

Guy's had some particular incentives to make the change. It was told bluntly that it would not get a new £30m ward block unless it got its spending under control. It had more peripheral units to close than the neighbouring St Thomas's district, which is currently £2.8m in debt with 137 beds shut and is going through the sort of fire Guy's experienced three years ago. Last week it too decided to introduce clinical directors.

From The Independent, *2 November 1988*

Hospital may opt out

By JENNY HOPE and JOHN DEANS

A premier teaching hospital is considering 'opting out' of National Health Service control, it was revealed yesterday.

Guy's Hospital in Southwark, South London, could be the first in the country to take the controversial step – which is expected to be made possible by the Government's long-awaited NHS review.

The review is to be published later this month, but some of the contents leaked out yesterday.

The boldest proposal is for hospitals to be allowed to 'opt out' of NHS bureaucracy and to become self-governing institutions while still remaining within the NHS as far as care of patients is concerned.

Under the personal direction of Mrs Thatcher, the review appears to favour changes that will increase efficiency and consumer choice and provide ways of raising extra cash for the NHS. It is also set to recommend the axing of local councillors from regional health authorities to reduce the possibility of political interference.

One way the 'opt out' system would work is for the Department of Health to provide 'core funding' in return for contracted services.

Eventually the hospital would pay its own way by selling services both to its local health authority and to private hospitals and patients. Guy's is an ideal candidate for 'opting out' as it has demonstrated already that it can run its own affairs, following an internal management shake-up over the last five years.

In place of the old management system, 14 'mini-hospitals' dealing with particular specialties were set up.

Each has its own budget, and doctors and nurses have considerable freedom provided they stay within it. The 'mini-hospitals' report monthly to a monitoring board.

Guy's provides highly specialised services to patients from all over Britain – about one in two are believed to come from outside the local health district – and there has also been growing concern that funding for the hospital does not take this into account.

Professor Elaine Murphy, district general manager for Lewisham and North Southwark health authority, which covers Guy's, confirmed that consultants and senior officers at the hospital had discussed the 'exciting possibilities' of the latest plan.

'But the hospital would remain within the NHS,' she said. 'It would not be going private and there are considerable problems that would have to be overcome.'

Senior Whitehall officials stressed yesterday that Mrs Thatcher's NHS blueprint was still in draft form and was 'subject to change'.

Experiments within the NHS will explore the potential for hospitals and health authorities to sell each other services.

The blueprint includes a scheme to enable family doctors to buy services from NHS hospitals, and a decision has to be taken on whether to give new tax incentives to pensioners to take out private health insurance.

The chairman of the National Association of Health Authorities, Mr Martyn Long, said the NHS would benefit from reform while remaining free at the point of delivery and being funded mainly from taxation.

But Labour's spokesman, Mr Robin Cook, claimed hospitals would be motivated by profit and not the needs of patients in their areas.

From the Daily Mail, *5 January 1989*

More choice means little voice for patients

I WAS interested to see that Prof Ian McColl has told the Centre for Policy Studies that his plan to opt Guy's Hospital out of Health Authority control would not be to the detriment of local people (February 3).

It seems to this Community Health Council that the people of Bermondsey are the best judges of what is good for them. We have therefore written to the Management Board at Guy's asking for a guarantee that any such proposals will be subject to the agreement of local people.

The fact is that most of the ballyhoo about Guy's opting out is the product of Prof McColl and a tiny group of like-minded consultants.

In their anxiety to present this scheme as a foregone conclusion they seem to have failed to consult even the majority of their medical and nursing colleagues, let alone the people whom they are supposed to serve.

As discussions on this scheme proceed it will be interesting to see if it really commands support.

Those who have accepted Prof McColl's repeated claims to speak for Guy's Hospital as a whole may be in for a shock.

Norman Lazenby.
Chairman,
Lewisham and North Southwark Community Health Council,
13 Catford Broadway,
London, SE6.

From the Guardian, *8 February 1989*

GUY'S Hospital has been called 'the noblest institution in London founded by one man.' The man in question was a 17th century publishing tycoon who made a fortune selling Bibles, tripled it by speculating on the South Sea Bubble, and left his money to found a hospital which became one of the most famous medical centres in the world.

That original conjunction of commerce and care seems relevant enough at a time when Guy's is at the centre of the row over the role of market forces in the British health service. But the arguments at Guy's have been less about the detailed issues raised by the White Paper than about what some consultants see as an attempt by the Government to 'capture' the hospital as a totem in its campaign to convince the profession and the public of the wisdom of the changes it wants to introduce.

To understand the background to the upheaval at Guy's you have to go back to 1985. Throughout the early eighties the hospital had lurched from crisis to crisis as doctors, responding to the growing demand for the hospital's services, overspent their budgets. Administrators then had to step in to cut spending and close wards, producing an insane medical stop-go process.

Guy's needed a saviour, and it found one in the person of Cyril Chantler, professor of pediatric nephrology and a vigorous critic of the old system. He presided over a revolution. The model was the Johns Hopkins hospital in Baltimore, with which Guy's had ties and where many consultants had worked on exchanges. Chantler persuaded Peter Griffiths, the NHS district manager, to back a version of the Baltimore model and the two men won the approval of the ministry. Chantler became chairman of a management board consisting of himself, and 14 (later 15) directors of specialties, together with senior administrators, accountants, and nurses. The directorates were management units consisting of a doctor assisted by an administrator and a nurse.

Whatever else it was, the 1985 revolution amounted to a decisive recapture of power by the doctors, who now assumed unquestioned command both in the departments and in the hospital as a whole. And the Chantler system worked. It ended the dichotomy between cost-conscious administrators who rarely visited a ward or a clinic and care-conscious doctors who as a matter of principle ignored such mundane considerations as staff levels or the price of drugs. Now that doctors were in charge cuts and changes that would have been unthinkable under lay administrators alone went through, and Guy's became a much more efficient hospital in a very short time. Between 1984 and 1988, expenditure was cut by 15 per cent, staff by 17 per cent, and beds by 28 per cent, but the number of patients treated increased and the waiting lists went down by 38 per cent.

This was not done democratically: Chantler refused to accept elected

(continued over)

directors, and the new board was also untrammelled by governors or trustees. 'It was autocratic government,' says Michael Laurence a consultant orthopaedic surgeon 'but it was popular because it was achieving things that everybody wanted.'

Chantler had given himself three years to re-structure the hospital. In April 1988 he handed over as chairman to Dr Hugh Saxton, a radiologist and an able medical manager, but a man without Chantler's charm or persuasive powers. A month before this, Margaret Thatcher had held a meeting at Chequers with her confidential medical advisers, including Ian McColl, director of surgery at Guy's, to discuss the ideas that were to lead to the White Paper on the future of the Health Service. Even Ian McColl's friends describe him as wilful and verging on the arrogant. As one said: 'He sees himself as a knight on a white charger, with the task of bringing home the grail for Margaret Thatcher.'

By the time the White Paper came out, the general impression of board members was that Dr Saxton had become a definite advocate of independent status, and that he believed that the way to get the best deal for Guy's in the new system was to give the government what it wanted. An early application for self government, without too many nit-picking reservations, would bring rewards. Foot dragging, it was implied, could bring the opposite.

This brings us to the question of 'Phase Three', the £90 million new building programme upon which the hospital is due to embark soon. The opponents of the White Paper at Guy's are convinced that the Government has indicated that the hospital could lose the funding for the programme if it does not come through on independent status. There is evidence that they are right. In the minutes of the management board meeting for April – the very meeting at which the decision on independence was taken – the following phrase occurs: 'Dr Saxton (said) . . . if we said No to self governing there might be trouble over Phase Three.'

Early in the year, press reports which his critics say mainly emanated from Ian McColl suggested that Guy's was already itching to 'opt out'.

Professor Harry Keen, director of general medicine, says: 'I believe Ian McColl offered Guy's in those meetings as the lead hospital for the self-governing scheme and then came back and talked to Cyril Chantler and Hugh Saxton. I'm not sure how committed those two were at that early stage, but what was really extraordinary was that a single consultant was playing this kind of role.'

It seems clear, in any case, that by sometime last summer it had been decided that Guy's was a perfect choice to spearhead the Government reforms.

Consultants outside the management board were [. . .] amazed and angry. As one said: 'It began to look as if the hospital was to be committed to a course of action on which nobody had been

(continued over)

consulted.' This impression was massively reinforced when it was soon afterward learned that Peter Griffiths, then head of the Regional Health Authority for the South-East – and the hospital's old friend from 1985 – had been asked to be the chief executive of Guy's in the run-up to independence. He had already been asked to be the Department of Health's man looking into applications for independent status. The money to pay Griffiths for the Guy's part of his job was to be supplied by Sir Philip Harris, the carpet magnate, a generous benefactor of the hospital, and, it was immediately rumoured, the man most likely to be the chairman of the Trust that would oversee an independent Guy's.

From the Guardian, *17 May 1989*

I WAS DELIGHTED to read Martin Woollacott's article regarding the possible future independent status of Guy's Hospital (Guardian Tomorrows, May 17). As an employee of the hospital, I have been taking a keen interest in the recent developments and the autocratic attitude of two consultants who, as you so rightly say, seem to have made the momentous decision to 'opt out' with minimal and occasionally no consultation.

The atmosphere amongst those staff who oppose the notion is one of despair that is beginning to lead to apathy with the fear of the inevitability of 'opting out'. It is, perhaps, due to this apathy that little more than half of the consultants voted on May 9. Obviously a truer representation of the opinions would have resulted from a 'three-line whip' vote but those in favour of the plan may have been happier with a poor turn-out so as to avoid majority rejection. It should not be forgotten, however, that two thirds of those who did vote opposed premature consideration of independent status.

That the Government could even hint at bribery regarding the construction of Phase III is alarming, though not in the least surprising.

I am continually amazed at the apparent shortsightedness of the general public who are either diffident or ignorant that the implementation of the White Paper would bring us one step nearer an American-type health 'care' structure and further away from providing a National Health Service with equal care for all. Most employees of the NHS are now aware that we need to impose tighter budgetary controls but that it is impossible to equate cost with health care. It would seem resource management is the way to successfully tighten budgetary control and many more hospitals are soon to commence resource management.

In 1977 the Government set up a group to look at the budgetary control of the health service. Its report, entitled Inequalities In Health – The Black Report, said that a positive health strategy depends on political and economic priorities. The choice of these priorities is partly a question of arguing that health deserves to have a higher place in the claims that can be made on the nation's resources. This is what was decided by Aneurin Bevan and the then Labour Government. If our present Government had been open in its intention to fragment and erode the NHS, it is possible that it would not have been celebrating a decade in power.

The newspaper shop had sold out of the Guardian by 9.30 on the morning of the article and the grounds were buzzing – with some of us jumping for joy.

Name withheld.
Guy's Hospital,
St. Thomas Street,
London SE1.

From the Guardian, *19 May 1989*

Setback for NHS reform as Guy's man quits

The Government received a serious setback over its National Health Service reforms yesterday when a senior manager withdrew from his pioneering role of steering Guy's hospital to self-governing status.

Mr Peter Griffiths, general manager of South East Thames region, was appointed earlier this year to spearhead the development of self-governing hospitals nationally at the Department of Health. The £70,000 post, funded by Sir Philip Harris, of the Queensway furnishing business, was to be combined with that of being shadow chief executive of Guy's Hospital, south London, as it moved to become self-governing.

Yesterday, however, Mr Griffiths told Lewisham and North Southwark Health Authority that he had decided to withdraw from his post at Guy's.

Many consultants at Guy's have made clear they are opposed to the idea of self-governing status and resented Mr Griffiths' appointment. It is understood that he decided not to press on with preparing the hospital to become self-governing mainly because of the medical profession's hostility.

Mr Griffiths' move pre-empted a decision to be taken by the health authority last night on whether he should be allowed to work with the hospital. The vote was widely expected to go against the idea. He said that in the light of the number of expressions of interest in self-governing status submitted to the Government, he would have to work full-time in his national role for the foreseeable future.

'I will be concentrating on my national commitments, so I will not spend more time supporting Guy's than any other self-governing trust.'

Consultants described Mr Griffiths' announcement as a victory for those opposed to self-governance and a serious setback for the Government.

From The Times, *27 June 1989*

Guy's staff poll rejects hospital independence

STAFF at Guy's Hospital in London, regarded by the Government as the leading contender for becoming a self-governing trust, have voted 9–1 against any change of status, it was announced yesterday. But in the ballot of all 3,000 workers from consultants to cleaners, only 33 per cent bothered to vote.

The ballot was conducted by the staff, with advice from the Electoral Reform Society, after the hospital management refused to cooperate in organising a poll.

Although the hospital has formally applied to become self-governing, a spokesman said no decision had been made on whether to go ahead, and the result of the ballot would be influential in determining the outcome.

'We are awaiting the result of the Judicial Review and that will have a strong bearing on our decisions,' he added.

In the action for Judicial Review in the High Court last week, consultants led by Prof Harry Keen, Guy's director of medicine, sought a declaration that the Government had acted illegally in allotting funds to prepare for self-governing status in advance of legislation.

Judgment was reserved by Lord Justice Woolf and Mr Justice Pill and a decision is expected soon.

Guy's has always been the flagship hospital for self-governing status, being the most prestigious of the six hospitals first chosen by the Department of Health to implement resource management, an essential pre-requisite for becoming self-governing.

The ballot result is a blow to the hopes of Mr Clarke, Health Secretary, to see the speedy introduction of self-governing status in leading hospitals.

Although he has always ruled out staff ballots as a way of deciding the future of any hospital, he has said that they would not become self-governing against the wishes of their consultants.

From The Daily Telegraph, *9 February 1990*

Opt-out questions anger Guy's staff

MANAGERS at Guy's hospital in London were last night accused of issuing staff a heavily-loaded questionnaire on whether the hospital should opt out of health authority control.

One of the 10 questions asks staff, in effect, if they would like to be paid more. Another asks if doctors and nurses should have more influence on policy.

Scott Bowman, who chairs the Hands off Guys! group campaigning against opting-out, said: 'It's so biased and bent that I can't believe they think anyone is going to take it seriously.'

Guy's has always been regarded as the flagship of the fleet of self-governing trust hospitals planned by the Government, despite opposition from many staff.

Last month, a ballot organised by Mr Bowman's group produced a majority of 90.8 per cent against opting-out on a turnout of about 33 per cent. A local health authority ballot starts next week.

Staff yesterday received two brochures from the management, one entitled Getting the Facts Straight, with the questionnaire.

Answers to the 10 questions score one point if they favour opting-out and two if they favour management not by the health authority but by a 'commissioning authority'. Staff are told that a score of 13 or less means 'you will probably prefer to work for an NHS trust'.

Question 1 says: 'If the changes go through, Guy's can either be run by a commissioning authority or control our own affairs. Which would you prefer?'

Question 2 is: 'We would have no choice in the people appointed to the commissioning authority, but we could suggest members of the trust. Which gives you the greater say?'

Three of the remaining questions deal with pay. One says: 'An NHS trust will be able to pay more than national rates to keep staff and our trust will not pay less than (national) rates. Would you like to be able to negotiate for more pay?'

Mr Bowman said it would be almost impossible for any rational person to score more than 13. He contrasted the questions with what he described as the impartiality of his group's ballot, which asked if staff were in favour of Guy's 'seeking to become a self-governing trust'.

Dr Hugh Saxton, chairman of the Guy's management board, said the questionnaire was intended to make staff think about the issues.

'If people want to send their forms in, once they have completed them, it would be interesting for us to see what their views are. It is not an official ballot.'

From the Guardian, *24 March 1990*

Guy's budget under the knife

GUY'S hospital trust yesterday announced cuts of £12.8 million as it became the first of the opted-out hospitals to take drastic measures to try to guarantee its survival in the National Health Service market-place.

The trust, which includes the renowned Guy's hospital and Lewisham district hospital in south London, is to cut 10 per cent of its budget and drop entire clinical specialisms at Guy's where it feels it lacks a market advantage.

About 800 jobs are likely to go, including those of doctors whose specialisms will not be retained.

Peter Griffiths, the trust's chief executive, said: 'The days are gone of it being just the porters and the cleaners who are the first and only people to go.'

Guy's has been regarded as the flagship of the first 57 self-governing trusts, which came into operation this month. However, it has debts of £6.8 million and wants to find £6 million to reinvest in services it regards as strengths and to improve staff pay above NHS levels.

What is behind the Guy's move is the prospect of a fight to the death among the London teaching hospitals. Overcapacity will be exposed from next April, when initial restrictions on the market workings of the new-style NHS will be relaxed.

The assumption of health planners is that authorities outside London will withdraw contracts from costly teaching hospitals and refer patients instead to cheaper local general units.

Mr Griffiths, until recently deputy chief executive of the NHS, said that shrinkage of the service in London was inevitable, and it was vital to prepare Guy's so it would not be driven to the wall.

From the Guardian, *26 April 1991*

People who look glum may lose their jobs

HOSPITAL staff who look glum have been told they may be at risk of losing their jobs under guidelines drawn up by managers at Guy's Hospital, London.

'Always looking in a bad mood' is one of several criteria by which managers will judge staff when considering redundancies in a cost-cutting exercise.

Trade union leaders at Guy's rejected the criteria at a meeting with management last Wednesday, claiming: 'It would be funny if it wasn't so sad.' One member of staff said: 'We deal with death and despair on a daily basis and we're supposed to look happy or get the sack. How absurd.' The personnel department at Guy's and Lewisham Hospital Trust proposed that staff should be rated in three categories when redundancies are considered – good, standard and poor.

Under a section on appearance, staff will be rated as poor if they are 'messy, grubby and always look in a bad mood'. Other criteria likely to land staff in the 'poor' category are 'does their work as though there is no customer who will benefit', 'acts as though the organisation exists for their own benefit', and 'upsets everyone with their manner'.

Criteria by which staff are judged to be good include 'smiling at customers', 'welcoming attitude to all', 'can be counted on to get the job done', and 'always works to provide a service for customers'. Mr Andy Young, joint union secretary for Guy's and Lewisham hospitals, said: 'If the criteria about upsetting people was applied to managers, we'll be minus a few of them.'

The threat of redundancy, however, applies only to porters, cleaners and other manual workers. Mr Young added: 'These criteria could easily be used to get rid of trade union representatives who take issue with managers and are not able to go round beaming all the time. The whole thing is totally subjective and very dangerous for people who are perfectly good at their job, but are not in favour with the bosses.'

Mr Roger Harris, Guy's associate general manager, said: 'These are draft proposals under discussion with the trade unions.'

Guy's and Lewisham Hospital Trust is shedding 400 jobs to overcome a budgetary deficit. More than 300 jobs will be lost through non-replacement, but up to 100 are expected to go through compulsory redundancy.

From The Daily Telegraph, *22 June 1991*

Guy's expects to balance budget

By Alan Pike

GUY'S HOSPITAL in London, the most controversial of the government's self-governing trusts, yesterday announced that it expected to balance its books and increase staff pay above nationally agreed levels.

Sir Philip Harris, trust chairman, and Mr Peter Griffiths, chief executive, said that a £7m overspend predicted early in the financial year had been almost eliminated. They now say that the trust will end the year within its budget.

The government's policy of allowing NHS hospitals to become self-governing trusts came under fierce fire in April when Guy's announced job cuts to prevent overspending.

Sir Philip said the trust management had taken tough decisions at the beginning of the financial year to bring costs down and, as a result, had no plans for cost-cutting ward closures this winter.

Mr Griffiths said yesterday that the changed position had largely been achieved by improved productivity. The number of patients treated had increased by 10 per cent. At the same time unit costs had been reduced by between 6 per cent and 8 per cent, £5m had been cut from labour costs, and more use was being made of cost-effective day surgery techniques.

The trust management plans to reward its lower-paid staff with £6-a-week pay supplements above the nationally agreed Whitley levels. About 20 per cent of staff will benefit from the increase which will be introduced in January. They will also receive £30 Christmas bonuses.

The £7m deficit at Guy's caused concern in the Department of Health, but Sir Philip denied that the trust had received extra funds from the government to help it balance its books. It does, however, expect to raise £2m from a building sale and lease-back arrangement.

From The Financial Times, *14 November 1991*

St Thomas's Closure Recommended in Leaked Report

ST THOMAS'S teaching hospital in London came a step nearer to closure yesterday as a leaked report recommended a critical review of the services that it provides.

The South East Thames Health Authority submission to the government enquiry into London's health care considers the split of services between St Thomas's and Guy's hospitals and recommends one of the two should cease activities. It is widely interpreted as signalling the closure of the politically more vulnerable St Thomas's.

Geoff Martin, director of the pressure group London Health Emergency, said that the report's message was unequivocal. 'You can rule out Guy's. Basically they are saying St Thomas's will close. This is probably its death warrant.'

The health authority said this was only one interpretation of the report, which will be submitted next week to Sir Bernard Tomlinson, who is leading the enquiry. 'It will be for Sir Bernard to make recommendations to the health secretary, Virginia Bottomley, and then for her to consider what he says.'

A health department spokesman said that any claims that the hospital would close were pointless speculation. He added: 'What counts is what Sir Bernard's report says on London as a whole and what decisions ministers take.'

From The Times, *28 July 1992*

Guy's goes into profit

After a year of controversies as diverse as redundancies, baby deaths and stripograms, Britain's biggest, most complex and certainly most colourful NHS trust this week reported a profit [. . .].

To the undoubted relief of Government ministers, the Guy's and Lewisham trust in south London said it had overcome the financial problems that dogged it at the start of its first year of self-government and had turned in an £87,000 surplus.

With the NHS ever more businesslike, the first annual results of the Guy's trust were those most eagerly awaited by the health market and market-watchers. As the flagship of the first wave of trusts which started trading in April last year, it had often seemed in danger of going down with all hands. For a while, it even looked like taking others with it.

Only four weeks after opting out, Guy's announced £6.8 million cuts and hundreds of job losses in a disastrously timed move thought to have cost the Conservatives dear at the local government elections just days later.

Parting company with its then finance director, it then staggered from one embarrassment to another. Within five months of opening for business, it was confirming a fresh £800,000 deficit. Last November, it had to shelve plans to raise £2m through the sale of some hospital buildings after it emerged that it had omitted to seek the necessary consent of the Department of Health.

Neither were all the problems financial: at Christmas, the hiring of scantily-clad female entertainers for official trust parties brought further publicity; in August, wards at Guy's had to be closed after two babies died from infection after heart surgery.

So it was with grim satisfaction that Sir Philip Harris, the trust's chairman, and Peter Griffiths, its chief executive, told their annual meeting on Monday night that the first-year report was good. The number of patients treated as in-patients or day cases was up 11.6 per cent on the previous year, though the number of out-patients was down, and there had been a trading surplus of £2.7 million on total income of almost £180 million, of which £87,000 was carried forward after payment of dividends and other adjustments.

Mr Griffiths said: 'If we had not taken early action, we could have been facing a problem of the order of £7 million which could have meant large-scale closures of services. To end the year with an increase in patients treated I think has been remarkable.'

Whether the smiles on the faces of the Guy's top brass will stay quite so broad for very long is another matter. The report of the Tomlinson inquiry into the NHS in London, expected to be published in the next few days, may throw the trust's long-term future into considerable doubt.

From the Guardian, *21 October 1992*

Hospital Trust Trailblazer Loses Job in Merger

The manager who blazed a trail for the Government's National Health Service shake-up has lost his job as part of the cuts in London hospitals, it was yesterday announced.

Peter Griffiths, chief executive of the Guy's hospital trust, the flagship of the first opted-out hospitals, has been passed over in favour of Tim Matthews, his opposite number at St Thomas's hospital, in the appointment of a chief executive for the trust to be formed by the two south London units.

Mr Griffiths, who will have no role in the merged trust, was the NHS's most prominent advocate of the market-style changes introduced to the service in 1991. He joined Guy's from the Department of Health, where he was NHS deputy chief executive and one of the architects of the shake-up.

His salary, more than £90,000 plus a car for himself and one for his wife, reflected the importance attached to making a success of the Guy's trust in its early days when it was the focus of media scrutiny.

In its first year the trust reported an 11.6 per cent increase in patients treated and a cash surplus of £87,000 on income of almost £180 million.

However, Mr Griffiths courted controversy. Within four weeks of opting out, and just days ahead of the 1991 local government elections, he announced £6.8 million cuts and hundreds of job losses, putting ministers' backs to the wall and triggering an investigation by the Commons health committee. At Christmas 1991, the trust was again in the headlines when scantily clad entertainers were hired for trust parties.

Mr Matthews, meanwhile, was quietly turning St Thomas's from a hospital viewed as one of the weakest in London into one which could compete on equal terms with Guy's in the merger recommended by the Tomlinson report on the capital's health services.

His appointment was made last Friday after a run-off with Mr Griffiths. The selection panel was chaired by Lord Hayhoe, the former Conservative health minister who is to chair the new trust, and also comprised four of the trust's proposed non-executive directors, two of whom came from Guy's.

Observers were yesterday speculating that Mr Griffiths had in part been a victim of hostility from doctors, particularly general practitioners whom Lord Hayhoe had recently met.

Mr Matthews said his appointment should not be interpreted as a signal that the merged trust would be based at St Thomas's rather than Guy's. Ministers have asked for a recommendation later this year on which site will be chosen.

Although the salary for the new post had not been fixed, Mr Matthews said he expected it to be 'broadly the same' as that paid by Guy's.

Mr Griffiths said in a statement: 'I have no doubt that working together, Guy's and St Thomas's hospitals will be a world-beating combination. I will continue to provide maximum support to Tim in planning for the successful launch on April 1 of the new trust, subject to approval by the secretary of state.'

From the Guardian, *2 March 1993*

Guy's Falls Victim to Changes

Guy's yesterday became the second of London's world-famous teaching hospitals to fall victim to the Government's overhaul of health care in the capital.

Virginia Bottomley, the Health Secretary, announced that Guy's would be stripped of in-patient and specialist services in favour of St Thomas's, its south London neighbour. It would be turned into a teaching and research campus, retaining only residual health services for local people.

In a statement in the Commons, Mrs Bottomley said that having resolved previously to merge the two, it had been decided to concentrate their clinical services on one site.

'Our judgment was that the St Thomas's site overall offers a better location and environment as a hospital and serves a bigger population. The need to safeguard what is the largest and one of the busiest accident and emergency departments in London was also crucial to the decision.'

Space vacated by Guy's clinical teams will be taken up by the move there of departments of King's College Hospital, south London, but the decision leaves a question mark over Philip Harris House, a £140 million clinical centre which was about to open at Guy's and was partly funded by £44 million from charities. Mrs Bottomley told reporters that up to 80 per cent of the new building would be used for the purposes originally intended, and that it was highly unlikely the charities would ask for any money back.

Local MPs remained angry with the decision. Simon Hughes, Liberal Democrat member for Bermondsey, described it as the biggest U-turn on health. 'This is a government that one year launches a flagship and builds a state of the art building, and the next year evacuates the flagship and says: "You can have your building, but with hardly any beds in it".'

From the Guardian, *11 February 1994*

PART 2

ISSUES

'Issues' seemed the most appropriate term to cover some of the knotty problems and dilemmas that occur one way or another in most organizations, and to which there are no easy or complete solutions. Often the more lurid examples of organizational failure seized on by the popular press arise from attempts at handling such dilemmas that are not so different from what commonly happens elsewhere but with less unfortunate results. Problems cannot always be avoided and a deeper understanding is needed than the language of neglect and 'incompetence' provides. The selection covers a range of problem areas and the different ways of coping with them. The intention was to help those who work in organizations to see their own efforts and experience in a wider context, and realize they are not alone in finding that certain matters are seldom very satisfactorily resolved. Some of these issues are perennials, endemic in organizations – like the satisfactions and dissatisfactions of work, and the problems of 'misunderstandings' – while the others are more topical. But in each case, whether we are managers or managed, most of us will meet these issues in some form, and have to find ways of making the best of them.

CHAPTER 6

The Meaning and the Satisfactions of Work

The following extracts have been taken from a book which consists of verbatim records of ordinary people talking about their work. They present many issues as starkly as any organizational theorist could.

One of the themes of the book from which these extracts have been taken is that very few people find satisfaction in their work. Even fewer regard their work relationships as a source of satisfaction. There are clues about what the individuals want from work in most of the extracts, as well as some accounts of special moments that make all the rest seem worth while . . .

Working

S. TERKEL

INTRODUCTION

This book, being about work, is, by its very nature, about violence – to the spirit as well as to the body. It is about ulcers as well as accidents, about shouting matches as well as fistfights, about nervous breakdowns as well as kicking the dog around. It is, above all (or beneath all), about daily humiliations. To survive the day is triumph enough for the walking wounded among the great many of us.

The scars, psychic as well as physical, brought home to the supper table and the TV set, may have touched, malignantly, the soul of our society. More or less. ('More or less', that most ambiguous of phrases, pervades many of the conversations that comprise this book, reflecting, perhaps, an ambiguity of attitude toward The Job. Something more than Orwellian acceptance, something less than Luddite sabotage. Often the two impulses are fused in the same person.)

It is about a search, too, for daily meaning as well as daily bread, for recognition as well as cash, for astonishment rather than torpor; in short, for a sort of life rather than a Monday through Friday sort of dying. Perhaps immortality, too, is part of the quest. To be remembered was the wish, spoken and unspoken, of the heroes and heroines of this book.

There are, of course, the happy few who find a savor in their daily job: the Indiana stonemason, who looks upon his work and sees that it is good; the Chicago piano tuner, who seeks and finds the sound that delights; the bookbinder, who saves a piece of history; the Brooklyn fireman, who saves a piece of life . . . But don't these satisfactions, like Jude's hunger for knowledge, tell us more about the person than about his task? Perhaps. Nonetheless, there is a common attribute here: a meaning to their work well over and beyond the reward of the paycheck.

BABE SECOLI

She's a checker at a supermarket. She's been at it for almost thirty years. 'I started at twelve – a little, privately owned grocery store across the street from the house. They didn't have no cash registers. I used to mark the prices down on a paper bag.

'When I got out of high school, I didn't want no secretary job. I wanted the grocery job. It was so interesting for a young girl. I just fell into it. I don't know no other work but this. It's hard work, but I like it. This is my life.'

We sell everything here, millions of items. From potato chips and pop – we even have a genuine pearl in a can of oysters. It sells for two somethin'. Snails with the shells that you put on the table, fanciness. There are items I never heard of we have here. I know the price of every one. Sometimes the boss asks me and I get a kick out of it. There isn't a thing you don't want that isn't in this store.

You sort of memorize the prices. It just comes to you. I know half a gallon of milk is sixty-four cents; a gallon, $1.10. You look at the labels. A small can of peas, Raggedy Ann. Green Giant, that's a few pennies more. I know Green Giant's eighteen and I know Raggedy Ann is fourteen. I know Del Monte is twenty-two. But lately the prices jack up from one day to another. Margarine two days ago was forty-three cents. Today it's forty-nine. Now when I see Imperial comin' though, I know it's forty-nine cents. You just memorize. On the register is a list of some prices, that's for the part-time girls. I never look at it.

I don't have to look at the keys on my register. I'm like the secretary that knows her typewriter. The touch. My hand fits. The number nine is my big middle finger. The thumb is number one, two and three and up. The side of my hand uses the bar for the total and all that.

I use my three fingers – my thumb, my index finger, and my middle finger. The right hand. And my left hand is on the groceries. They put down their groceries. I got my hips pushin' on the button and it rolls around on the counter. When I feel I have enough groceries in front of me, I let go of my hip. I'm just movin' – the hips, the hand, and the register, the hips, the hand, and the register . . . (As she demonstrates, her hands and hips move in the manner of an Oriental dancer). You just keep goin', one, two, one, two. If you've got that rhythm, you're a fast checker. Your feet are flat on the floor and you're turning your head back and forth.

Somebody talks to you. If you take your hand off the item, you're gonna forget what you were ringin'. It's the feel. When I'm pushin' the items through I'm always having my hand on the items. If somebody interrupts to ask me the price, I'll answer while I'm movin'. Like playin' a piano.

I'm eight hours a day on my feet. It's just a physical tire of standing up. When I get home I get my second wind. As far as standin' there, I'm not tired. It's when I'm roamin' around tryin' to catch a shoplifter. There's a lot of shoplifters in here. When I see one, I'm ready to run for them.

When my boss asks me how I know, I just know by the movements of their hands. And with their purses and their shopping bags and their clothing rearranged. You can just tell what they're doin' and I'm never wrong so far.

It's meats. Some of these women have big purses. I caught one here last week. She had two big packages of sirloin strips in her purse. That amounted to ten dollars. When she came up to the register, I very politely said, 'Would you like to pay for anything else, without me embarrassing you?' My boss is standing right there. I called him over. She looked at me sort of on the cocky side. I said, 'I know you have meat in your purse. Before your neighbors see you, you either pay for it or take it out.' She got very snippy. That's where my boss stepped in. 'Why'd you take the meat?' She paid for it.

Nobody knows it. I talk very politely. My boss doesn't do anything drastic. If they get rowdy, he'll raise his voice to embarrass 'em. He tells them not to come back in the store again.

Years ago it was more friendlier, more sweeter. Now there's like tension in the air. A tension in the store. The minute you walk in you feel it. Everybody is fightin' with each other. They're pushin', pushin' – 'I was first.' Now it's an effort to say, 'Hello, how are you?' It must be the way of people livin' today. Everything is so rush, rush, rush, and shovin'. Nobody's goin' anywhere. I think they're pushin' themselves right to a grave, some of these people.

A lot of traffic here. There's bumpin' into each other with shoppin' carts. Some of 'em just do it intentionally. When I'm shoppin', they just jam you with the carts. That hits your ankle and you have a nice big bruise there. You know who does this the most? These old men that shop. These *men*. They're terrible and just *jam* you. Sometimes I go over and tap them on the shoulder: 'Now why did you do this?' They look at you and they just start *laughin'*. It's just hatred in them, they're bitter. They hate themselves, maybe they don't feel good that day. They gotta take their anger out on somethin', so they just *jam* you. It's just ridiculous.

I wouldn't know how to go in a factory. I'd be like in a prison. Like this, I can look outside, see what the weather is like. I want a little fresh air, I walk out the front door, take a few sniffs of air, and come back in. I'm here forty-five minutes early every morning. I've never been late except for that big snowstorm. I never thought of any other work.

I'm a couple of days away, I'm very lonesome for this place. When I'm on a vacation, I can't wait to go, but two or three days away, I start to get fidgety. I can't stand around and do nothin'. I have to be busy at all times. I look forward to comin' to work. It's a great feelin'. I enjoy it somethin' terrible.

PHIL STALLINGS

He is a spot welder at the Ford Assembly plant on the far South Side of Chicago. He is twenty-seven years old; recently married. He works the third shift: 3.30 p.m. to midnight.

'I start the automobile, the first welds. From there it goes to another line, where the floor's put on, the roof, the trunk hood, the doors. Then it's put on a frame. There is hundreds of lines.

'The welding gun's got a square handle, with a button on the top for high voltage and a button on the bottom for low. The first is to clamp the metal together. The second is to fuse it.

'The gun hangs from a ceiling, over tables that ride on a track. It travels in a circle, oblong, like an egg. You stand on a cement platform, maybe six inches from the ground.'

I stand in one spot, about two- or three-feet area, all night. The only time a person stops is when the line stops. We do about thirty-two jobs per car, per unit. Forty-eight units an hour, eight hours a day. Thirty-two times forty-eight times eight. Figure it out. That's how many times I push that button.

The noise, oh it's tremendous. You open your mouth and you're liable to get a mouthful of sparks. (Shows his arms.) That's a burn, these are burns. You don't compete against the noise. You go to yell and at the same time you're straining to manoeuver the gun to where you have to weld.

You got some guys that are uptight, and they're not sociable. It's too rough. You pretty much stay to yourself. You get involved with yourself. You dream, you think of things you've done. I drift back continuously to when I was a kid and what me and my brothers did. The things you love most are the things you drift back into.

Lots of times I worked from the time I started to the time of the break and I never realized I had even worked. When you dream, you reduce the chances of friction with the foreman or with the next guy.

It don't stop. It just goes and goes and goes. I bet there's men who have lived and died out there, never seen the end of that line. And they never will – because it's endless. It's like a serpent. It's just all body, no tail. It can do things to you . . . (Laughs.)

Repetition is such that if you were to think about the job itself, you'd slowly go out of your mind. You'd let your problems build up, you'd get to a point where you'd be at the fellow next to you – his throat. Every time the foreman came by and looked at you, you'd have something to say. You just strike out at anything you can. So if you involve yourself by yourself, you overcome this.

I don't like the pressure, the intimidation. How would you like to go up to someone and say, 'I would like to go to the bathroom?' If the foreman doesn't like you, he'll make you hold it, just ignore you. Should I leave this job to go to the bathroom I risk being fired. The line moves all the time.

I know I could find better places to work. But where could I get the money I'm making? Let's face it, $4.32 an hour. That's real good money now. Funny thing is, I don't mind working at body construction. To a great degree, I enjoy it. I love using my hands – more than I do my mind. I love to be able to put things together and see something in the long run. I'll be the first to admit I've got the easiest job on the line. But I'm against this thing where I'm being held back. I'll work like a dog until I get what I want. The job I really want is utility.

It's where I can stand and say I can do any job in this department, and nobody has to worry about me. As it is now, out of say, sixty jobs, I can do almost half of 'em. I want to get away from standing in one spot. Utility can do a different job every day. Instead of working right there for eight hours I could work over there for eight, I could work the other place for eight. Every day it would change. I would be around more people. I go out on my lunch-break and work on the fork truck for a half-hour – to get the experience. As soon as I got it down pretty good, the foreman in charge says he'll take me. I don't want the other guys to see me. When I hit that fork lift, you just stop your thinking and you concentrate. Something right there in front of you, not in the past, not in the future. This is real healthy.

I don't eat lunch at work. I may grab a candy bar, that's enough. I wouldn't be able to hold it down. The tension your body is put under by the speed of the line . . . When you hit them brakes, you just can't stop. There's a certain momentum that carries you forward. I could hold the food, but it wouldn't set right.

Proud of my work? How can I feel pride in a job where I call a foreman's attention to a mistake, a bad piece of equipment, and he'll ignore it. Pretty soon you get the idea they don't care. You keep doing this and finally you're titled a troublemaker. So you just go about your work. You *have* to have pride. So you throw it off to something else. And that's my stamp collection.

It's gonna change. There's a trend. We're getting younger and younger men. We got this new Thirty and Out. Thirty years seniority and out. The whole idea is to give a man more time, more time to slow down and live. While he's still in his fifties, he can settle down in a camper and go out and fish. I've sat down and thought about it. I've got twenty-seven years to go. (Laughs.) That's why I don't go around causin' trouble or lookin' for a cause.

The only time I get involved is when it affects me or it affects a man on the line in a condition that could be me. I don't believe in lost causes, but when it all happened . . . (He pauses, appears bewildered.)

The foreman was riding the guy. The guy either told him to go away or pushed him, grabbed him . . . You can't blame the guy – Jim Grayson. I don't want nobody stickin' their finger in my face. I'd've probably hit him beside the head. The whole thing was: Damn it, it's about time we took a stand. Let's stick up for the guy. We stopped the line. (He pauses, grins.) Ford lost about twenty units. I'd figure about five grand a unit – whattaya got? (Laughs.)

I said, 'Let's all go home.' When the line's down like that, you can go up to one man and say, 'You gonna work?' If he says no, they can fire him. See what I mean? But if nobody was there, who the hell were they gonna walk up to and say, 'Are you gonna work?' Man, there woulda been nobody there! If it were up to me, we'd gone home.

Jim Grayson, the guy I work next to, he's colored. Absolutely. That's the first time I've seen unity on that line. Now it's happened once, it'll happen again. Because everybody just sat down. Believe you me. (Laughs.) It stopped at eight and it didn't start till twenty after eight. Everybody and his brother were down there. It was really nice to see, it really was.

GARY BRYNER

He's twenty-nine, going on thirty. He is president of Local 1112, UAW. Its members are employed at the General Motors assembly plant in Lordstown, Ohio. 'It's the most automated, fastest line in the world.' A strike had recently been settled 'for a time'.

The almighty dollar is not the only thing in my estimation. There's more to it – how I'm treated. What I have to say about what I do, how I do it. It's more important than the almighty dollar. The reason might be that the dollar's here now. It wasn't in my father's young days. I can concentrate on the social aspects, my rights. And I feel good all around when I'm able to stand up and speak up for another guy's rights. That's how I got involved in this whole stinkin' mess. Fighting every day of my life. And I enjoy it.

Guys in plants nowadays, their incentive is not to work harder. It's to stop the job to the point where they can have lax time. Maybe to think. We got guys now that open a paper, maybe read a paragraph, do his job, come back, and do something else. Keeping himself occupied other than being just that robot that they've scheduled him to be.

When General Motors Assembly Division came to Lordstown, you might not believe it, but they tried to take the newspapers off the line. The GMAD controls about seventy-five percent of the assembly of cars produced for the corporation. There's eighteen assembly plants. We're the newest. Their idea is to cut costs, be more efficient, take the waste out of working, and all that kind of jazz. To make another dollar. That's why the guys labeled GMAD: Gotta Make Another Dollar. (Laughs.)

In '70 came the Vega. They were fighting foreign imports. They were going to make a small compact that gets good milage. In the B body you had a much roomier car to work on. Guy's could get in and out of it easily. Some guys could almost stand inside, stoop. With the Vega, a much smaller car, they were going from sixty an hour to a hundred an hour. They picked up an additional two thousand people.

When they started up with Vega, we had what we call Paragraph 78 disputes. Management says, that on every job you should do this much. And the guy and the union say, that's too much work for me in that amount of time. Finally, we establish work standards. Prior to October, when GMAD came down, we had established an agreement: the guy who was on the job had something to say. When GMAD came in, they said, he's long overdue for extra work. He's featherbedding.

Instead of having the guy bend over to pick something up, it's right at his waist level. This is something Ford did in the thirties. Try to take every movement out of the guy's day, so he could conserve seconds in time, to make him more efficient, more productive, like a robot. Save a second on every guy's effort, they would, over a year, make a million dollars.

They use time, stopwatches. They say, it takes so many seconds or hundreds of seconds to walk from here to there. We know it takes so many seconds to shoot a screw. We know the gun turns so fast, the screw's so long, the hole's so deep. Our argument has always been: that's mechanical; that's not human.

The workers said, we perspire, we sweat, we have hangovers, we have upset stomachs, we have feelings and emotions, and we're not about to be placed in a category of a machine. When you talk about that watch, you talk about it for a minute. We talk about a lifetime. We're gonna do what's normal and we're gonna tell you what's normal. We'll negotiate from there. We're not gonna start on a watch-time basis that has no feelings.

When they took the unimates on, we were building sixty an hour. When we came back to work, with the unimates, we were building a hundred cars an hour. A unimate is a welding robot. It looks just like a praying mantis. It goes from spot to spot to spot. It releases that thing and it jumps back into position, ready for the next car. They go by them about 110 an hour. They never tire, they never sweat, they never complain, they never miss work. Of course, they don't buy cars. I guess General Motors doesn't understand that argument.

There's twenty-two, eleven on each side of the line. They do the work of about two hundred men – so there was a reduction of men. Those people were absorbed into other departments. There's some places they can't use 'em. There's some thinking about assembling cars. There still has to be human beings.

If the guys didn't stand up and fight, they'd become robots too. They're interested in being able to smoke a cigarette, bullshit a little bit with the guy next to 'em, open a book, look at something, just daydream if nothing else. You can't do that if you become a machine.

Thirty-five, thirty-six seconds to do your job – that includes the walking, the picking up of the parts, the assembly. Go to the next job, with never a letup, never a second to stand and think. The guys at our plant fought like hell to keep that right.

There was a strike. It came after about four or five months of agitation by management. When GMAD took over the plant, we had about a hundred grievances. They moved in, and where we had settled a grievance, they violated 'em. They took and laid off people. They said they didn't need 'em. We had over fourteen hundred grievances under procedure prior to the strike. It's a two-shift operation, same job, so you're talking about twenty-eight hundred people with fourteen hundred grievances. What happened was, the guys – as the cars came by 'em – did what's normal, what they had agreed to prior to GMAD. I don't think GM visualized this kind of a rebellion.

The strike issue? We demanded the reinstitution of our work pace as it was prior to the onslaught by General Motors Assembly Division. The only way they could do it was to replace the people laid off.

Assembly workers are the lowest on the totem pole when it comes to job fulfillment. They don't think they have any skill. Some corporate guy said, 'A monkey could do the job.' They have no enthusiasm about pride in workmanship. They could care less if the screw goes in the wrong place. Sometimes it helps break the monotony if the screw strips. The corporation could set up ways to check it so when the product goes to the consumer it should be whole, clean, and right. But they've laid off inspectors. 'Cause they could give a shit less. Inspectors are like parasites – they don't produce, they don't add something. They only find error. That error costs money to fix, so . . . they laid off, I don't know how many inspectors per shift. They want quantity.

The guys are not happy here. They don't come home thinking, boy, I did a great job today and I can't wait to get back tomorrow. That's not the feeling at all. I don't think he thinks a blasted thing about the plant until he comes back. He's not concerned at all if the product's good, bad, or indifferent.

Their idea is not to run the plant. I don't think they'd know what to do with it. They don't want to tell the company what to do, but simply have something to say about what *they're* going to do. They just want to be treated with dignity. That's not asking a hell of a lot.

I weave in on both sides of the assembly line. From the right side, the passenger's side, to the driver's side. Talking to guys. You get into a little conversation. You watch the guy, 'cause you don't want to get in his way, 'cause he'll ruin a job. Occasionally he'll say, 'Aw, fuck it. It's only a car.' It's more important to just stand there and rap. I don't mean for car after car. He'd be in a hell of a lot of trouble with his foreman. But occasionally, he'll let a car go by. If something's loose or didn't get installed, somebody'll catch it, somebody'll repair it, hopefully. At that point, he made a decision: It was just a little more important to say what he had on his mind. The unimate doesn't stand there and talk, doesn't argue, doesn't think. With us, it becomes a human thing. It's the most enjoyable part of my job, that moment. I love it!

TOM BRAND

He is plant manager at the Ford Assembly Division in Chicago. He has been with the company thirty years. [. . .]

There's a plaque on the desk: Ford, Limited Edition. 'That was our five millionth car. There are about forty-five hundred people working here. That's about 3,998 hourly and about 468 salaried.' Management and office employees are salaried.

You're responsible to make sure the car is built and built correctly. I rely on my quality control manager. Any defects, anything's wrong, we make sure it's repaired before it leaves the plant. Production manager takes care of the men on the line, makes sure they're doing their job, have the proper tools and the space and time to do it in. But the quality control manager is really our policeman. Quality control doesn't look at every item on the car. Some by surveillance. You take a sample of five an hour. Some, we look in every car. They make sure we're doing what we say we're doing.

Okay, we've got to build forty-seven an hour. Vega, down in Lordstown, had a hundred an hour. They got trapped with too much automation. If you're going to automate, you always leave yourself a loophole. I haven't seen their picture. I want to show it to all my managers. Okay, we build 760 big Fords a day. [. . .]

Three years ago, I had plenty of grievances. We had a lot of turnover, a lot of new employees. As many as 125 people would be replaced each week. Now with the economic situation, our last raises, and the seven days' holiday between Christmas and New Year's, this just changed the whole attitude. They found out it's a real good place to work. They're getting top dollar. Twelve paid vacation days a year, and they like the atmosphere. There was a lot of fellas would go in the construction industry about this time of the year. Less now.

I've had fellas come in to me and say, 'I'm not satisfied. Can I talk to you about it?' I say, 'Sure, come on in.' You can't run a business sitting in the office, 'cause you get divorced too much from the people. The people are the key to the whole thing. If you aren't in touch with the people they think, He's too far aloof, he's distant. It doesn't work. If I walk down the line, there'll be a guy fifty feet away from me. I'd wave, he'd wave back. Many of 'em I know by name. I don't know everyone by name, but I know their faces. If I'm in the area, I'll know who's strange. I'll kid with one of 'em. [. . .]

I don't think I'll retire at fifty. I'm not the type to sit around. Maybe if my health is good I'll go to fifty-seven, fifty-nine. I enjoy this work very much. You're with people. I like people. Guys who really do the job can spot a phony. When I walk out there and say good morning, you watch the fellas. There's a world of difference if they really know you mean it.

Doing my job is part salesmanship. I guess you can term it human engineering. My boss, so many years past, used to be a real bull of the woods. Tough guy. I don't believe in that. I never was raised that way. I never met a guy you couldn't talk to. I never met a man who didn't put his pants on the same way I do it in the morning. I met an awful lot of 'em that think they do. It doesn't work. The old days of hit 'em with a baseball bat to get their attention – they're gone.

If I could get everybody at the plant to look at everything through my eyeballs, we'd have a lot of the problems licked. If we have one standard to go by, it's easy to swing it around because then you've got everybody thinking the same way. This is the biggest problem of people – communication.

It's a tough situation because everybody doesn't feel the same every day. Some mornings somebody wakes up with a hangover, stayed up late, watched a late, late movie, missed the ride, and they're mad when they get to work. It's just human nature. If we could get everybody to feel great. [. . .]

LARRY ROSS

The corporation is a jungle. It's exciting. You're thrown in on your own and you're constantly battling to survive. When you learn to survive, the game is to become the conqueror, the leader.

'I've been called a business consultant. Some say I'm a business psychiatrist. You can describe me as an advisor to top management in a corporation.' He's been at it since 1968.

I started in the corporate world, oh gosh – '42. After kicking around in the Depression, having all kinds of jobs and no formal education, I wasn't equipped to become an engineer, a lawyer, or a doctor. I gravitated to selling. Now they call it marketing. I grew up in various corporations. I became the executive vice president of a large corporation and then of an even larger one. Before I quit I became president and chief executive officer of another. All nationally known companies.

Sixty-eight, we sold out our corporation. There was enough money in the transaction where I didn't have to go back in business. I decided that I wasn't going to get involved in the corporate battle any more. It lost its excitement, its appeal. People often ask me, 'Why weren't you in your own business? You'd probably have made a lot of money.' I often ask it myself, I can't explain it, except. . . .

Most corporations I've been in, they were on the New York Stock Exchange with thousands and thousands of stockholders. The last one – whereas, I was the president and chief executive, I was always subject to the board of directors, who had pressure from the stockholders. I owned a portion of the business, but I wasn't in control. I don't know of any situation in the corporate world where an executive is completely free and sure of his job from moment to moment.

Corporations always have to be right. That's their face to the public. When things go bad, they have to protect themselves and fire somebody. 'We had nothing to do with it. We had an executive that just screwed everything up.' He's never really ever been his own boss.

The danger starts as soon as you become a district manager. You have men working for you and you have a boss above. You're caught in a squeeze. The squeeze progresses from station to station. I'll tell you what a squeeze is. You have the guys working for you that are shooting for your job. The guy you're working for is scared stiff you're gonna shove him out of his job. Everybody goes around and says, 'The test of the true executive is that you have men working for you that can replace you, so you can move up.' That's a lot of boloney. The manager is afraid of the bright young guy coming up.

Fear is always prevalent in the corporate structure. Even if you're a top man, even if you're hard, even if you do your job – by the slight flick of a finger, your boss can fire you. There's always the insecurity. You bungle a job. You're fearful of losing a big customer. You're fearful so many things will appear on your record, stand against you. You're always fearful of the big mistake. You've got to be careful when you go to corporation parties. Your wife, your children have to behave properly. You've got to fit in the mold. You've got to be on guard.

When I was president of this big corporation, we lived in a small Ohio town, where the main plant was located. The corporation specified who you could socialize with, and on what level. (His wife interjects: 'Who were the wives you could play bridge with.') The president's wife could do what she wants, as long as it's with dignity and grace. In a small town they didn't have to keep check on you. Everybody knew. There are certain sets of rules. [. . .]

When the individual reaches the vice presidency or he's general manager, you know he's an ambitious, dedicated guy who wants to get to the top. He isn't one of the gray people. He's one of the black-and-white vicious people – the leaders, the ones who stick out in the crowd.

As he struggles in this jungle, every position he's in, he's terribly lonely. He can't confide and talk with the guy working under him. He can't confide and talk to the man he's working for. To give vent to his feelings, his fears, and his insecurities, he'd expose himself. This goes all the way up the line until he gets to be president. The president *really* doesn't have anybody to talk to, because the vice presidents are waiting for him to die or make a mistake and get knocked off so they can get his job.

He can't talk to the board of directors, because to them he has to appear as a tower of strength, knowledge, and wisdom, and have the ability to walk on water. The board of directors, they're cold, they're hard. They don't have any direct-line responsibilities. They sit in a staff capacity and they really play God. They're interested in profits. They're interested in progress. They're interested in keeping a good face in the community – if it's profitable. You have the tremendous infighting of man against man for survival and clawing to the top. Progress. [. . .]

To the board of directors, the dollars are as important as human lives. There's only yourself sitting there making the decision, and you hope it's right. You're always on guard. Did you ever see a jungle animal that wasn't on guard? You're always looking over your shoulder. You don't know who's following you. [. . .]

You have a nice, plush lovely office to go to. You have a private secretary. You walk down the corridor and everybody bows and says, 'Good morning, Mr Ross. How are you today?' As you go up the line, the executives will say, 'How is Mrs Ross?' Until you get to the higher executives. They'll say, 'How is Nancy?' Here you socialize, you know each other. Everybody plays the game.

A man wants to get to the top of the corporation, not for the money involved. After a certain point, how much more money can you make? In my climb, I'll be honest, money was secondary. Unless you have tremendous demands, yachts, private airplanes – you get to a certain point, money isn't that important. It's the power, the status, the prestige. Frankly, its delightful to be on top and have everybody calling you Mr Ross and have a plane at your disposal and a car and a driver at your disposal. When you come to town, there's people to take care of you. When you walk into a board meeting, everybody gets up and says hello. I don't think there's any human being that doesn't love that. It's a nice feeling. But the ultimate power is in the board of directors. I don't know anybody who's free. You read in the paper about stockholders' meetings, the annual report. It all sounds so glowing. But behind the scenes, a jungle.

DIANE WILSON

She works for the OEO. 'This is a section called PM & S. I can't for the life of me ever remember what it means. Sometimes they change it. They reorganize and you get another initial. (Laughs.)

'I'm a processing clerk. There are three of us in this one department. We send grants to grantees after field reps have been out to see these poverty-stricken people. The grantees are organizations of the poor. Maybe the Mobilization Centre in Gary, where I live – Grand Rapids Poverty Center, something for senior citizens, a day care center. They give 'em all names.

'We mail 'em out forms to sign so they can get the money from Washington. When they return the forms to us there's another process we go through. We have a governor's letter and a package in an orange folder that we send out to him. He has to give his consent. We have a little telegram we type up. He approves it or he doesn't. We send it on. That makes it official. There's a thirty-day waiting period. After that time we send out the package to Washington. . . .

You wish there was a better system. A lot of money is held up and the grantees who want to know why they can't get it. Sometimes they call and get the run-around on the phone. I never do that. I tell the truth. If they don't have any money left, they don't have it. No, I'm not disturbed any more. If I was just starting on this job, I probably would. But the older I get, I realize it's a farce. You just get used to it. It's a job. I get my pay-check – that's it. It's all political anyway.

A lot of times the grantee comes down to our audit department for aid. They're not treated as human beings. Sometimes they have to wait, wait, wait – for no reason. The grantee doesn't know it's for no reason. He thinks he's getting somewhere and he really isn't.

They send him from floor to floor and from person to person, it's just around and around he goes. Sometimes he leaves, he hasn't accomplished anything. I don't know why this is so. You can see 'em waiting – so long. [. . .]

Life is a funny thing. We had this boss come in from Internal Revenue. He wanted to be very, very strict. He used to have meetings every Friday – about people comin' in late, people leavin' early, people abusin' lunch time. Everyone was used to this relaxed attitude. You kind of went overtime. No one bothered you. The old boss went along. You did your work.

Every Friday, everyone would sit there and listen to this man. And we'd all go out and do the same thing again. Next Friday he'd have another meeting and he would tell us the same thing. (Laughs.) We'd all go out and do the same thing again. (Laughs.) He would try to talk to one and see what they'd say about the other. But we'd been working all together for quite a while. You know how the game is played. Tomorrow you might need a favor. So nobody would say anything. If he'd want to find out what time someone came in, who's gonna tell 'em? He'd want to find out where someone was, we'd always say, 'They're at the Xerox.' Just anywhere. He couldn't get through. Now, lo and behold! We can't find *him* anywhere. He's got into this nice, relaxed atmosphere. . . . (Laughs.) He leaves early, he takes long lunch hours. We've converted him. (Laughs.)

After my grievances and my fighting, I'm a processing clerk. Never a typist no more or anything like that. (Laughs.) I started working here in 1969. There was an emergency and they all wanted to work overtime. So I made arrangements at home, 'cause I have to catch a later train. Our supervisor's black. All of us are black. We'll help her get it out so there won't be any back drag on this. Okay, so we all worked overtime and made a good showing.

Then they just didn't want to give us the promotion which was due us anyhow. They just don't want to give you anything. The personnel man, all of them, they show you why you don't deserve a promotion. The boss, the one we converted – he came on board, as they call it, after we sweated to meet the deadline. So he didn't know what we did. But he told us we didn't deserve it. That stayed with me forever. I won't be bothered with him ever again.

But our grievance man was very good. He stayed right on the case. We filed a civil rights complaint. Otherwise we woulda never got the promotion. They don't want anybody coming in investigating for race. They said, 'Oh, it's not that.' But you sit around and see white women do nothin' and get promotions. Here we're working and they say you don't deserve it. The black men are just as hard on us as the white man. Harder. They get angry with you because you started a lot of trouble. The way I feel about it, I'm gonna give 'em all the trouble I can.

Our boss is black, the one that told us we didn't deserve it. (Laughs.) And our union man fighting for us, sittin' there, punchin' away, is white. (Laughs.) We finally got up to the deputy director and he was the one – the white man – that finally went ahead and gave us the promotion. (Laughs.) So we went from grade 4 clerk-typist to grade 5 processing clerk.

We had another boss, he would walk around and he wouldn't want to see you idle at all. Sometimes you're gonna have a lag in your work, you're all caught up. This had gotten on his nerves. We got our promotion and we weren't continually busy. Any time they see black women idle, that irks 'em. I'm talkin' about black men as well as whites. They want you to work continuously. [. . .]

Oh, we love it when the bosses go to those long meetings, those important conferences. (Laughs.) We just leave in a group and go for a show. We don't care. When we get back, they roll their eyes. They know they better not say anything, 'cause they've done nothing when we've been gone anyhow. We do the work that we have to do. The old timekeeper, she sits and knits all that time, always busy.

CHAPTER 7

Skilling and Deskilling

Like the rest of us, those engineers who design the equipment that other people use in their work have developed particular beliefs concerning how to go about their job and what constitutes an effective outcome. And those beliefs work well for them. The snag – and it has been obvious for years – is that very often a new generation of equipment drastically reduces the skills required among those who will use it. The following article looks at some ways that modern technology gives new twists to this old dilemma – and argues that deskilling is not inevitable.

Engineers and the Work that People Do

H. H. ROSENBROCK

1 INTRODUCTION

The phenomenon which I wish to discuss in this paper can be illustrated by a plant which was making electric light bulbs in 1979. Production was 800 bulbs an hour, of the type having a metallized reflector and the components of the glass envelope were made elsewhere. They travelled on a chain conveyor around the plant, which occupied an area about 30 feet by 10 feet and was quite new. It was noisy, and the large room which housed it was drab, but conditions were not unpleasant.

The plant was almost completely automatic. Parts of the glass envelope, for example, were sealed together without any human intervention. Here and there, however, were tasks which the designer had failed to automate, and workers were employed, mostly women and mostly middle-aged. One picked up each glass envelope as it arrived, inspected it for flaws, and replaced it if it was satisfactory: once every 4½ seconds. Another picked out a short length of aluminium wire from a box with tweezers, holding it by one end. Then she inserted it delicately inside a coil which would vaporize it to produce the reflector: repeating this again every 4½ seconds. Because of the noise, and the isolation of the work places, and the concentration demanded by some of them, conversation was hardly possible.

This picture could be matched by countless other examples, taken from any of the industrialized countries. Beyond the comment that the jobs were obviously bad ones, and that something should have been done about them, we are not likely to be surprised or to feel that the situation was unusual. Yet, as I shall hope to show, what has been described is decidedly odd.

2 A DESIGN EXERCISE

To prepare the way, let us take one of the jobs, say the second one, and suppose that in a first year engineering degree course it was proposed, as a design exercise, to automate it. Picking up bits of wire out of a box is obviously too difficult, but we can easily avoid it. Let the wire be taken off a reel by pinch rollers and fed through a narrow tube. At the end of the tube, let it pass through holes in two hardened steel blocks. Then we can accurately feed out the right length, and by displacing one of the steel blocks we can shear it off. If this is all made small enough, it can enter the coil, so that when the wire is cut off it falls in the right place.

So far, so good, but the coil may perhaps not be positioned quite accurately. Then, if we cannot improve the accuracy, we shall have to sense its position and move the wire feeder to suit. Perhaps we could do this by using a conical, spring-loaded plunger, which could be pushed forward by a cam and enter the end of the coil. Having found its position in this way, we could lock a floating carriage on which the plunger and wire feeding mechanism were mounted, withdraw the plunger, and advance the wire feeder.

There would be scope here for a good deal of mechanical ingenuity, but of a kind which might not appeal to all of the students. 'Why not,' one of them might ask, 'why not use a small robot with optical sensing? The wire feeder could be mounted on the robot arm, and then sensing the position of the coil and moving the arm appropriately would be a simple matter of programming.'

An experienced engineer would probably not find much merit in this proposal. It would seem extravagant, using a complicated device to meet a simple need. It would offend what Veblen[1] calls the 'instinct of workmanship', the sense of economy and fitness for purpose. Yet the student might not be discouraged. 'All that is true,' he might say, 'but the robot is still economically sound. Only a small number of these plants will be made, and they will have to bear the development costs of any special device we design. Robots are complicated, but because they are made in large numbers they are cheap, while the development costs will be much less.'

After a little investigation, and some calculation, it might perhaps turn out that the student was right. A plant might even be built using a robot for this purpose. What I would like to suggest, however, is that this would not be a stable solution. It would still offend our instinct of workmanship. The robot has much greater abilities than this application demands. We should feel, like the robot specialist,[2] that 'To bring in a universal robot would mean using a machine with many abilities to do a single job that may require only one ability.'

As opportunity served we might pursue one of two possibilities. We might in the first place seek to find some simpler and cheaper device which would replace the robot. Alternatively, having a robot in place with capacities which had been paid for but were not being used, we might attempt to create for it a task which more nearly suited its abilities. It might, for example, be able to take over some other task on a neighbouring part of the line. Or we might be able to rearrange the line to bring some other suitable task within the reach of the robot. At all events, as engineers we should not rest happy with the design while a gross mismatch existed between the means we were employing and the tasks on which they were employed.

3 THE APPLICATION

The drift of this fable will become clear. For robot, substitute man or woman, and then compare our attitudes. This I will do shortly, but first let me extend the quotation which was given above[2]: 'However, it is less obvious that robots will be needed to take the place of human beings in most everyday jobs in industry. . . . To bring in a universal robot would mean using a machine with many abilities to do a single job that may require only one ability.' There is a curious discrepancy here between the apparent attitudes to robots and to people, and it is this which I wish to explore.

It will be readily granted that the woman whose working life was spent in picking up a piece of aluminium wire every 4½ seconds had many abilities, and was doing a job which required only one ability. By analogy with the robot one would expect to find two kinds of reaction, one seeking to do the job with a 'simpler device', and the other seeking to make better use of human ability. Both kinds of reaction do exist, though as will be seen, with a curious gap.

First, one cannot read the literature in this field without stumbling continually against one suggestion: that many jobs are more fitted for the mentally handicapped, and can be better done by them. The following are some examples.

'Slight mental retardation . . . often enables a person to do tedious work which would handicap a "normal" worker because of the monotony.'[3]

'The U.S. Rubber Company has even pushed experimentation so far as to employ young girls deficient in intelligence who, in the framework of "scientific management" applied to this business, have given excellent results.'[4]

'The tasks assigned to workers were limited and sterile . . . the worker was made to operate in an adult's body on a job that required the mentality and motivation of a child. Argyris demonstrated this by bringing in mental patients to do an extremely routine job in a factory setting. He was rewarded by the patients' increasing the production by 400 per cent.'[5]

'Mike Bayless, 28 years old with a maximum intelligence level of a 12-year-old, has become the company's NC-machining-centre operator because his limitations afford him the level of patience and persistence to carefully watch his machine and the work that it produces.'[6]

Swain[7] remarks that 'The methodological difficulties of using this . . . approach to the dehumanised job problem cannot be glossed over,' the meaning of which, one hopes, is that society would utterly reject it. Nevertheless, the quotations should alert our instinct of workmanship to the gross misalignment between human abilities and the demands of some jobs. A much more respectable response to this misalignment is the one which appeals to many technologists and engineers – that is, to carry the process of automation to the point where human labour is eliminated.

This becomes easier in manual work as the robot becomes cheaper and more highly developed. So, for example, in the manufacture of automobile bodies spot-welding is now regularly done by robots, and spray-painting will also soon cease to be a human occupation. Similar possibilities for eliminating human labour in clerical work are opened up by the microprocessor.

When it is applied to jobs which are already far below any reasonable estimate of human ability, there can be no objection on our present grounds to this development. Difficulties begin when we consider jobs that demand skill and the full use of human ability. To automate these out of existence in one step is never possible. They have to go first through a long process of fragmentation and simplification, during which they become unsuitable for human performance.

The mismatch between jobs and human abilities has also been approached from the opposite side by social scientists. Seeing the under-use of human ability, they have developed their techniques[8] of job enlargement, job enrichment, and of autonomous groups. These take existing jobs, and redesign them in a way which makes more use of the human abilities of judgement and adaptability. For example, in an autonomous group the allocation of tasks among its members is not imposed from outside but is left to the group itself to decide. The jobs that result can be better matched to human abilities, within the usually severe constraints of the technology. As Kelly[9] has noted, the opening which is given for the exercise of judgement and adaptability within the group may account for some of the increased productivity that has been observed.

These, then, are the techniques available to us for eliminating the mismatch between jobs and human abilities. There are two which reduce the abilities deployed, one of them inadmissible and the other stemming from engineering. There is a group of techniques which seek to use the abilities of people more fully, and these stem from the social sciences. So far as I know there are no others of significance; and what is remarkable is that engineers and technologists have not produced any methodology for using to the full the abilities and skills of human beings.

The designer of the lamp plant, for example, had made its operation automatic wherever he could do so conveniently. Where he could not, he had used human beings. He might perhaps have used robots, and if so he would have been concerned to use them economically and to make full use of their abilities. He felt, it appears, no similar concern for the full use of human abilities. We may say, paradoxically, that if he had been able to consider people as though they were robots, he would have tried to provide them with less trivial and more human work.

4 A PARADIGM

The conclusion we have reached discloses the oddity which was mentioned at the beginning of this paper. It is one that becomes more strange the more one considers it, and we are bound to ask how it arises.

The question has two parts: how do individual engineers come to adopt the view we have described, and how did this originate and become established in the engineering profession? As to the individual, engineers in my experience are never taught a set of rules or attitudes which would lead to this kind of view, nor do they base their actions on a set of explicit principles incorporating it. Instead, we have to imagine something like a 'paradigm' discussed by Thomas Kuhn.[10] This is the name he gives, in the sciences, to a matrix of shared attitudes and assumptions and beliefs within a profession.

The paradigm is transmitted from one generation to another, not by explicit teaching but by shared problem-solving. Young engineers take part in design exercises, and later in real design projects as members of the team. In doing so, they learn to see the world in a special way: the way in fact which makes it amenable to the professional techniques which they have available. Paradigms differ from one specialization to another within engineering, so that a control engineer and a thermodynamicist, for example, will see a gas turbine in slightly different ways. Effective collaboration between them will then demand a process of mutual re-education, as many will have discovered from this or other kinds of collaboration.

Seen in this way, as a paradigm which has been absorbed without ever being made fully explicit, the behaviour of the lamp-plant designer becomes understandable. We still have to ask how this paradigm arose. This is a question which deserves a more extended historical study than any I have seen. Tentatively, however, I suggest the following explanation, which has been given elsewhere[11] in somewhat greater detail.

Looking back at the early stages of the industrial revolution we tend to see the early machines as part of one single evolution. Examples of the machines themselves can be found in museums, and in looking at them we see the family resemblance which they all bear, deriving from the materials that were used and the means by which they were fashioned. They were made of leather and wood, and of wrought and cast iron, and in all of them these materials were fashioned in similar ways.

What I wish to suggest is that there were in fact two quite different kinds of machine, similar only in their materials and their construction, but with opposed relationships to human abilities. One of them can be typified by Hargreaves's spinning-jenny, which he invented for his own or his family's use. It is a hand-operated machine, deriving from the spinning-wheel, but allowing many threads to be spun at the same time. To use it demands a skill, which is a natural development for the skill needed to use the spinning-wheel. This skill in the user is rewarded by a great increase in his productivity. Samuel Crompton's spinning-mule was a similar kind of machine, and even when it was driven mechanically it needed the skilled cooperation of the spinner.

The other type of machine can be typified by the self-acting mule which was invented by Richard Roberts in 1830. What Roberts set out to do was not, like Hargreaves or Crompton, to make skill more productive. Rather he set out to eliminate skill so that the spinner was no longer needed except to supervise a set of machines. Fragments of his job remained, such as mending broken threads or removing threads which had been spun. These jobs were given largely to children, and they began to resemble the jobs around the lamp-making plant.

For reasons which were valid enough in the early nineteenth century, and which are well documented by Ure[12] and Babbage,[13] the second course proved more profitable for the inventor and the manufacturer than the first. When the engineering profession arose later in the century it therefore inherited only one attitude to the relation between machines and human skill, which is essentially the one described above.

Whether this attitude is appropriate at the present time is something which I should question. In a broad economic sense, the under-use of human ability is clearly a loss. Some of the reasons which made it nevertheless profitable for an early manufacturer no longer apply with the same force. Unskilled labour is still cheaper than skilled,[13] but much less so than it was at an earlier period. Once only skilled workers could strike effectively,[12] but the less-skilled now, by their numbers, may have even greater industrial strength.

Under present conditions, the motivation of workers may be a major preoccupation of managers. By 'quality circles' or other means they may strive to engage the abilities of the workers outside their jobs. By the social scientists' techniques of job-redesign they may seek to make the jobs themselves less repugnant to human ability. For engineers to spend effort and money at the same time on fragmenting jobs and reducing their content seems neither rational nor efficient, if there is any alternative.

5 AN ALTERNATIVE PARADIGM

If Hargreaves and Crompton could develop machines which collaborated with the skills of workers in the eighteenth century, can we not do the same in the twentieth century, using the incomparable power and flexibility of new technology? A major difficulty is that the problem is not generally posed as a choice between two alternative routes along which technology could develop. The engineering paradigm is not explicit, and it prevails not by a conscious choice, but by suppressing the ability to see an alternative. It is therefore useful to construct an example to show how a valid choice could indeed be made. This is not easy. At least 150 years of engineering effort have been given to one alternative, while the other has been ignored. One path is therefore broad, smooth and easy, the other narrow, difficult and rough. The example, however, need not be taken from engineering. What has been said applies equally to all technology, and will take on a new force as the advance of the microprocessor affects newer and wider areas.

What proves easiest is to choose as example an area where high skill exists, and where the encroachment of technology upon skill has hardly yet begun. In this way, both possible routes which technological development could follow are placed upon an equal basis. Following an earlier account,[11] the example of medical diagnosis will be used.

Feigenbaum[14] has recently described a computer system called PUFF for the diagnosis of lung diseases. It uses information about patients obtained from an instrument and from their past history. The information is matched against a set of 'rules' which have been developed by computer scientists in collaboration with medical specialists. In the rules is captured the knowledge of the physician, part of which he was explicitly aware of knowing. Another part was knowledge which he used unconsciously and which only became explicit as he compared his own response with that of the computer.

Though still in an early stage of development, the system gave agreement of 90 to 100 per cent with the physician, according to the tests which were used. There is no difficulty in supposing that this and similar systems can be improved until they are at least as good as the unaided physician.

One way in which they might be used is to make the skill in diagnosis of the physician redundant. The computer system could be operated by staff who had not received a full medical training, but only a short and intensive course in the computer system and its area of application. There might then be no difficulty in showing that the quality of diagnoses was as good as before, and possibly even better. The cost would be reduced, and a better service could be offered to the patient.

Alternatively, diagnosis might still be carried out by the physician, but he could be given a computer system to assist him in his work. Much that he had carried in his mind before would now be in the computer, and he would not need to concern himself with it. The computer would aid him by relieving him of this burden, and would allow him to carry on his work more effectively.

Under this second system, the physician would usually agree with the computer's diagnosis, but he would be at liberty to reject it. He might do so if, for example, some implicit rule which he used had not yet found its way into the computer system; or if he began to suspect a side effect from some new drug. Using the computer in this way, the physician would gradually develop a new skill, based on his previous skill but differing from it. Most of this new skill would reside in the area where he disagreed with the computer, and from time to time more of it might be captured in new rules. Yet there is no reason why the physician's skill in using the computer as a tool should not continually develop.

This is all speculation, but I believe not unreasonable speculation. Which of these two possible routes would be the better? The first leads, step by step, towards the situation typified by the lamp plant. The operators, having no extensive training, can never disagree with the computer, and become its servants. In time, the computer might be given more and more control over their work, requesting information, demanding replies, timing responses and reporting productivity. A mismatch would again arise between the abilities of the operators, and the trivialized tasks they were asked to perform. Social scientists might then be invited to study their jobs, and to suggest some scheme of redesign which would alleviate the monotony or the pressure of the work.

The second path allows human skills to survive and evolve into something new. It cooperates with this new skill and makes it more productive, just as Hargreaves's spinning-jenny allowed the spinner's skill to evolve and become more productive. There seems no reason to believe that this second path would be less economically effective than the first.

The example can be readily transposed into engineering terms. It applies with little change to the future development of computer-aided design. It suggests also that if we re-thought the problems, the operator's job on an NC machine tool need not be fragmented and trivialized, to the point where 'slight mental retardation' becomes an advantage. The task of making a part, from the description produced by a CAD system, could be kept entire, and could become the basis of a developing skill in the operator.

As I have said elsewhere,[15] the task of developing a technology which is well matched to human ability, and which fosters skill and makes it more productive, seems to me the most important and stimulating challenge which faces engineers today. If they are held back from this task, it will not be so much by its difficulty, as by the need for a new vision of the relation between engineering and the use of human skill. That I should pose such a problem to engineers will indicate, I hope, the very high position which I give to the role of engineering.

6 POSTSCRIPT

My paper could end at that point, but some readers may (and I hope will) feel a sense of unease. The argument which is developed above is in essence a broadly economic one. The skills and abilities of people are a precious resource which we are misusing, and a sense of economy and fitness for purpose, upon which we justly pride ourselves as engineers, should drive us to find a better relation between technology and human ability.

Yet economic waste is not the truest or deepest reason which makes the lamp plant repugnant to us. It offends against strong feelings about the value of human life, and the argument surely should be on this basis.

I wish that it could be, but my belief at present is that it cannot, for the following reasons. To develop such an argument we need a set of shared beliefs upon which to build the intellectual structure. Medieval Christianity, with its superstructure of scholastic philosophy, would once have provided the framework within which a rational argument could have been developed. By the time of the Industrial Revolution, this had long decayed, and nineteenth-century Christianity did not unequivocally condemn the developments I have described.

Marxism provides an alternative set of beliefs, and a philosophical superstructure, and it utterly condemns the misuse of human ability: but only when it is carried on under a capitalist system. If it is carried on under socialism then Marxism seems not to condemn it unequivocally, and those are the conditions under which Marxism can have the greatest influence. In support, it is only necessary to say that the lamp plant was in a socialist state, and is in no way anomalous there.[16]

Humanism might serve as another possible basis, with its demand[17] 'that can make use of all the potentialities he holds within him, his creative powers and the life of the reason, and labour to make the powers of the physical world the instruments of his freedom'. This indeed underlies much of the thought in the social sciences, yet again it seems that no conclusive argument can be based on it.

The difficulties are twofold. First, no system of beliefs is as widely disseminated as industrial society. Therefore if a conclusive argument could be based on one system of beliefs, it would have only a limited regional force. Secondly, and almost axiomatically, if there is a system of beliefs from which some of the prevalent features of industrial society can be decisively condemned, it will not be found as the dominant set of beliefs in an industrialized country.

My own conclusion is that rejection of trivialized and dehumanized work precedes any possible rationalization. Tom Bell[18] tells the following story of his mate who, day after day, sharpened needles in Singer's Clydebank works. 'Every morning there were millions of these needles on the table. As fast as he reduced the mountain of needles, a fresh load was dumped. Day in, day out, it never grew less. One morning he came in and found the table empty. He couldn't understand it. He began telling everyone excitedly that there were no needles on the table. It suddenly flashed on him how absurdly stupid it was to be spending his life like this. Without taking his jacket off, he turned on his heel and went out, to go for a ramble over the hills to Balloch.'

No very large part of the population so far has turned on its heel and gone for a ramble over the hills, though a mood akin to that does exist. If industrial society ever comes to be decisively rejected, it seems to me that it will be in this way and for these reasons, rather than as the result of a logically argued critique. The thought, if valid, takes on a special significance at the present time, when we are engaged in determining the kind of work which men and women will do in the area of the microprocessor.

REFERENCES

1. Veblen, T. (1898) 'The instinct of workmanship and the irksomeness of labor', *American Jour. of Sociology*, 4, 2, pp. 187–201.
2. George, F. H. and Humphries, J. D. (eds) (1974) *The Robots are Coming*, NCC Publications, p. 164.
3. Swain, A. D. (1977) (quoting Tinkham, M. L. (1971) 'Design of industrial jobs a worker can do', in Brown, S. C. and Martin, J. N. T. (eds) *Human Aspects of Man-Made Systems*, Open University Press, p. 192.
4. Friedmann, G. (1955) *Industrial Society*, Free Press of Glencoe, p. 216.
5. Herzberg, F. (1966) *Work and the Nature of Man*, World Publishing, p. 39.
6. *American Machinist* (1979), 123, 7, July, p. 58.
7. Swain, A. D., loc. cit.
8. Drake, R. I. and Smith, P. J. (1973) *Behavioural Science in Industry*, McGraw-Hill.
9. Kelly, J. E. (1978) 'A reappraisal of sociotechnical system theory', *Human Relations*, 31, pp. 1069–1099.

10. Kuhn, T. S. (1970) *The Structure of Scientific Revolutions*, Univ. Chicago Press, *passim* but especially pp. 181–187.
11. *New Technology: Society, Employment and Skill* (1981), Council for Science and Society.
12. Ure, A. (1835) *The Philosophy of Manufactures*, Charles Knight, London. Also *The Cotton Manufacture of Great Britain* (1836), Charles Knight, London.
13. Babbage, C. (1832) *On the Economy of Machinery and Manufactures*, reprinted 1963, Kelley, New York.
14. Feigenbaum, E. A. (1979) 'Themes and case studies of knowledge engineering', in Michie, D. (ed) *Expert Systems in the Micro-electronic Age*, Edinburgh Univ. Press, pp. 3–25.
15. Rosenbrock, H. H. (1977) 'The future of control', *Automatica*, 13, Pergamon, pp. 389–392.
16. Haraszty, M. (1977) *A Worker in a Worker's State*, Penguin Books.
17. Maritain, J. (1977) *True Humanism*, Geoffrey Bles, Centenary Press, p. xii.
18. Meachams, S. (1977) *A Life Apart*, Thames and Hudson, p. 137, quoting Tom Bell.

CHAPTER 8

Misunderstandings

If one had to choose a single problem that people in organizations bemoan more often than any other it would surely be the 'poor communication' and 'misunderstandings' that are more or less endemic in all but the smallest and most stable organizations. But in referring to such problems, managers and administrators often imply that they result from no more than carelessness – and that in a well run organization such things would not occur. In fact, the issue runs very much deeper than that, as the following piece makes very plain. It is a slightly condensed version of the first two chapters of an important and valuable book that deals with these difficulties. It goes on in later chapters to describe some novel ways of tackling these problems in the particular context of consultancy relationships. But it is obvious that much of what the authors say about the relationship between clients and 'helpers' applies equally to other organizational relationships, especially those between staff or service personnel, and line managers.

Understanding Problems and the Problem of Understanding

C. EDEN, S. JONES AND D. SIMS

Consider the following account.

John Smith is a marketing manager in a division of a large manufacturing company, Ian Brown the division's newly appointed marketing director. John Smith had just been to a meeting of the marketing department, the first with its new director. The appointment had not been a great surprise. Most people had assumed that Ian would get the job after his predecessor Brian Jones had been promoted to Head Office. In the three years since he had joined the division, Ian's area had been particularly successful, with two major and successful new product launches. He also had exactly the right kind of personality, John mused, aggressive, dynamic, self-confident. Personally John did not like him and thought he could be an 'absolute bastard' at times, but John had to admit that he was good at his job. Furthermore, with the successor to Ian's old job still undecided it would be stupid to 'get on the wrong side' of the man, even if his own chances of getting the job were, at this stage, remote. Anyway, he thought, the meeting had not been the exciting event everyone had been expecting, although the fact that no announcements had been made about the successor would be bound to get everybody talking. In the meeting Ian had just gone over the future plans and there was nothing new, the usual policy statements about the fact that the division was strong in some markets, weak in others and efforts to find new products would continue to have a high priority.

Peter Williams, responsible for the industrial products section, had put forward his usual argument that the problems in his area had little to do with the division's (i.e. his) efforts and much more to do with overall adverse market conditions. There was no doubt that he was probably right and Ian had not openly disagreed, though he had cut Peter short in the middle of his 'spiel'. (Peter did tend to go on a bit.)

As John walked down the corridor Martin Evans, the promotions co-ordinator, came up to him. 'What did you think of that, then?' he asked. 'O.K.', John grunted, guardedly, turning into his office. Martin was one of those people he disliked and distrusted. His efforts to impress Ian in the meeting had been so obvious as to be almost amusing, John thought.

As John sat down Alan Dixon came in. Alan was the new-products manager and a good friend both in and outside work. He was looking anxious. 'Didn't like the sound of all that,' he said. 'I reckon we are all going to be under the microscope now. Did you notice how he looked at me when he said we should pay more attention to exploiting existing names in development? (John hadn't.) You know how much trouble I had convincing Brian that we should keep separate identities for products in different market segments. I thought I had won that one. Now it looks as if I'll have to go through it all over again. I tell you, if he starts trying to change things radically in my area, it will be a disaster. And what about the way he was getting at Peter. I think he is definitely going to try to give Peter the push . . .'

Although this scene is an imagined one, we hope that what it describes believably captures some of the flavour of organizational life as most of us experience it.

We left John and his friend Alan in the middle of discussing what had 'gone on' in the meeting they had both just attended. It is clear that Alan had placed an interpretation upon the events occurring in that meeting, in terms of potential significance for him, quite different from that belonging to John. His interpretation had led him to feel distinctly anxious about the future behaviour of the new marketing director. John, on the other hand, had found the meeting rather uneventful. We may even suppose that he had been disappointed that it had not been more exciting. Are we 'rigging' the story? Of course. Yet we would ask you to consider how often when 'comparing notes' with colleagues after a meeting you find that each person will recall different aspects of the meeting, place different emphases on different aspects, or interpret the implications of the meeting in different ways. Sometimes the differences can be so significant that it hardly seems that the same meeting is being discussed.

The point that we wish to make here is so obvious that it appears almost trivial. Different people interpret situations in different ways. We have much in common with others in our social worlds – language, shared beliefs about the nature of things and relationships between them, and shared norms about what we should or should not do. Many of these come to have a meaning so institutionalized that they are taken to be 'matters of fact'.[1] Nevertheless our individual histories are unique to each of us. Different people interpret situations in different ways because they bring to a situation their own particular mental 'framework' of personal beliefs, attitudes, hypotheses, prejudices, expectations, personal values and objectives, with which they can make sense of (place an interpretation upon) the situation.[2] Thus they pay attention to certain things, ignore others, and regard some as having a particular significance for themselves in the future.

Returning to our example, this perspective would lead us to suggest that different recollections of a meeting by different individuals have less to do with one person having a 'better' memory than another than with how those individuals differently made sense of the meeting in terms of their particular mental frameworks. That is to say, individuals' recollections of a meeting and interpretations of what was significant within it come from their own beliefs and expectations – for example, about the world of things and people in general, about meetings in their organization, about the people there and their intentions – and from the future implications they see in the meeting for themselves in terms of their values and objectives. [. . .]

AN ORGANIZATION OF HUMAN BEINGS

Much of a person's hypothesizing about his world will be about the other human beings that make up that world. He will be concerned to understand what makes other people 'tick' as much as is enough for him to manage his interactions with them to his own satisfaction.

In the scenario described earlier we learned that John, the main protagonist, disliked his new boss but respected him for his competence, disliked and distrusted one of his colleagues and therefore avoided discussing his feelings about the meeting with him, but was involved in a close and friendly relationship with another who had dropped in immediately after the meeting for a 'post-mortem' on it. The point we wish to draw out here is that individuals in organizations are involved, as elsewhere, in complicated social relationships where they dislike, like, care about, find boring, are rude to, dismiss, fear, even fall in and out of love with, other members of the organizations. Much of their energy is spent in handling these relationships and in developing some understanding of those others in order to do so (and a large proportion of time is spent in, and enjoyment derived from, gossiping about other people).

So-called 'irrationalities' of personal evaluations of other people as those who 'get up my nose' or 'bore the pants off me' have a great deal more influence on decisions which involve those people than perhaps we would care to admit. Thus, for example, we know that being liked by the boss is at least as important as being seen by him as competent, in terms of what we might be able to persuade him to do.[3] Most of the time our own behaviour and that of others is not reflected upon or managed in a particularly self-conscious way. We are usually as human beings extremely competent in dealing with all the nuances, variations, surprising twists and turns of interactions with other people. Brief discontinuities, moments of uncomfortableness in an otherwise satisfactory or, to us, unimportant relationship rarely represent serious problems for us.

However, there clearly are times when we see events in relationships with others as having significant implications that we do not like. Indeed there is a large body of professional practice concerned with teaching about, or intervening in, 'interpersonal' problems in organizations. Often it is assumed that there is some relatively straightforward demarcation between such 'interpersonal' problems and other kinds of problems. That such a demarcation is rarely, if ever, clear cut is one of the points we hope our example illustrates.

POLITICAL CONCERNS

John and his friend Alan had been ruminating about what Ian Brown, the new director, being the sort of man they believed him to be, and in the light of the things he had said in the meeting, might do in the future which would have implications for their life in the organization. In his new role Ian had suddenly become someone of much greater significance than in the past. The meeting had left Alan feeling anxious and we can readily imagine him spending no small amount of mental energy on attempting to predict exactly what Ian's future actions might be with respect to himself. He will probably attempt to 'suss' out the opinions and feelings of various colleagues. He will probably consider what strategies he might use to prevent Ian from interfering in ways that he does not like, and so on. We are touching here upon that category of activities in which individuals engage with respect to one another known as organizational politics. Specifically, self-consciously and according to some strategic sense of a desired end to be served, they seek to gain other people's support for, or prevent them from hindering, certain states of affairs relating to those ends.

To do this, individuals will seek to ensure that other people hold the definition of a situation that they want them to hold. They can do this in several ways. For example they will sometimes attempt to persuade through the power of 'rational' argument, or through the self-evident merit of their image of desired ends or means, or by appeal to their own 'superior' expertise. Sometimes they will lie, cheat and attempt to manipulate. In either case they will be selective about what information they reveal and order its presentation in particular ways according to their own understanding of what is likely to be most persuasive to the particular people concerned. They will usually present their argument as reflecting a concern for the 'good' of the organization, or at least of those particular people. Often they will believe this to be so, sometimes they will not, but to admit otherwise would be to break one of the cardinal rules of the organizational political game – that of admitting to 'selfish' motives. The essence of this rule is not that people actually believe others to be unselfish, indeed usually quite the opposite. Simply that there appears to be an almost 'fact of the matter' norm among members of most organizations that it is illegitimate to admit to personal ends.

Because individuals with distinct perspectives and political concerns rarely reach complete agreement about ends and means, compromise outcomes are often negotiated or bargains struck about favours to be exchanged at different times.[4] Alliances will be formed, some relatively stable and enduring, others relatively short term. The energetic will spend considerable effort and time in finding out what others do want and think on a particular issue. (Often this involves a game-like process in which both parties know what is going on, are ready to be involved in what is going on, but do not acknowledge openly that they are participating in a lobbying process.) They will 'chat up' those they regard as powerful, not for any particular purpose but still with some strategic conception that such activities will bear fruit later in some particular context.[5] And they will do these things because they seek, as reasonable men and women, to pursue what they regard as right and best. It is important to be clear that organizational politics is not the sole territory of self-interested manipulators, megalomaniacs or charlatans. [. . .]

To take this perspective seriously means that it is impossible to assume, self-evidently and non-problematically, that the way other people interpret a situation is the same as, or even similar to, the way we interpret that 'same' situation. An event which you or I might see as a major crisis for a particular reason may be seen as a major crisis by someone else for completely different reasons, by another person as a minor difficulty, and yet other people may not even have noticed it at all. No situation is inherently, 'objectively' a problem. A problem belongs to a person; it is an often complicated, and always personal (albeit in some part shared with some others) construction that an individual places on events. [. . .]

THE EXPERIENCE OF PROBLEMS

We can usually give some sort of an answer to the question 'What is the problem?'[6], but it may not be an answer that convinces us, and we often feel we have only been able to give a rather limited description. So it is quite common that the only descriptions we can find for problems are, without in any way being intended to be lies, not descriptions that we feel contain the most important truths about our problems.

Now this is a common feature of the experience of many people, that the step between feeling some sort of discomfort or dissatisfaction, feeling that there is some problem somewhere, and being able to say 'The problem is such-and-such' is a very big step. In fact quite often we find that if we can say what the problem is we have gone a long way towards solving it. This seems to be true with any kind of problem, whether it be some technically oriented work problem, a relationship problem at home, or anything in between.

One of the properties of problems with which helpers have found it quite hard to grapple is the extent to which all problems are personal; different persons see different problems in what other people would take to be the same situation. This is an important point in our argument, and it is fairly well accepted in everyday 'common sense'. This point does not seem to raise much disagreement when it is expressed theoretically, but it is often rather more difficult to bear it in mind and act upon it in practice. For this reason, we shall give three examples of what different people seeing different problems may look like.

Suppose that a student reported himself as feeling tired and listless, generally not very well, and that he did not feel he could be bothered to do anything. A students' union officer might conclude that the student's problem was depression, and might probe to find out more about the depression by asking the student how long it had been going on. The doctor at the university medical centre might say that the problem was a cold, that there were a lot of them about and that she had just had one herself. The student's academic tutor might think that the student was not absorbing himself sufficiently in his work, and that a bit more application and hard work would make still more application and hard work easier. The campus radical might think that the problem was classical anomie and alienation, brought on by the death throes of the capitalist system, and the student counsellor might start from the belief that the problem must lie with the student's sex life. Each of these people finds a different problem in the situation, at least in part because they are each inclined to attribute different causes to events.

For another example, think of a board of directors in a medium-sized manufacturing firm, confronted with a set of figures which show that they 'have a problem of' their market share declining. In this case, the people involved might agree this label for their problem, but might have quite different interpretations of that agreed problem label. The production director may think that the problem is a hopeless advertising campaign that the marketing department have bought, the marketing director may think that the problem is the inflexibility of the production department, which prevents them from being able to offer customers the delivery dates and special options that competitors can achieve. The finance director may think that the problem is excessive conservatism on the part of both the marketing and the production directors in continuing with rigid quality control even though it means that their product is a little more expensive than others on the market.

It is by no means always the case that people assume that problems stem from others rather than themselves. For example, on a magazine, it would be quite possible for an editor to think that they are losing readers because the features editor has become fascinated by some subject which bores most of their readers, while the advertisement controller may attribute loss of readers to a decrease in the number of advertising pages. Both people might believe that it is really their contribution that the magazine depends on, and so any serious problems must stem from their own function.

When we talk about problems, we are not necessarily thinking of problems in the negative sense – our definition was that a problem was a situation where someone wanted something to be different from how it was and was not quite sure how to go about making it so. Thus opportunities for building on strengths and making positive improvements, openings that you feel are there to be exploited but you cannot quite see how at the moment, are also counted as problems for our purpose. The same point about how different people see different problems still applies. The editor and the advertisement controller of a successful magazine may well see different problems in the sense of different opportunities for their magazine, where the editor may think that there is an opportunity to expand the editorial content by a few pages, and thus bring in large numbers of extra readers, ensuring the health, future and profitability of the magazine. The advertisement controller may at the same time see an opportunity to tie the editorial matter more closely to the advertising material, and increase the number of pages of prestige advertising, thus enabling them to increase the rate per page for advertising there, and so ensuring the health, future and profitability of the magazine!

So different people see different problems, and in this sense problems are made and not born. To some extent we believe we can generalize about the kinds of problems that people of different roles, personalities and cultures define for themselves. For example, there is a frequent generalization in the Health Service that, while physicians see everything (not just patients) as complicated and needing a lot of thought, surgeons see all problems as much more cut and dried. Some personalities seem to find the running of a large business to be something which they just get on with and which they do not see as problematic, while others find it a very difficult problem to decide what to eat for lunch. In some cultures, possession of a certain kind of problem seems to be very important to people. For some people in British engineering companies, for example, to have no problem of stress and over-working suggests to them that they are slacking, or unimportant, or in some other way deficient. With some people it seems that if they are short of problems at work they manage to devise themselves the most amazingly complicated problems to do with how they go on holiday.

All these differences in the kinds of problem that different people see do not necessarily imply that any of them are wrong, or that they are deceiving themselves, but rather that almost any situation that a person might be dissatisfied with can be seen as having multiple causes, and any one of those causes may be taken as the central point to hang a problem around. If a person is dissatisfied with the amount of money they have, they may say that the problem is too much taxation, or that their company pays them too little, or that their financial aspirations are too high, or any of a huge number of possible tags could be used to describe the problem that they are experiencing. They may say all of these things, and mean them, which means that it is very important not to take the first verbal tag offered as being 'the problem', but only as an initial indicator that there may be a complicated interlocking mess of problems there to be investigated.[7]

When we are in a situation which is complex and worrying, we are usually too busy and too anxious and too involved with that situation to perceive such choices of what we might see the problem as being; they are often visible only from the outside.

THE HELPER AND PROBLEMS

Problems, then, are very individual things in the sense that different persons might see quite different problems in the same situation. The individual may find it helpful to remember that another person might construct a quite different problem, or even no problem at all, if they were in the same situation; this fact may be of some help in letting a person think more laterally about their problems.

The argument becomes much more significant, however, when we think about problems with which several persons are concerned, because in that case those persons might have quite different views of the problem, both because they have different ways of understanding what is going on around them, and also possibly because they have different interests, responsibilities, duties, and relationships, which lead them to quite different concerns. [. . .]

It would not be untypical in an organization for a person to feel unease or disquiet about something, and for them then to need the agreement of their colleagues and their boss before they can talk to a helper about it. When they talk to their colleagues and boss, they will almost certainly have to answer questions from them about 'What is the problem?' They will need to give them some answer to that question, which shows that the problem is of a type that they need help with, but which also does not suggest that they need help because they are incompetent (presuming they do not want to be thought imcompetent), and also probably which suggests to them that it is in their interests too to have help with this problem; so the person might well choose to state their problem in a way that implies that a solution to it might also solve problems that they suspect some of their colleagues have. They will also almost invariably feel the need to talk about this problem in terms of not being satisfied over the things that are publicly regarded in their organization as legitimate values; this means that a lot of problems which might initially have had nothing to do with such concepts end up being talked about in the teams of the persons who have them in terms of profits, efficiency, ensuring future markets and so on. Even within a team of managers who get on reasonably well and trust each other, it would be unusual for a problem to be phrased in more personal and less legitimate terms such as promotion, making life easier for oneself, or gaining some advantage over another department in the organization.

Not only will the person who introduces the problem produce a carefully doctored version in this way, but also the other members of the team will want to have their say, and so produce further and possibly drastic changes, as the problem is discussed and negotiated within the team. Once again, the points they make are edited by them in line with years of hard-earned and successful experience in that organization, as to what sort of things they need to say in order to get what they want and maintain a favourable image with one another. The skills which all of us who work in organizations develop mean that, without anyone being in the least untruthful or deliberately deceitful, the discussion is almost bound to be quite some way removed from a frank and open discussion of what it is that is eating us. [. . .]

All this, it should be noted, presumes good will and no intention to mislead on the part of anybody. We are for the moment ignoring such situations as when a person presents a problem which they intend to lead to the downfall and removal of one of their colleagues, or where someone lays claim to a problem which they do not actually feel, but they think will impress their colleagues, or where a helper is brought in to talk about a problem in the hope that they will fail, so that the problem concerned can be shown to be of huge proportions and unassailable. A current favourite is to put a problem to a helper in such a way that you get a report back from him which can then be argued as a case for making people redundant: 'we deeply regret this, but the study that has been carried out by independent consultants has shown that . . .', and the helper, by being set a carefully selected problem, has produced a predictable answer which can then be used by the clients as a pseudo-objective justification for the action they were going to take anyhow.

For another example, two departments in an oil company both retained operational research consultants to look at the question of how much storage tankage should be built at a particular refinery. Both groups set out to produce profit-maximizing answers to the question. Each group was given the context of the issue by its employing department, and both groups came up with answers which were in the interests of their department; the two answers conflicted sharply. Even in this case, it seems unlikely that the persons concerned thought they were distorting anything. Much more likely is that they thought they were giving the 'right' description of the problem. So how does a helper begin to be helpful in such a complicated situation?

The first answer to this question that we have found useful is to find ways to help clients to talk as directly as they can about what it is that is concerning them. If the helper is labelled as an operational researcher, clients may feel that they should quantify as much as they can of what they say to him. Nothing wrong with that, of course, if they were already thinking of it all quantitatively, but quite often they may not have been doing so, the quantities they give may be an afterthought; they do not feel very confident in the quantification, and therefore however good the rest of the helper–client interaction, they will not feel very confident in the outcome of whatever work the helper does. They know that it was all based on doubtful data in the first place. So it is important that the client should feel able to talk about things in non-quantitative ways.

Similarly, a lot of factors that are significant in many of the more important organizational decisions are not seen by the decision maker as being definite points, but rather are feelings, or hunches, or theories. When talking to helpers they are quite likely to feel that they should not spend their time telling a 'management scientist' about feelings and theories, but should rather stick to the 'facts'. It is our experience that the things that are seen as objective, hard 'facts' around problems that are really concerning people are often fairly trivial compared with the subjective, soft 'feelings' or 'theories' that they see as central to it. This is scarcely surprising, because people who are dealing with complicated and large issues will have built up a body of experience and wisdom over time which probably incorporates more different things than they would know how to separate out or talk about; their 'feelings' are actually based on a huge number of 'facts', but because they cannot remember and describe those facts individually, they may not regard the resulting feeling as a worthy topic to talk about in front of a helper. Helpers who let such an inhibition persist will be deprived of most of their clients' important thinking about their situations. [. . .]

Thereby the helper does not find out what is really bothering his clients. They work together on a problem which either neither of them, or just the helper 'owns'. In these circumstances often neither of them feels satisfied with the outcome as, for example, when a helper works, with the best of intentions and effort on a problem he thought his client had only to find out afterwards that his recommendations have been quietly ignored and the client is acting in ways that make no sense with respect to the problem the helper heard about; while the client, while acknowledging that the helper has done his best, is confirmed in his belief that the helper can only provide assistance with particular, and limited, aspects of problems.

NOTES

1. For a detailed and important analysis of the relationship between 'subjective' and 'objective' realities and knowledge see Berger, P. L. and Luckmann, T. (1966) *The Social Construction of Reality*, New York, Doubleday. Another useful but difficult book in this context is by Silverman, D. (1970) *Theory of Organizations*, who describes and evaluates several different perspectives for understanding organizations, including his own orientation to the nature of actions as arising from the meaning individuals ascribe to events (see particularly Chapter 6).
2. For a discussion of the nature of beliefs and values, see Chapter 3 in Eden, C., Jones, S. and Sims, D. (1979) *Thinking in Organizations*, London, Macmillan. See also Young, M. (1977) *Society, State and Schooling*, and Rokeach, M. (1973) *Nature of Human Values*.
3. For a discussion of the significance of personal relationships and what he terms 'particularism' in organizational decision-making, see Perrow, C. (1972) *Complex Organizations*.
4. For an interesting analysis of the difficulty in distinguishing between means and ends in the pursual of goals and objectives, see Ackoff, R. L. (1979) 'The future of operations research is past', *Journal of the Operations Research Society*, 30, pp. 93–104.
5. For a book which describes in detail the internal political aspects of organizational decision-making using the case study of the purchase of a computer, see Pettigrew (1973) *Politics of Organizational Decision Making*. Another fascinating case is described, almost in the form of a novel, by Jones, R. and Lakin, C. (1978) *The Carpet Makers*, Maidenhead, McGraw-Hill.
6. For further discussion of this question, see Eden, C. and Sims, D. (1979) 'On the nature of problems in consulting practice', *Omega*, Vol. 7, 2, pp. 119–27; Sims, D. (1978) 'Problem construction in teams', Ph.D. Thesis, University of Bath; and Sims, D. (1979) 'A framework for understanding the definition and formulation of problems in teams', *Human Relations*, Vol. 32, 11, pp. 909–21.

7. The idea of problems being found in 'messes' comes from Ackoff, R. L. (1974) *Redesigning the Future*, who describes a mess as a 'system of problems'. Kepner, C. H. and Tregoe, B. B. (1965) The Rational Manager, New York, McGraw-Hill, use on page 63 a different definition of mess, very similar to our definition of 'problem'.

CHAPTER 9

Equal Opportunities

The drive to offer equal employment opportunities was directed initially at eliminating unjust discrimination – the employee, or potential employee, was the victim. Only latterly have discriminatory employment practices been seen as acting against organizational interests – the organization is itself the victim when self-sealing beliefs prevent recognition of talent and diverse experience. The first reading examines how the assumptions we all make about people are perpetuated by uncriticized experience. The second reading raises some interesting questions about women's experiences in organizations. The secretary's role, which is itself perceived in terms of gender stereotypes, is a role whose stereotype influences the experience of many women in organizations. Both readings come from a book where analysis is alternated with vignettes of organizational life. These vignettes are all the funnier for being so painfully true to experience.

9A

But Some Are More Equal Than Others: Socialization and Attribution

R. RICHARD RITTI

George Orwell's classic *Animal Farm* is an allegorical tale of social stratification, of the demise of an attempt to establish a classless society. The creatures of *Animal Farm*, having overthrown their masters, live by seven commandments, the last of which is simply, 'All animals are equal'. All comes to naught, however, when the deceitful and ambitious pigs establish themselves as the new ruling stratum and amend the final commandment to read:

BUT SOME ANIMALS ARE MORE EQUAL THAN OTHERS

Most of us working in organizations think of social stratification in organizations as an okay thing, a necessary thing. Achievement is rewarded by promotion, and there has to be a hierarchy of command. There have to be executives, managers, and workers. But we think it's okay mostly because *we'll* be up there in that hierarchy some day, after working hard to achieve that status and the rewards that accompany it. In a similar manner, we understand that lower organizational participants are also there for reasons of merit – or lack of it. The net result in societies and organizations is a stratification into various ranks or statuses, arranged from top to bottom.

If you are well socialized into your organizational culture and are asked to account for the fact that a particular person holds a particular rank in the organizational hierarchy, chances are you will come up with answers that involve the *attribution* of traits and motives. Research in attribution theory tells us that, typically, when asked to account for some action they have taken, *actors* will explain their behavior as stemming from the *situation* in which they found themselves. *Observers*, on the other hand, usually invoke some explanation involving the personal *traits or motives* of the actor. And this is especially true when the situation is one of failure rather than success.[1] We thus attribute abilities and motives to upwardly mobile managers in accordance with the status they have achieved. These attributions enhance perceptions of the correctness of managerial decisions. And these perceptions, in turn, are self-fulfilling, for the soundness of the decision may ultimately rest on the willingness of subordinates to carry it through. 'They must know what they're doing – they wouldn't be there if they didn't.'

The myth, symbol, and ritual of organizational culture both signify and solidify attributions. Ritual imparts objective reality to myth and prescribes the behavior through which organizational participants enact the myth. Remember that myths are accounts of the origins of things, as well as unquestioned beliefs about the practical benefits of certain techniques and behaviors. I think it crucially important here to distinguish between the actual *practice* of those techniques and behaviors, and the *mythology* that supports that practice. It is entirely possible for a member of the organization to subscribe completely to the myth and still recognize that in *this* situation the practice supported by the myth is flawed. Take the myth of performance as an example. All corporate cultures hold to the myth that the only thing that counts toward promotion is performance. The myth further states that superiors have full knowledge of their subordinates' work and that this knowledge is carefully quantified in the performance appraisal (ritual). Ergo, the deserving and talented are promoted, others are not. But the fact that the performance appraisal ritual is supported by the myth in no way guarantees that it was carried out appropriately in a given case. The myth *encourages* that belief, but that is all. Put another way, its possible that you may feel mad as hell that you got reviewed unfairly in this instance, but that only reveals your unquestioning acceptance of the myth of the ritual.

Symbols of rank also signify and solidify attributions – larger offices, better furniture, windows, rugs, and so on. And symbolic communication sometimes occurs in odd forms. I recall the day that Arthur K. 'Dick' Watson brought a talking mynah bird to the executive floor of IBM World Headquarters – as it was then called. Although it is true that the bird was suitably attired in charcoal gray, this was still a most 'unIBMmanagerlike' thing to do. It was, however, most symbolic of the fact that the Chairman of the Board's brother is above the usual corporate restraint on managerial behavior.

Up to now, we have been talking about earned statuses only, what sociologists term *achieved* statuses. But sociology tells us that there is yet another kind of status that accounts for social stratification – *ascribed* status. Thus, some members of society are assigned (ascribed) lower social statuses because of beliefs that society holds about them by reason of sex, race, religion, or ethnic background.

Examples? In 1960, many doubted that a Catholic, John F. Kennedy, could be elected President. Somewhat later, in the 1984 election, there was doubt whether Geraldine Ferraro could stand up to the heat of public debate against a man. [. . .] Indeed, women were among the most doubtful, a significant point about culturally formed social expectations. Some people are accorded lower ascribed social statuses than others, and we don't elect low-status people to our most prestigious national office. [. . .]

Let's look at ascribed status more carefully and see what it means for us in organizations. Not too many years ago you would have observed that most professionals, almost all middle managers, and all executives were white males. On the other hand, most clericals and almost all secretaries were females, mostly white. As a white male professional entering the organization, you might simply have taken this situation for granted. And if asked to explain the situation, you probably would have said, 'That's just the way it is.' If pressed further, chances are you would again come up with answers involving the attribution of traits and motives. In this case, though, your attribution of abilities, traits, and motives would not be to individuals, but to females or blacks *as a class*. These explanations would likely have something to do with motives and goals, based on the assumption that these people are where they are because that is what they want, or because they lack some of the qualities necessary for success. Thus, you would probably attribute the status – the organizational situation – of these people to personal characteristics like ability, motivation, values, and goals, rather than the situation in which they have been placed. [. . .]

So pervasive are these explanations invoking personal characteristics that, when we witness a case to the contrary, we again resort to individual explanations to account for this departure from the general rule. She is an exceptional woman – 'thinks like a man', someone will say by way of preserving the more general account. It used to be said of a successful black man that he was a 'credit to his race'. This again by way of preserving the general stereotype that blacks as a class are generally unwilling or unable to make the effort to succeed. [. . .]

Having established these explanations, the principles of perception outlined in the previous section help us see what we expect to see, and we interpret accordingly. Women are emotional, passive, and nurturing; blacks flamboyant, aggressive, and undependable. Perceptual distortion and 'filling in' provide abundant support for our beliefs.

We thus begin to treat people as though the things we've assumed about them are actually true. We protect them from emotional upsets; we protect them from failure; we protect them from stressful responsibility and treat them differently in thousands of other little ways that we don't realize ourselves.

The final act of this ongoing organizational drama is the observation that people start behaving in *fact* the way we expect them to behave. How could our expectations have that much effect? Well, a number of research studies have been conducted on the effect of situational expectations on behavior. Two of these merit brief mention.

In the first, people were assigned at random to one of two experimental groups. These groups differed only in that one learned that their 'jobs' were less important and less interesting than those assigned to the other group; furthermore, there was no hope of 'upward' movement for them. The other group, given similar information about the nature of their 'jobs,' learned that 'upward' movement was possible, depending on how well they performed. The results? The randomly selected group with no hope of movement spent considerably more time socializing among themselves and criticizing the actions of 'management'. Although the experimental situation was rigged so that the two groups were otherwise treated identically, the 'not promotable' group started behaving just as we expect lower ascribed status employees to behave.[2]

In the second and more dramatic experiment, two groups of college students were randomly assigned the roles of prisoner and prison guard. They began behaving so realistically, so brutally, that the experiment had to be terminated a week early. The experimenter called off the experiment because of his horror upon this realization:

> I could easily have traded places with the most brutal guard or become the weakest prisoner . . . Individual behavior is largely under the control of social forces and environmental contingencies rather than personality traits . . . We thus underestimate the power and pervasiveness of situational controls over behavior because: a) they are often . . . subtle; b) we can often avoid entering situations where we might be so controlled; c) we label as 'weak' or 'deviant' people in those situations who do behave differently *from how we believe we would* [italics added].[3]

[. . .]

NOTES

1. Lawrence S. Wrightsman, *Social Psychology*, 2nd Ed., Belmont, CA: Wadsworth (1977): 100.
2. Arthur R. Cohen, 'Upward communication in experimentally created hierarchies,' *Human Relations II*, (1958): 41–53.
3. Philip G. Zimbardo, 'Pathology of imprisonment,' *Society* 9 (1972): 6.

9B
Cat In The Hat

R. RICHARD RITTI

Stanley was sitting peacefully in Lesley's office waiting for her to return from an early afternoon meeting. He hadn't talked with her since she'd been moved to her new responsibility in Corporate Communications. The new position looked like a real opportunity to move ahead, so naturally Stanley wanted to find out how it was going.

Stanley and Lesley had been friends in The Company for quite a while now. Still, he wasn't quite prepared for what was about to happen. But wait, here comes Lesley now.

'You! You're probably just like the rest of 'em. Another sexist! Another male chauvinist!'

'Me?' was about all Stanley could reply weakly.

'Probably.' Lesley's tone softened. 'Oh, no. I don't really mean that. I know you're okay, Stan. It's just that . . . listen, *listen* to this. Here I am at this meeting. We're getting a project group together to cover Marsh's big research lab dedication next month. We're going to do a whole series for . . .' Lesley described her excited anticipation of the new job and of how the meeting had progressed.

They are waiting for the Corporate Director to arrive so that the meeting might get underway. And here she is, sitting at one side of the table, prepared as usual with her handful of sharp pencils and a fresh yellow pad. Being new, and knowing hardly anyone there, she's not saying much.

Okay, here's the Director. Let's get on with the job.

Now at this point, and according to Company ritual, the host manager takes orders for coffee; five black, two sugar only . . .

'Then he turns to me, *to me*, and says in this unctuous voice, "Would you get these for us, honey. The machine's down the hall to the left".'

'Get these for us, honey?! Who the hell does he think he is? Why the hell should I get his lousy coffee? Just 'cause I'm the only "lady" in the room? I don't even *drink* the damn stuff!' Lesley was greatly exercised.

Unfortunately, Stanley didn't help much, 'Did you?' he asked. It was an innocent enough question, but Stanley just managed to dodge the phone book that sailed his way.

'Yes!' Lesley almost shrieked the answer.

'But why? . . .'

'I just didn't know what else to do. I . . .'

Hearing the commotion, Pat Jones (The Company's Director of Human Resources Research) poked her head in the door and caught the last of the conversation. 'Sounds like you're having fun. Look, I apologize for listening in, but I really couldn't help hearing your story. Would you like some advice?'

Lesley nodded.

'I've worked with these guys for years now, and they're really not that bad a bunch. But you can see for yourself, it's like a men's club around here. Sure, there are women around, but almost all of us are clerks, secretaries, you know. I'm the odd ball. And whether or not you and I like it, those clerks and secretaries do little extra things for them like . . .'

'Like getting coffee!' Lesley cut in, 'So that big jerk figured I was just another secretary! Why?'

'What did you expect? How would he know otherwise?' Then Pat added with a chuckle, 'He's more to be pitied than censured, you know. He just assumed that you were there to take notes.'

'But what do I do?' said Lesley, 'I can't go around introducing myself and saying that I'm not a secretary.'

'Oh,' replied Pat, 'You could. But it isn't necessary. Next time when you're with strangers, just make sure you wear a hat.'

'A hat? I don't even *own* a hat.'

'Then buy one,' Pat countered.

'For heaven's sake why?' asked Lesley.

'Ever see a secretary at one of these meetings in a hat?' was Pat's simple answer.

'No, that would be absurd,' said Lesley.

'Exactly. Important women wear hats at important events. The boys may not know who you are, but at least they'll understand you're not the one to get the coffee.'

What's that you say? You think that's silly advice? Well, maybe so. I really didn't intend it as a serious suggestion, though indeed that was Pat Jones's advice. But the point is clear enough, isn't it? Old ways of doing things die hard, and male managers still expect female secretaries to get the coffee and to perform other petty non-work tasks. And, by and large, they expect secretaries to be females and vice versa. That's what they're used to. Consequently, as a pencil-wielding, yellow-pad-carrying female, they assume that Lesley (a) is a secretary, (b) is ready and willing to get the coffee, (c) is waiting to be told what to do, and (d) has the primary job interest of pleasing male authority figures.

Lesley's problem is to short-circuit the process and avoid the accompanying discomfort for all involved by providing unmistakable cues that she is not a secretary or other lower participant. And though she probably would not wear a hat, other dress cues are also important. For example, carrying an expensive leather briefcase would be an unmistakable sign of professional status. Finally, in situations where she does not expect to be known, she might plan ahead, arrive early, and introduce herself by name and position to each new arrival. You know, that might not be a bad idea for all of us.

CHAPTER 10

Managing Technological Change

The benefits of new technology can be something of a 'promised land': you have to pass through a veritable wilderness of sensitive, ferociously complicated, terrifyingly expensive and far-reaching decisions to get there. There is no guarantee that the system will work as you hoped, once you arrive. Indeed for every major blessing it brings, it is as likely to bring a clutch of nasty little curses. The new system may be infuriatingly difficult to get working. It may be even more infuriating once it is. Many organizations have passed through the first wave of the 'information technology revolution' only to find themselves exiled again as their systems become outdated by improvements in the technology. The following article gives a clear account of these familiar problems: as relevant today as when it was first written. It argues for an evolutionary and participative approach to system design but is commendably frank about the difficulties. As usual, there are no easy answers . . .

The Process of Introducing Information Technology

K. D. EASON

1 THE AGE OF INFORMATION TECHNOLOGY

We are constantly being bombarded with the news that we are entering a new information technology era which will revolutionize the office, bring robots to our production lines, change the face of our high streets and bring information services of all kinds into our own homes (Evans 1979, Forester 1979, Toffler 1980). We are also forcefully told of the threat this revolution poses for employment (Jenkins and Sherman 1979) but nevertheless we are exhorted to embrace the technology speedily because unless we do our companies will lose their competitiveness.

Close behind the reports of the wonders of the new technology are reports of the slow rate at which companies are responding to the challenge. Zermeno *et al.* (1979) for example, documents the slow march of robots into British manufacturing industry whilst Mackintosh (1981) reports a survey of top UK industrial managers which shows that they know something is going on but are 'either incapable or unwilling to learn about its strategic implications for their own organizations'.

Why are we being slow to adopt information technology? Many reasons can and have been advanced. One argument is that we are in a recession and when the main preoccupation is survival there is no point in making long-term plans to introduce new technology. A second argument is that within organizations, and especially within management, there is a deep-rooted ignorance of this technology and its significance. This argument leads to efforts to increase the computer literacy of management and to schemes such as the regional centres of the National Computing Centre in the UK which will provide advice to local businessmen.

A third argument is that, whilst information technology may have many potential benefits, it is not easy to realize these benefits. Most reasonably sized organizations have made some use of computers and found it very difficult to achieve the promised results. Some systems were never implemented; others that were implemented became sources of inertia and inflexibility within their organizations. In a recent study (Lyne and Davis 1981) we found that management were very suspicious of the claims of computer salesmen and were being very cautious with their money. There is also a widespread recognition that introducing information technology creates human, social, political and organizational problems which have to be solved before implementation can be successful. The increasing awareness of trade unions of these implications serves to make management more wary. If they are unsure of the benefits claimed and are aware of the potential problems, it is small wonder managers are slow to venture into the information technology revolution.

Of these arguments the one that is receiving most attention at the moment is the need to improve the level of computer literacy: to show people the technology and help them to understand it. I believe this to be a necessary but not sufficient condition for the successful implementation of information technology. It leaves potential users with a wide variety or problems concerning the choice of a system which will meet their specific needs and how to implement the system with the minimum of negative ramifications within their organization. In this paper my intention is twofold; to consider in more detail the nature of the problems to be overcome and then to consider how best organizations may be assisted to cope with these problems.

2 THE IMPACT OF COMPUTERIZATION

We can conveniently divide these issues into two groups:

1. Issues concerning the functions to be performed by the technology.
2. Consequential effects of implementing the system within the organization.

2.1 The functions of information technology

Computer-based technology is potentially very flexible. However before it can be used by the non-specialist it has to be programmed to perform very specific activities. If these activities are what is required by the organization, all may be well. If the activities performed by the system differ even slightly from what is needed major problems can develop; either the system is rejected or perhaps is only partly used (where the 'fit' is best) or the organization modifies what is required (the 'tool' defines the 'task') (Eason *et al.* 1974). The experience of the latter is of a system rigidly shaping how activities are undertaken; representatives of the organization and their customers find their freedom to behave appropriately to their task constrained by 'what the computer will allow'. Over time, as the task of the organization changes a badly fitting and rigid system can become a major obstacle to the organization's ability to respond adaptively. Far from becoming a major vehicle to facilitate change, the system can become a major source of inertia.

These problems point to many issues which concern the would-be user of information technology. What are his needs and how unique are they? Can he get a good fit from a package or does he need special purpose software? How flexible is the software and how readily can it be modified as organizational needs change? To answer these questions the user must obviously understand the potential of the technology but he must also and pre-eminently be able to assess his own needs.

Even if a system has the potential to serve a user's needs, the potential may not be realized. The user may find the system difficult to use, difficult to understand, takes too much of his time or involves unacceptable and unnatural behaviour from him. These issues make up the problem of 'usability' or 'user acceptance' and Eason (1981a) has described how the strategies users adopt when confronted by these problems can mean that a new system remains unused. When introducing a new system, therefore, it is necessary to consider not only the user's needs but also the forms of answering these needs which will be acceptable to him.

2.2 Consequences of implementing information technology

In some ways the information flows in an organization can be compared with the nervous system in a body. To install a new means of processing information is rather like providing the body with a major transplant. We know that an organ transplant in the body may be unsuccessful in two ways; it may be rejected as foreign tissue or it may lead to severe complications because of the adaptations it necessitates in interdependent systems. The body is a collection of systems which need to work in some degree of harmony. Similarly an organization is a collection of systems which have to achieve a degree of harmony if useful work is to be produced. The insertion of a computer system in the role of purveyor of information between systems can disrupt the harmony. The result may be a rejection of the system or serious negative complications elsewhere in the organization which effectively dissipate the gains made by introducing the system.

Figure 10.1 presents a sociotechnical systems view of an organization showing the many different subsystems which have to operate within it, any of which may be disrupted by the injection of a computer system into a central information processing role. A considerable volume of research has been conducted to show where and in what form the knock-on effects of

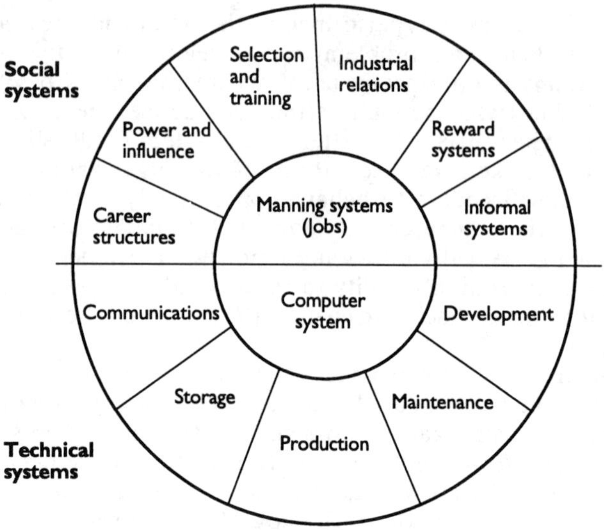

Figure 10.1 The organization as a complex sociotechnical system

computer technology are likely to show themselves. The following is a brief summary of the major effects that can occur in the social systems identified in Figure 10.1.

2.2.1 JOB NUMBERS

There is frequently a change in the number of jobs required within the organization. Perhaps the largest perceived threat of computer technology is that it will lead to a massive loss of jobs. This is sometimes the case but there are also many examples of increases in job numbers. However, it is often the case that the new jobs will require different skills from the old ones and many people may be displaced because they are deemed unsuitable for the new jobs (Gotlieb and Borodin 1973).

2.2.2 JOB CONTENT

Contrary to many popular views, people are still needed when computers are in use. What they do will almost certainly change. One view has man freed of dull routine and able to become the creative problem solver of the organization. Another view has man in dull repetitive jobs serving the computer by providing input for it. In practice both kinds of jobs have been created and there is often considerable potential for designing appropriate kinds of jobs (Eason and Sell 1981).

2.2.3 HEALTH ISSUES

There is growing awareness that the use of visual display units might be a health hazard. The evidence for serious impairments is by no means conclusive and appears to relate primarily to full-time users engaged in routine work. There is plenty of evidence for more transitory health problems e.g. visual fatigue and postural problems, such as backache (Pearce 1980a,b, 1981).

2.2.4 SKILLS AND TRAINING

Changing jobs means changing skills and therefore new training programmes. Obviously this will mean the development of keyboard skills or learning the procedures of the computer systems but in practice it often goes much further than this and affects the way people perceive their jobs and the way they learn to exploit the facilities of the computer system to perform the job differently.

2.2.5 FORMALITY

Perhaps the most commonly found consequence of computerization is an increase in the formality of organizational procedures. The functioning of a computer depends upon formal programs and their use demands a degree of formality. As a result formality and discipline spread into the organizational procedures which surround the system. Whether this becomes a useful source of order and efficiency or an inhibiting source of rigidity and inflexibility depends upon how the organization manages this effect (Bjorn-Andersen and Eason 1980).

2.2.6 POWER AND INFLUENCE

Information often leads to power, influence and status. There has long been an argument that computerization will lead to a further centralization of power, as senior managers with better sources of information are better able to control their organizations. However, the evidence from empirical studies, whilst showing this as a prevalent trend, also shows decentralization and lateral transfers of power and influence (Bjorn-Andersen and Rasmussen 1980).

2.2.7 PERSONNEL POLICIES AND INDUSTRIAL RELATIONS

Changes in job content and skills have knock-on effects for other personnel policies. Payment systems have to be rethought, grading systems for new and changed jobs evaluated and career patterns replanned. The industrial relations practices of the organizations may suddenly need amendment; for example demarcation agreements may be rendered irrelevant. The attitude and actions of trade unions to these changes may be vital to the success of technological change.

2.3 Consequences for systems design

Other ramifications, particularly for interdependent technical systems, have not been listed. Suffice it to say that any change in the ground rules by which an organization operates will have many effects. The purpose of cataloguing these effects is to make four points:

1. Whilst it is necessary to understand the new technology, there are a host of other issues which must also be understood before technical change can be successful.
2. Whilst there are many ramifications, there is very little that is unidirectional or inevitable about them. Jobs may be lost but jobs may also be gained, poor jobs or good jobs may be created, etc. *The choice of system and the choice of the way it is integrated into the organization will determine the kinds of effects that are found.*
3. If systems selection and design is conducted largely on technical and economic criteria (as has tended to be the case) without explicit recognition of these organizational issues, the process will be one of fighting many fires as they become apparent. It will also be one in which the sociotechnical system created has not been designed but has arisen in an *ad hoc* way. It may in fact lead to a form of organization ineffective for organizational purposes and unwanted by the personnel of the organization.
4. There is a wide choice of systems and ways in which they may be implemented and therefore, to a large extent, the effects can be controlled and guided. We need forms of systems design which explicitly tackle these issues if we are not to be surprised by the obstructions to technological progress and unhappy with the results.

3 STRATEGIES FOR CONSIDERING ORGANIZATIONAL CONSEQUENCES IN SYSTEMS DESIGN

As a member of the HUSAT Research Group at Loughborough University of Technology I have been working on the human and organizational ramifications of computer systems for over a decade. This group has contributed to research on the effects of systems but much of our work has also been to help organizations confront these ramifications and plan for them during systems design. Initially we worked within the normal systems design framework and found it difficult to ensure appropriate attention to human and organizational issues. Gradually we have evolved a different approach which is now becoming popular in the organizations with whom we have worked. In the sections that follow I trace the changes in approach we have found necessary and document the strategies we are now following.

3.1 Stage 1: Human factors in a traditional systems design process

In the early stages of our efforts to help organizations consider the human ramifications of systems during the design process we found ourselves operating within what might be considered a traditional design process and this is probably still the dominant approach in use today. The major elements of this approach are presented in Figure 10.2. In this approach the dominant theme is putting together a working technical system. The system

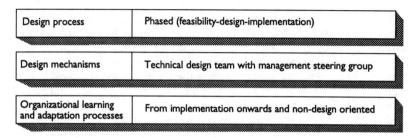

Design process	Phased (feasibility-design-implementation)
Design mechanisms	Technical design team with management steering group
Organizational learning and adaptation processes	From implementation onwards and non-design oriented

Figure 10.2 The design elements in technology-led systems design

is usually created by a design team consisting of technical experts with senior management in a steering role concerning themselves with cost-benefit aspects of the system. The design process usually consists of some kind of feasibility study followed by a phase in which equipment is purchased and software purchased and/or designed. Finally the working and tested system is implemented.

Our role is primarily to help the organization and its employees learn about the system and its consequences and to take appropriate action to achieve the benefits and avoid or minimize the negative effects. This proved to be a quite difficult feat. Under the technology-led approach the end users of the system did not become involved until the system was implemented. The end users are the people best able to predict the consequences of a specific system because (a) they have an intimate knowledge of the nature of the work and (b) they understand the workings of the many related systems that may be affected. An outsider can point to where effects may occur but it takes a detailed knowledge of the specific organizational fabric to judge what form they will take.

Our work in this kind of systems design process was therefore confined to helping people appreciate the issues of a system that had already been designed. Their new learning could not be used to develop a system with different effects: it could only be used to ameliorate the effects by accommodating them within other organizational systems and by adaptation of the users themselves. The situation is summarized in Figure 10.3.

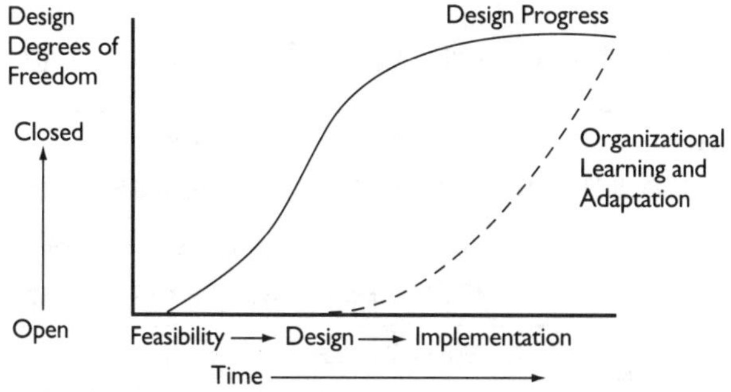

Figure 10.3 Design closure and organizational learning in technology-led systems design

We can look upon the design process as one of progressive 'firming up'. Initially the technology can in theory do everything but in practice can do nothing. By a succession of design decisions a system is gradually developed which can achieve something specific but at the same time it loses the rest of its potential. In this systems design process the design of the technical systems is virtually frozen before users become sufficiently aware of the ramifications of the system to take action. They can then only take action within the interrelated systems of the organization or can reject the system or minimize its use.

3.2 Stage 2: User involvement in systems design

During the 1970s it becamed apparent to many people that the traditional systems design process was not an adequate vehicle for taking full account of the organizational issues surrounding the implementation of new technology. There was a movement, particularly strong to Scandinavia (see, for example, Bjorn-Andersen 1980) towards involving users much earlier in the design process in order that they could affect the design of the systems they were to use. In the Scandinavian countries these moves have been given the backing of a legal framework. In the UK, we promoted similar approaches as did many others, notably Enid Mumford (Mumford and Henshall (1979).

The general change in approach is summarized in Figure 10.4. The major change is that the mechanisms by which the system is created are expanded to include end users at both the steering level and at the detailed design level. There are many ways of accomplishing this ranging from co-opted user representatives in the technical design team to 'user design' in which users effectively develop their own system (a classification of alternative forms of user involvement is given by Damodaran and Eason (1981)). The overall aim of such schemes is always, however, to encourage users to participate in the creation of the system throughout the design process.

There has now been considerable experience of user-involvement schemes and one general point emerges; it is an essential feature for many reasons but it is exceptionally difficult to manage effectively. The main problems encountered are as follows.

3.2.1 INFLUENCE AND CONTROL

There is always the question of how much of a voice users have in design decisions. If they find they can have little influence and are there merely

Design process	Phased (feasibility-design-implementation)
Design mechanisms	User involvement at design team and steering group level
Organizational learning and adaptation processes	Throughout the design process

Figure 10.4 The design elements in systems design with user involvement

because a gesture towards consultation was supposed to smooth implementation, they can become disenchanted and resistant. On the other hand if they have a major voice, the technologists or management may feel they have been robbed of their prerogatives and may become resistant to user involvement.

3.2.2. UNDERSTANDING SYSTEMS TERMINOLOGY

The nature of the technology and the terminology of systems design is initially a mystery to most users. It is especially difficult in the early stages of design when there is only an abstract version of the system available. It is very difficult for users to comment meaningfully on a flow-chart or a system specification. They need time and help before they can make their contribution. It is much easier to comment when a working system becomes available but by then it is too late to make changes.

3.2.3 STEPPING OUT OF DAY-TO-DAY WORK

Regular work may mean the user has the necessary experience to judge the ramifications of system proposals, but he often needs help to go from an action role to a reflective and predictive role in which he can summarize his experience in useful ways. Again time and help are needed.

3.2.4 CHOOSING BETWEEN ALTERNATIVES

There are many options in the way a system is designed and how it is implemented. Choosing between them means deciding what is desirable and what is undesirable, trading-off different criteria and predicting what will be necessary and worth while in the future. The users may be the best placed to make these decisions but it is not a familiar exercise and they frequently need help to make explicit the aspirations of themselves and their organizational units.

3.2.5 CONFLICT MANAGEMENT

There will inevitably be conflict of interest and disagreement about what is needed and how it should be implemented. Some conflicts are obvious and there will probably be institutional ways of dealing with them, e.g. industrial relations procedures for dealing with redundancies. There are, however, also likely to be many conflicts between different groups of users about the services provided by the system, the siting of terminals, who shall have access to information, etc., and such conflicts must be resolved during the design process.

3.2.6 TAKING TECHNICAL DECISIONS DURING USER INVOLVEMENT

It will be apparent that users come ill-equipped to contribute to systems design and they need time and help before their experience is available in a usable form. In the meantime technical designers are trying to establish a hardware specification and make decisions about software, etc. If users are to influence systems design, the output from users must be available before the design is frozen. Unfortunately the length of time it takes for users to learn and adapt and for conflicts to be resolved often exceeds design deadlines which either means delays in schedules or decisions taken without the full contribution of the users. It is frequently the case that, in practice, user involvement makes little contribution to systems design but helps to ameliorate the effects of the system elsewhere as users see the ramifications and help plan for them.

The situation is summarized graphically in Figure 10.5. As a result of user involvement, the influence of users has moved to an earlier phase of the design process. However, because of the problems listed above, they inevitably need time before they are capable of making an effective contribution. During this time the design of the system is gradually being frozen and there is only a limited 'window' during which users can influence design decisions. In many situations it is a time when the users are still ill-equipped to make their contribution. As a result the process remains largely technology-led although the impact of user involvement has helped to predict and plan for the organizational ramifications.

3.3 Stage 3: Evolutionary design for organizational learning

User involvement has made it possible for us to plan for the organizational ramifications of new technology. We are still however a long way from the ideal situation in which the members of an organization are able to proceed through the following three steps:

1. Determine the future opportunities and/or demands on their organization.
2. Establish the most desirable way in which they should be organized for their future tasks.
3. Select appropriate forms of technology to support the chosen form of organization.

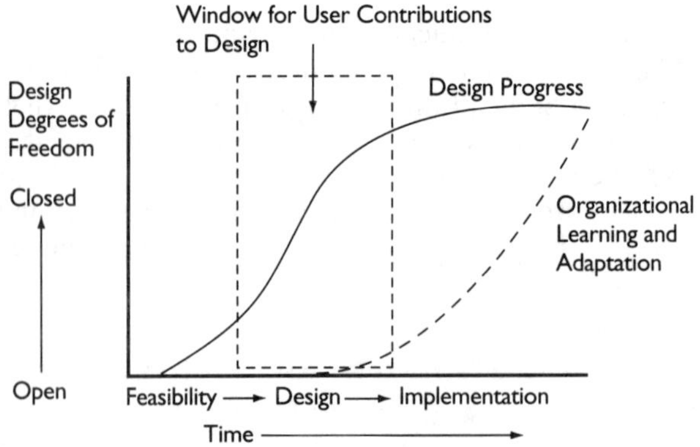

Figure 10.5 The design closure and organizational learning in user involvement

At present decisions made upon technical criteria tend to make this process operate in reverse. It is of course possible for technologists to determine the appropriate form of organization and to select technological systems that support it but (a) they have a more limited understanding of the organization than those who run it and work in it and (b) they will not have to live with the consequences of the decision.

In our view we need systems design methods which enable potential users to work through this process to ensure that the technology chosen supports the kind of organization they conclude they need. We have been working on various schemes to facilitate user and organization learning so that they are better able to contribute to design decisions but inevitably it takes time. This technique can never be wholly successful if we are always faced with a limited period before the degrees of freedom in design are lost. We have therefore turned our attention to design methods in which this does not happen; to evolutionary design.

In this approach a system is gradually put together from small beginnings always with the possibility that parts of it may be modified, withdrawn or elaborated. Rather than being an entity which is conceived and built at one time and implemented to remain that way for its operational life, the system is now conceived as something that will grow and change over time as the needs of the organization change. This is a very different concept and fortunately there have been developments in the technology which make it an increasingly practical proposition. The advent of microelectronics means hardware is cheap and portable and that a small standalone system can be implemented quickly, the facilities of which can be added to later with the possibility of linking it to other systems. Similarly developments in software mean that the service the user receives can be changed with relative ease. Indeed it is quite possible for the interface to be 'personalized' so that the same system provides tailor-made services to a variety of users.

These changes mean that we can rewrite the way many systems are developed in order to give users a much greater say in what is being created in their name. In Figure 10.6 and 10.7 this approach to design is summarized and its implications highlighted.

Figure 10.6 identifies the main features we require in an evolutionary design process. We need a form of technology which will permit growth and change and design mechanisms in which there is a regular transmission

Design process	An evolutionary process preserving flexibility of change
Design mechanisms	Regular user feedback to design team
Organizational learning and adaptation processes	Evolutionary and continuous

Figure 10.6 Design elements in evolutionary design

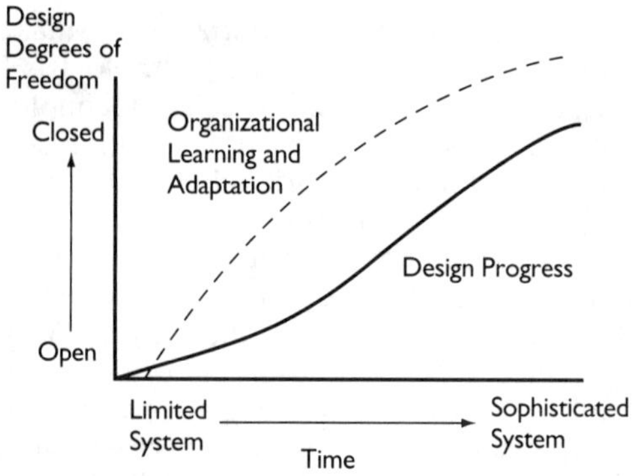

Figure 10.7 Organizational learning and evolutionary systems design

of information about needs and problems from users to design staff. In order that this flow of information can be valid and relevant, we also need to facilitate an evolution of learning by the users about system facilities and how they may be exploited.

Figure 10.7 expresses what we might hope to achieve if we seek the goals expressed in Figure 10.6. Recognizing that organizational learning about technology and adaptation must begin slowly and progressively evolve, we can hope to ensure that systems development follows a similar pattern so that organizational learning can inform systems development. It is also important that systems development never reaches complete closure, that there is always potential for change, because the organizational learning and change process will never end.

We have been working with a number of organizations to implement design processes with these features. We cannot claim to have developed a complete methodology but many elements of the strategy are emerging and are described in the next section.

4 METHODS OF PROMOTING PARTICIPATIVE AND EVOLUTIONARY SYSTEMS DEVELOPMENT

The strategy we have evolved identifies three strands to the systems development process:

1. A technical system undergoing development and evolution.
2. System usage which is also growing with time.
3. Forms of user involvement which serve the dual functions of enabling the users to participate in design activities and to be supported in system usage.

In our view these three strands are mutually dependent. For example, users need experience of a real system before they can participate fully and effectively and systems evolution depends upon continued input from users about their emerging needs. . . . some of the major activities . . . in the systems development process are . . . described below.

4.1 Involvement

If there is to be effective user involvement, mechanisms need to be established which will provide for involvement. This may mean the establishment of working parties with briefs for different facets of the development, the selection of user representatives, etc. There can be no single answer to the form these structures could take because each organization will have a unique array of user groups, a culture which creates certain expectations about participation, a set of industrial relations procedures, etc., and these will shape the structures that are appropriate to carry user involvement. The general rules should be (a) to ensure all 'stakeholders' (i.e. everyone who will be affected by the system) are involved in some capacity, (b) to ensure representatives maintain good contact with those they represent and (c) to arrange that users are involved in those aspects of design upon which they have expertise and about which they have a keen interest. This means that some users may be involved in broad strategic discussions about the kind of system to be developed whilst the involvement of others may concern questions of office layout.

4.2 Pilot systems

The people working within the user-involvement structures need real experience of relevant systems before they can take informed decisions. The existence of cheap and easily implemented small-scale systems based on minis and micros means that it is possible for organizations to implement systems for experimental and learning purposes. The system should be either a package which provides a relevant service to an important function in the organization or should be a 'prototyping' system, i.e. a flexible system which can be rapidly shaped to provide a relevant service. The objective of these systems is *not* to test and prove the service so that it might be more widely implemented. The objective is to provide users with an experience which will enable them to delineate the service they require. It is important therefore to dispel any expectations that the initial system will be permanent in the form it is first implemented.

4.3 Trials and experiments

Pilot systems provide the vehicle for the user-involvement structures to consider many different design issues as well as for users to become familiar with system usage. Figure 10.8 lists some of the possibilities.

In an environment where their manifest purpose is to examine the system to determine their needs of such a system, users can learn to cope with the system without the anxieties which usually accompany the learning of a system they have to master to retain their jobs. The learning process can also be used to catalogue the issues and problems which will have to be covered by user-support structures, e.g. manuals, in-system aids, training schemes, etc. More centrally to design issues the pilot system can be used to test task matches with tasks of the organization. Users may be encouraged to 'stress test' the service of the system by examining how well it would

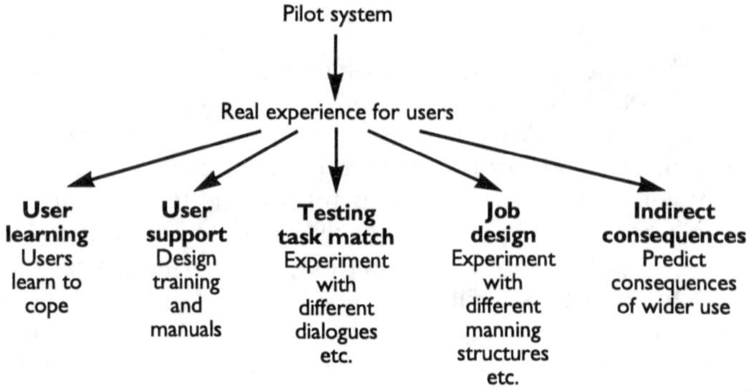

Figure 10.8 Trials for user learning and design

support the variety of forms their tasks take, i.e. the normal and the abnormal. If the system is of the prototyping form it should be possible to change the form of the interactive dialogues, the data-base structures, the forms of output, etc., to examine how well alternatives can meet user needs.

In addition to examining the form the technical system might take, it is also possible to use the pilot system to examine alternative forms that might be taken by the organization. The users might, for example, examine different forms of job design, i.e. different ways of manning the system and allocating responsibilities. They might, for example, create a specialist job of terminal operation or share terminal operations across all users (Eason 1981b). The system may also provide a basis for thinking through the wider consequences of system usage for skills, job number, job grades, careers, payment systems and the relations between sections of the organization. In one organization, for example, staff within three branches used a pilot system to examine the implications of co-ordinated action through the systems upon their individual autonomy.

4.4 Structured design exercises

Trials with pilot systems can provide relevant user experience upon which decisions can be based but we have found it necessary to structure the process by which this experience is used to take decisions. The reason for this is that it is very easy for the user experience to become unrelated to the decision process; it may not, for example, be fed to those taking the decisions, or the people concerned may not be able to make the jump from specific experience to general requirement. We therefore use the four-stage design exercise procedure depicted in Figure 10.9 as a means of focusing user experience on design decisions. This procedure is in a general form which can be used to debate the wide variety of decisions which concern users; from alternative systems the organization might employ to alternative sites for a VDU in an office. The initial stage is to elicit alternative solutions. This can be a problem because people tend to be limited by the current position or by the organization of the pilot system. If it has been possible to examine a variety of options in the pilot these barriers may

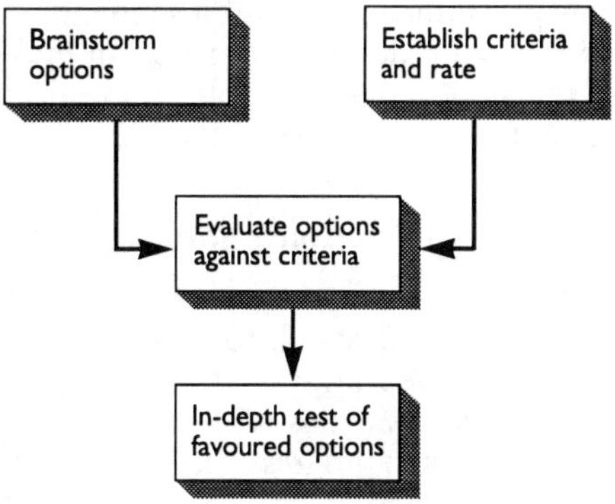

Figure 10.9 Structured design exercises for users

already have been removed. If not it may be necessary for external agents to identify other options and to encourage users to contribute other ideas. It is often appropriate to treat the generation of alternatives as a brainstorming exercise in which anything goes, i.e. not to permit criticism of any idea that is advanced. This is especially important in circumstances where the users may be anxious about the presence of more senior staff or clever systems staff who might reveal their ideas to be nonsense.

A parallel activity to the generation of options is the generation of criteria which will be used to evaluate options. This is again a sensitive procedure because different groups may put priority on quite different criteria, e.g. for one group the important issue may be the recency of information, for another it may be the computational facilities, for another it may be security and privacy of the data base. The eliciting of criteria and their placement in rank order can be a very revealing process for all concerned and can reveal deep splits in the demands being made on the system. It is important that these splits come to light before design rather than being revealed afterwards when some users find their requirements have been disregarded. Where there are major differences and objectives, the help of experts in group dynamics may be necessary to seek effective ways of meeting the conflicting demands.

The next stage is to relate the option to the leading criteria that have been identified and to judge how each option will perform. This is a stage when the experience of the users in the pilot study and more generally in their task environment can be very useful in judging the viability of an option. It may also be possible to try out some of the options if the design issue is, for example, concerned with dialogues or the siting of terminals.

The final phase is to elaborate and test favoured options. In our work we have found that our detailed knowledge of the human implications of many systems can be fed into all the stages of this procedure without prejudicing the rights of users and systems designers to take their own decisions. It is possible, for example, to suggest options, to identify criteria others have found relevant, to show how others have sought to resolve conflicts, to help identify areas where options may have implications and to identify ways of detailing and testing favoured options.

The objective of this procedure is to offer a sequence of activities within which those involved in taking design decisions can make the best use of their knowledge and the knowledge available from other sources in order to make the best decisions for their circumstances.

4.5 Progressive implementation of facilities

From the viewpoint of the user, a computer system consists of a set of facilities which he gradually comes to understand, to master and to exploit. A pilot system will usually have a limited array of facilities and there are difficult questions about how to move from this stage to a more permanent, operational system. One possibility is to progressively replace pilot system facilities with improved facilities and to elaborate the system by adding further facilities as it becomes apparent they are needed. The learning that comes from the trials and experiments and the structured design exercises can provide the evidence for the facilities that are required. Similarly the output from the user evaluation studies and from user support (see below) provides continuing evidence for changes in required facilities. The provision of facilities is therefore a continuing process if the system is to evolve as the users' learning and, therefore, their definition of their needs, evolves. Establishing a technical system which can be continually amended and elaborated poses many difficult questions beyond the scope of this paper. They are being debated elsewhere and some of the issues are, for example, examined by Edmonds (1981).

It might be assumed that the process of making more or different facilities available to users of necessity means progressively adding more hardware and software to an initially small system. This is not inevitably the case. An alternative is to employ a large-scale system which is sufficiently flexible to permit the tailoring of facilities to users' needs as they become apparent and to permit users progressively greater access to facilities as they become more experienced with the system.

4.6 User evaluation studies

The principle of evolutionary systems design is that the system will continue to be modified and elaborated in accordance with emergent user needs. An essential ingredient is a feedback loop from the users to system managers and designers (see Figure 10.10) and we have found remarkably few systems where this is a regular, institutionalized procedure. In a number of the organizations with whom we have worked we have organized evaluation studies in which we have conducted semi-structured interviews with users to explore their experiences of systems. The interviews make assessments on a series of system acceptability measures (Damodaran 1981) which range from assessments of the quality of the information service (task fit), through evaluations of ease of use and the effectiveness of user support, to assessments of the effects upon job content and other indirect consequences. A relatively formal evaluating procedure of this kind is necessary to ensure that the organization learns from pilot schemes but it is also needed during the subsequent life of the system if there is to be informational feedback to show how the system should evolve.

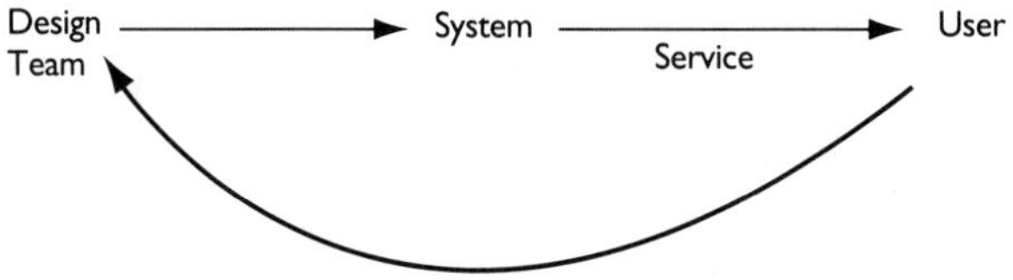

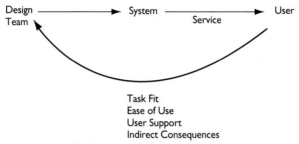

Figure 10.10 Evaluation of user responses to systems

4.7 User support and organizational learning

It might be thought that once a user understands the procedures of a computer system, he has mastered it. However, real mastery comes when the user begins to perceive how the system can and could be used by him and by his organization to perform organizational tasks in different and more effective ways. This kind of learning tends to come a considerable while after the system is first implemented and sometimes never occurs because the conditions do not exist to promote such continuous development. To promote these developments the technical system needs to be complemented by a social system dedicated to its use and its development. This social system consists in part of user support staff (liaison staff, training staff, etc.) whose function is to help users find new ways of exploiting the system (in effect, to promote continuous user learning) and to carry information about system inadequacies and the need for system development back to system designers. Another part of the social system consists of those system designers whose function is to maintain and develop the system. In the traditional systems-design process the assumption is that the design team breaks up when the system is implemented leaving only a skeletal team to operate and maintain it. An evolutionary concept requires that a design capability is retained through the life of the system.

As Figure 10.11 illustrates, this support structure is a vehicle for providing evaluative feedback and for providing user support. In its support role, not only does it provide staff who can give support but it is responsible for the provision of other support methods (training, in-system aids and manuals). The support can be considered to be of two types: compensatory and developmental. It is normal for there to be provision of compensatory support, e.g. what do I do when the system goes down? I do not understand a command, I've got an error message I do not understand, etc. What is often missing is a forum in which the user can discuss a new need and be helped to see how the system could be used to meet it or indeed the system can be revised to meet it.

5 CONCLUSIONS

If one examines closely the radical and far-reaching consequences of introducing information technology, it is small wonder that organizations are

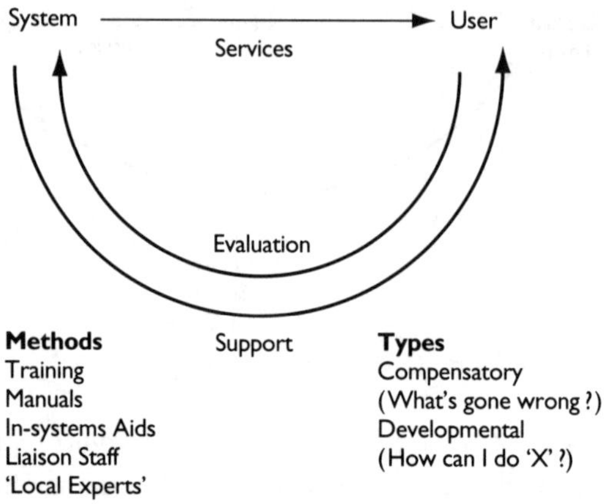

Figure 10.11 User support for organizational learning

slow to embrace the new technology. Our traditional systems-design methods tend to be technology led and often lead to implementation problems. In trying to help organizations plan systems design we have found it difficult to obtain adequate attention for human factors issues in this traditional approach. The move to user involvement in systems design provides the potential for fuller consideration of organizational ramifications. However, users confronted by the need to make a contribution need time and opportunities to learn about the intended system and its effects. Frequently they are only able to see the ramifications clearly when it is too late to change the system. Their contribution therefore becomes confined to amelioration of the system's negative effects.

In our view if we are to achieve the desirable goal of permitting organizational needs to define the nature of the technology, we need to change the way we approach systems design. In our work with organizations we have been moving away from 'one-shot implementation' towards a more evolutionary way of introducing a system, which is never regarded as finished. The nature of modern computer technology means this approach is now a practicable proposition and it means users have the time and opportunity to gather experience before they have to specify the systems they regard as desirable. In working with organizations we have tried to promote learning for design decisions by creating temporary design bodies, implementing pilot studies specifically for learning purposes, developing user design exercises, instituting regular evaluation procedures and creating social structures for user support and system evolution. It is our view that only by adopting such practices within organizations can we give members of the organization the confidence and knowledge to take on new technology and exploit it to the full.

Acknowledgements

The concepts reported in this paper have been developed as a result of working with Professor Brian Shackel, Leela Damodaran, Susan Pomfrett and other colleagues in the HUSAT Research Group. I am happy to acknowledge their contribution to the development of the strategy for introducing new technology which is outlined in this paper. The strategy has emerged as a result of our close collaboration with a number of organizations and I also acknowledge the pioneering spirit of the staff of these organizations without which our ideas could not be tested.

REFERENCES

Bjorn-Andersen, N. (ed) (1980) *The Human Side of Information Processing*, North-Holland, Amsterdam.

Bjorn-Andersen, N. and Eason, K. D. (1980) 'Myths and realities of information systems contributing to organizational rationality', in Mowshowitz, A. (ed) *Human Choice and Computers Vol 2*, North-Holland, Amsterdam, pp. 97–100.

Bjorn-Andersen, N. and Rasmussen, L. B. (1980) 'Sociological implications of computer systems', in Smith, H. T. and Green, T. R. G. (eds) *Human Interaction with Computers*, Academic Press, London.

Damodaran, L. (1981) 'Measures of user acceptability', in Pearce, B. G. (ed) *Health Hazards of VDUs? Vol 3*, Loughborough University of Technology, Loughborough, pp. 61–70.

Damodaran, L. and Eason, K. D. (1981) 'Design procedures for user involvement and user support', in Coombs, M. and Alty, J. (eds) *Computer Skills and the User Interface*, Academic Press, London.

Eason, K. D. (1981a) Manager–computer interaction. A study of a task–tool relationship. Ph.D. Thesis, Loughborough University of Technology.

Eason, K. D. (1981b) 'Job design and VDU operation', in Pearce, B. G. (ed) *Health Hazards of VDUs? Vol 3*, Loughborough University of Technology, Loughborough, pp. 71–88.

Eason, K. D., Damodaran, L. and Stewart, T. F. M. (1974) A survey of man–computer interaction in commercial applications, LUTERG No. 144, Loughborough University of Technology.

Eason, K. D. and Sell, R. G. (1981) 'Case studies in job design for information processing tasks', in Corlett, E. N. and Richardson, J. (eds) *Stress, Work Design and Productivity*, Wiley, Chichester.

Edmonds, E. A. (1981) 'Adaptive man–computer interfaces', in Coombs, M. and Alty, J. (eds) *Computer Skills and the User Interface*, Academic Press, London.

Evans, C. R. (1977) *The Mighty Micro*, Hodder & Stoughton, Sevenoaks.

Forester, T. (ed) (1979) *The Micro-electronics Revolution*, Blackwell, Oxford.

Gotleib, C. C. and Borodin, A. (1973) *Social Issues of Computing*, Academic Press, New York.

Jenkins, C. and Sherman, B. (1979) *The Collapse of Work*, Eyre Methuen, London.

Lyne, M. and Davis, R. (1981) 'A microprocessor in Lincoln' *National Electronics Review 1980/1*, pp. 55–9.

Macintosh, I. M. (1981) Letter to the *Guardian*, 10 April.

Mumford, E. and Henshall, D. (1979) *A Participative Approach to Computer System Design*, Associated Business Press, London.

Pearce, B. G. (ed) (1980a) *Health Hazards of VDUs? Vol. 1*, Loughborough University of Technology, Loughborough.

Pearce, B. G. (ed) (1980b) *Health Hazards of VDUs? Vol. 2*, Loughborough University of Technology, Loughborough.

Pearce, B. G. (ed) (1981) *Health Hazards of VDUs? Vol 3*, Loughborough University of Technology, Loughborough.
Toffler, A. (1980) *The Third Wave*, Collins, London.
Zermeno, R., Moseley, R. and Braun, E. (1979) 'The robots are coming – slowly', in Forester, T. (ed) *The Micro-electronics Revolution*, Blackwell, Oxford, pp. 184–197.

CHAPTER 11

Planning and Strategy

Planning is an issue because, although nearly everyone wishes they could do it better, there is virtually no agreement on how it should be done or, indeed, whether it can or should be done. In considering the difficulties, it's important to remember that planning poses both organizational and intellectual problems. Of the three readings that follow, the first is more concerned with the organizational aspects and makes very clear why planning is not something one can leave to 'the planners'.

The second piece was created by savage editing of a long, comprehensive and, in places, somewhat technical review of the literature relevant to forecasting and planning (which cited no less than 175 references). The original paper surveyed a considerable body of psychological literature concerning human biases in information-handling and decision-making, as well as reviewing the various studies that have attempted to evaluate forecasting and planning. What follows presents some of the principal findings and conclusions but scarcely does justice to a paper that anyone closely involved in planning should have at their bedside.

The final piece reflects recent scepticism about planning. The rapid pace of change makes formal planning difficult. Flexibility, guided by a 'vision', may be more appropriate. This article presents some of the practical wisdom that managers use to take advantage of the interplay between the vision and everyday tasks.

11A
The Challenge of Corporate Planning

D. E. HUSSEY

[. . .] While most organizations purport to practise corporate planning and it is possible to find planners in most large companies, there is considerable research evidence, supported by the opinions of informed observers, that very few companies obtain optimum benefit from their planning efforts. Many plan very badly. The pitfalls in planning are well documented, but despite this many companies approach planning from somewhere deep down in the elephant trap.

[. . .] The building of corporate planning is made difficult by the nature of the job. Planning is not a profession, such as accountancy or chartered secretaryship. Although it has an able association in the Society for Long Range Planning, it does not have examinations or professional qualifications. It does not generally offer a career in itself, but positions in a total general management career. It attracts good people, most of whom get promoted very quickly to other jobs. The result is breadth rather than depth of experience: several people in an organization with some planning knowledge, but too few with very much. [. . .]

The 10 Major Traps in Corporate Planning

1. *Top management's assumption that it can delegate the planning function to a planner.*
2. *Top management becomes so engrossed in current problems that it spends insufficient time on long-range planning, and the process becomes discredited among other managers and staff.*
3. *Failure to develop company goals suitable as a basis for formulating long-range plans.*
4. *Failure to obtain the necessary involvement in the planning process of major line personnel.*
5. *Failure to use the plan as standards for measuring managerial performance.*
6. *Failure to create a climate in the company which is congenial and not resistant to planning.*
7. *Assuming that corporate comprehensive planning is something separate from the entire management process.*
8. *Injecting so much formality into the system that it lacks flexibility, looseness and simplicity, and restrains creativity.*
9. *Failure of top management to review with departmental and divisional heads the long-range plans which they have developed.*
10. *Top management's consistently rejecting the formal planning mechanism by making intuitive decisions which conflict with formal plans.*

(Adapted from a study of 215 companies by George Steiner, published as Pitfalls in Comprehensive Long Range Planning, *Planning Executives Institute, 1972.)*

Figure 11.1 tracks the evolution of planning concepts, and at once illustrates some of the problems of improving planning in the UK. Each of the forms of planning illustrated is still practised by some organizations even though the process of development has moved on. Many of the organizations which claim to practise corporate planning are in fact using what are outdated concepts, some of which no longer fit the social environment in which we operate. They may still benefit the organization, but at a suboptimal level.

The figure of course simplifies. There are variations within each of the labelled boxes, and some overlapping of concepts. Also the evolution is of

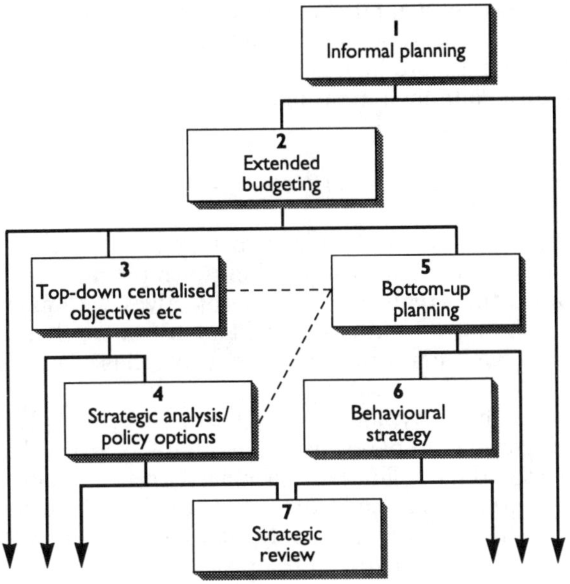

Figure 11.1 Evolution of planning approaches

planning thinking, not a process through which every organization must pass. Most join at a particular point on the evolutionary tree. It must also be stressed that success may result from any of the stages: the argument of this article is that the aim should be to do even better, rather than being satisfied with current levels of success. The right approach to corporate planning can bring the additional degree of success.

Let me explain the stages in Figure 11.1.

1 INFORMAL PLANNING

This is the state known to everybody, where top management keeps its plan in its heads, and does not attempt to make a formal plan for the organization. It works, often very well, for the autocratic, opportunistic entrepreneur with flair. Unfortunately many who approach their planning by this method also lack flair. It is an approach which becomes increasingly untenable under modern pressures for more participation.

2 EXTENDED BUDGETING

Hesitating steps were taken on the road to corporate planning when organizations began to extrapolate the annual budget into the future. Usually an accounting exercise, it represented an attempt to see the logical future consequences of the chosen course of action. It fails because it is unresponsive to environmental changes, carries an implicit and incorrect assumption that present policies will continue into the future, and has a tendency to become a mere figures exercise. Few organizations practise it in its extreme form, although it has not become extinct.

3 TOP-DOWN PLANNING

Here we begin to follow the first of two forks, which might loosely be termed 'analytical' and 'behavioural'. Top-down planning involves only a few at the top of the organization, sets objectives without the involvement of those who have to attain them, and is frequently dominated by OR approaches and corporate models (not that these are bad in themselves).

Three forms might be typified: 'ivory tower', where a planner remote from the organization prepares the plans, 'tablets from the mountain' where objectives and guide lines are produced on the assumption that all wisdom is concentrated in head-office, and 'boffin' where the corporate model produces all the answers, but only the expert can operate the model. These types of planning are still widespread, despite the fact that lack of involvement ensures that plans are rarely implemented.

4 STRATEGIC ANALYSIS/POLICY OPTIONS

The analytical branch evolves into a more rational approach at strategic thinking, moving to a planning role of presenting management with policy options, rather than one-solution plans. It uses very worthwhile techniques like portfolio analysis, and is responsive to environmental changes. Many organizations would benefit by getting this far along the evolutionary tree: comparatively few have. Its main danger is under-rating the significance of human behaviour.

5 BOTTOM-UP PLANNING

The rationale for this style of planning is to involve those who are concerned with implementing the plans. A very common sub-form is the 'church collection method'. It works like this. Everyone in the organization is asked to write a plan for his own area. His contribution is dropped into the corporate hat. Someone adds it all up, rejecting a few obvious faked coins, but usually accepting with gratitude what is donated. This becomes the plan.

It fails because the boardroom ignores it and carries on with strategies which are outside of the plan, and because the involvement is a sham: it is too narrow to be real. Another version attempts to combine top-down with bottom-up by issuing objectives as edicts and inviting managers to say in detail how they will attain them. Variations of bottom-up planning are very common.

6 BEHAVIOURAL STRATEGY

This attempts to broaden the degree of involvement of managers in planning. There are various approaches. One is a form of planning conference where all managers identify and work through the issues facing the company, aiming to produce an outline plan as its end product. Another is a carefully structured organizational development approach to strategy, which encourages individual creativity and wide involvement.

Philips Eindhoven have been leading exponents of an OD approach. The weaknesses of the behavioural approach are the difficulties of reconciling the actions from the initiative with the top management strategy, the problem of quick response to changing circumstances, and the fact that measures such as this tend to become less effective as they are repeated in successive years.

7 STRATEGIC REVIEW

Finally we have the latest stage in the evolution, a deliberate attempt to take what is best from each branch and blend analysis with behavioural in a structured way. Typically the approach defines objectives and strategic guidelines in a participative way, but ensures that the decisions taken are founded on sound analysis. Those who are interested can find a case study of the approach in 'Corporate planning at Rolls-Royce Motors Ltd', by R. Young and D. E. Hussey, *Long Range Planning*, April 1977.

Government could take a lead in improving the quality of corporate planning in the UK. So far its approach has been largely through the planning agreements initiative. One of the biggest difficulties this faces is the practical one. Many organizations either do not have corporate plans and therefore have nothing which they can agree with government, or they produce plans in which top management has little confidence. To have a planning agreement one presumably needs a plan.

My feeling is that government has gone down the wrong road. What it should be doing is getting the process of planning more widely discussed and practised. One way of doing this is by an enquiry into corporate planning, to do for planning what the Sandiland's Committee did for inflation accounting.

The purpose of such a study might be to examine the research evidence on good and bad planning, to study alternative approaches, to examine how corporate planning can be made more participative, to see what the business schools and professional bodies are teaching in this area, and to establish the things that should be done to help the entire country improve its corporate planning efforts.

Something needs to be done.

11B

Forecasting and Planning: an Evaluation

R. M. HOGARTH AND S. MAKRIDAKIS

Intuitive forecasting and planning are not new phenomena. On the other hand *formal* Forecasting and Planning (F & P) activities have risen to prominence in business, nonprofit, and public organizations within only a few decades. Furthermore, annual expenditure related to F & P now involves billions of dollars.

The utility of these activities has, however, been questioned (e.g.(7), (33)). The purpose of this paper, therefore, is to assess forecasting accuracy and planning effectiveness in organizations and to provide guidelines to calibrate expectations. [. . .]

FORECASTING AND PLANNING: EMPIRICAL EVIDENCE

[. . .] *Long-range forecasting and planning.* Long range forecasting (two years or longer) is notoriously inaccurate. Ascher (4) has examined the predictive accuracy of forecasting (and indirectly, planning) in the fields of population, economics, energy, transportation, and technology. His conclusions are pessimistic. Ascher found errors varying from a few to a few hundred percentage points, as well as systematic biases. He also stated that one could not specify beforehand which forecasting approach, or forecaster, would have been right or wrong. Furthermore, because policymakers are supplied with so many varying forecasts, the problem of 'choosing' a forecast can be as difficult as making one's own. Parenthetically, it should be noted that the fields examined by Ascher are characterized by much experience and expertise in making forecasts as well as readily available data. One can therefore imagine the situation in other fields with data less 'suitable' for forecasting (i.e. with less aggregation and greater fluctuations).

Ascher's conclusions are echoed by opinions expressed in the long-term forecasting literature (e.g. (8)). It is difficult to assess the size of forecasting errors; unforeseen changes in trends can occur; discontinuities are possible; and new events or conditions emerge. Moreover, past data can provide contradictory clues to future trends (6). For instance, while growth of some products in an industry can occur in one way, others follow different patterns (5).

[. . .] Despite many fervent proponents, there is concurrently much disappointment in long-range planning as presently practised (6) (7) (11) (26) (31) (33). Long-range planning, it is claimed, has fallen short of its promises and fundamental changes are necessary both in conception and execution. This has given rise to 'strategic planning' (see (2), (10)). In practice, however, 'many managers use the phrases strategic planning and long-range planning interchangeably' (10 p. 24). Long-range planning, it should be noted, grew and flourished in the sixties (21), a period characterized by relative stability and high growth rates. Furthermore, forecasting errors tended to be positive (i.e. actual values exceeded forecasts). Thus, even if plans proved to be 'wrong', few complained of the direction of the errors. However, this did not occur in the seventies when forecasting was on occasion grossly in error in the opposite direction.

Medium-term forecasting and planning. Medium-term plans (three months to two years) are theoretically derived from long-term plans and incorporate medium-term forecasts, estimates of available resources, constraints and competitive considerations. The most common forms are operational budgets which also serve the important function of control mechanisms.

Considerable misconceptions exist concerning the ability of economists and business forecasters to predict important changes either in the general level of economic activity or for a given industry, firm or product. Cyclical turning points, in particular, are notoriously difficult to forecast (22), (23). The problem faced by economists and planners is two-fold: first, unanticipated recessions occur: second, predicted recessions fail to materialize. Furthermore, the timing of economic recessions and accelerations is frequently missed. Finally, as with long-term forecasts, there are many different forecasts available from which people can choose those that best fit their preconceptions. [. . .]

Forecasters and planners have shown systematic deficiencies in their predictions and plans for the future; furthermore, in a majority of cases their estimates are less accurate than those of simple quantitative models (however, for exceptions see the finance literature, e.g. (5)). [. . .]

Short-term forecasting and planning. There is considerable inertia in most economic and natural phenomena. Thus the present states of many variables are predictive of the short-term future (i.e. three months or less). Rather simple, mechanistic methods such as those used in time series forecasting can often make accurate short-term forecasts and even outperform more theoretically elegant and elaborate approaches used in economic forecasting (3) (22).

Short-term planning is characterized by several operations essential to basic business functions, e.g., establishment of schedules for production, distribution and employment, cash management, etc. It is the only form of F & P for which forecasts can be reasonably accurate and where real gains can be made consistently. However, it typically receives less attention than it merits.

The comparative studies indicate both systematic biases and large errors; quantitative models outperform judgemental forecasts; in addition, simpler models are often at least as accurate as sophisticated ones; even random walk models sometimes outpredict the alternative formulations. Moreover, simple decision rules can often be as effective as elaborate F & P procedures (see also below).

General examination of forecasting and planning. [. . .]
In an important study, Grinyer and Norburn (9) attempted to relate measures of corporate financial and management performance to planning

activities. They examined 21 companies in a variety of industries. No significant relationship was found between extent of planning and financial and management measures. Indeed, the only significant relationship detected was 'between the number of items of information used in reaching decisions on appropriate action and financial performance.' Further studies have also indicated lack of relationships between planning and various measures of financial performance (17). On the other hand, studies by Karger and Malik (16), Herold (12), and Thune and House (32) concluded that formal planning was positively related to financial performance: in addition, a study by Ansoff *et al.* (1) indicates that mergers were managed more effectively with explicit planning. The evidence is unclear and was recently well summarized by Wood and LaForce (34): 'The review of the available empirical studies disclosed conflicting findings in the planning evaluation area' (p. 517). More studies are, therefore, urgently needed despite the inherent methodoligical problems of isolating the effects of formal planning systems from other variables. [. . .]

FORECASTING AND PLANNING: IMPLICATIONS AND RECONCEPTUALIZATION

[. . .] There is uncanny similarity between the history of F & P and experiments concerning the 'illusion of control' (18) (19). Observation of successes in predicting the outcomes of known random processes (e.g. coin tossing) can lead to unfounded beliefs of control in experimental situations. Similarly, the successes met by F & P in the sixties caused by under- as opposed to over-prediction seem to have led to analogous real-world illusions of control which have been shattered by subsequent events. None the less, people have a tendency to attribute success to their own efforts and failure to external factors (14). Indeed, both animals and humans have sometimes been shown to develop more effective decisions if they do have 'illusions of control' – the illusion leads to more proactive and self-fulfilling behaviour (25). The issue that is not clear, however, is the extent to which such illusions are functional.

Linked to the illusion of control are tendencies to see patterns where none exist (29). These are further related to extensive findings indicating that intuitive notions of probabilistic concepts are deficient. Experiments show that people often lack the concepts of independence between random events and sampling variability (15): in addition, they frequently underestimate the uncertainty inherent in the environment (13) which leads, inter alia, to mistaken confidence in judgment (20). For F & P, the implications involve the all too frequent surprises by unforeseen events which, in turn, discredit F & P.

Paul Samuelson has probably best captured the inability of forecasters and planners to understand the full extent of uncertainty: 'I think that the greatest error in forecasting is not realizing how important are the probabilities of events other than those everyone is agreeing upon' (28 p. 51).

A further important psychological finding is that although the availability of additional information increases confidence in judgment, it does not necessarily increase predictive accuracy (24) (30). This has serious implications for F & P given the tendency to consult and subscribe to many forecasting services, and to create huge data banks. Furthermore, since people have a tendency to retain information selectively in accord with their prejudices and to reject possible disconfirming evidence, the potential dysfunctional consequences of collecting data from many often differing sources is disturbing. As more information becomes available, it is increasingly easier to 'prove' what one wishes. Emshoff and Mitroff (7) emphasize this point in relation to problems engendered by large strategic MIS: 'Access to more information results in its selective use to support preconceived positions . . . They [managers] assume that the quality of decisions has improved because of the amount of information that support it' (p. 50). [. . .]

We have already said much about human limitations. Of particular importance is the need to develop appropriate attitudes for facing the uncertainty inherent in the future. People should heed Russell's admonition to learn 'how to live without certainty, and yet without being paralysed by hesitation' (27, p. 14). Forecasting must therefore be used to identify sources of uncertainty in the environment. Planning should concern itself with developing policies which acknowledge the uncertainties and are on the efficient frontier. Planning cannot assume forecast accuracy.

Some argue that executives and policymakers do admit the inherent deficiencies of planning but recognize functional side-effects such as improvements in communication and coordination, educating people to think explicitly about the future, and the use of planning as a mechanism for motivation and control. However, the question that should be raised is whether these side-effects could not be achieved more effectively through direct means.

The specificity of goals and forecasts should be linked to the time-frame. Long- and medium-term plans involve periods for which action–outcome–feedback loops are necessarily deficient and where learning is problematic. However, objectives that define direction are necessary. The precision with which such direction is specified should, we argue, be an inverse function of the length of the planning horizon. Whereas textbooks advocate precise goals, there are many advantages to deliberate ambiguity. [. . .]

Given the limitations of F & P, what should be done from a practical viewpoint? Would it be better, for example, to abandon formal F & P and rely solely on intuitive procedures? We do not think so.

First, intuitive procedures do not have an impressive record. Second, in the short-term, 'traditional' F & P are not only feasible but can be accurate. Indeed, we believe that few organizations avail themselves of the considerable benefits to be had in this domain. For instance, evidence has been cited that quantitative, and particularly simple models can outperform humans in a wide range of situations. Quite simple models can provide comparable, and often better results than more sophisticated models. Formal F & P can and should be used in 'traditional' mode for short-term situations. On the other hand, more careful analysis is needed concerning longer F & P horizons. [. . .]

Although it may be comforting to seek additional information to improve specific forecasts, the possibility of increasing forecast accuracy and the corresponding costs and benefits should be assessed. The *value of information* is, paradoxically, often overestimated by unaided intuition with the result that the search for additional information brings no more than false psychological comfort. For example, a recent case that came to our attention was the expenditure of $20 million to plan and forecast a $160 million investment. However, a detailed analysis of the situation and possible errors in forecasts indicated that even perfectly accurate forecasts would not be worth anything like $20 million. In some situations, even perfect knowledge of the future has relatively little value. [. . .]

One of our major arguments is for realism in F & P. Illusions and limitations need to be recognized; the use of F & P for control, motivation and communication accepted for what they are, and the extent of future uncertainties both appreciated and appropriately incorporated in plans. F & P can be useful, but current practices need to be changed. [. . .]

11c
The Tactics of Strategic Opportunism

DANIEL J. ISENBERG

Responding to today's needs doesn't necessarily preclude tomorrow's visions. Consider this comment from a chief executive officer (CEO) in the midst of a corporate turnaround: 'I like to fuzz up time scales completely. At the same time I'm talking about rigorous cost cutting, I'm also talking about the possibility of a major acquisition that would completely restructure our company. People get very upset by that, but I feel that you can do those two things at the same time.'

These words express what I call 'strategic opportunism', (35) the ability to remain focused on long-term objectives while staying flexible enough to solve day-to-day problems and recognize new opportunities. In several studies of senior executives, I have discovered that effective managers strike this balance (36). How? They consistently employ certain habits – ways of searching for and processing information and ways of acting on ideas – that help them bridge the gap between short-term demands and long-term direction.

A senior manager's most important role, management theory tells us, is to chart a long-term, strategic course for a company and keep the company moving in that direction. But success in this role can elude managers, since goals are often static while the business environment rarely is. Each day brings an incessant stream of surprises, new information, opportunities, and what one CEO called 'the chaotic intrusion of short-term problems.'

As a result, many executives' daily agendas are diffuse and reactive, rather than logical extensions of a global, long-term plan. Indeed, some believe that the daily demands of their jobs force them to give short shrift to formal planning. A division president in a communications company, for example, described his working style this way: 'I flitter a lot from one thing to another, but this business sometimes dictates that. You never get anything done if you don't have at least two or three things going on at the same time.'

Failing to think strategically has a price, of course, as the communications executive acknowledged: 'Sometimes I feel like a rhinoceros who doesn't see well and whose power of concentration is terrible; he charges at something that's a long way off, then forgets where he's going and stops to eat grass.' On the other hand, managers who concern themselves only with charging at long-term goals may overlook something promising – or threatening – lurking somewhere in the grass along the way.

The challenge for senior managers, then, is to maintain both flexibility and direction. This article describes some of the habits of thinking and ways of acting that managers use to meet this challenge. While no magic formula exists for balancing today's to-do list against the five-year plan, strategic opportunism can be an effective way to respond to immediate concerns while setting and pursuing long-term goals.

HABITS OF THINKING

Few executives would deny the necessity of strategic planning, but many fear that a strategic plan can become a straitjacket if followed too rigidly. Indeed, these managers perceive their strategic course not as a constraint on their activities but as a general framework within which they can take advantage of the unexpected. They try to stay receptive to new information and opportunities – to eventualities not accounted for in the strategic plan.

COLLECTING IDEAS

The metaphors these executives use to describe what they do suggest the ways they seek out new ideas. One manager told me that he saw himself as a beachcomber, examining the spoils of high tide and deciding whether to pick up a piece of flotsam, leave it, or throw it back – perhaps to study later, when it washes up again at a different place and time. Another chief executive likened himself to a frog on a lily pad waiting for flies to buzz by. He chooses his vantage point carefully so as to attract the fattest and slowest flies.

In combing the beach or watching for flies, senior managers often collect ideas whose relationship to strategic goals may appear murky at first. The idea-gathering process is iterative and often indirect, as one division general manager explained: 'You're looking for ways to get at problems, so that when the thing hits you, you say, "My God! Here's one that looks pretty good." Sometimes that forces somebody else to make a little modification, and then you say, "I like that one too," and then you grab that one.' The ideas constitute an inventory of possibilities; ultimately, the manager will adopt some and reject others.

One way that managers sift through and evaluate new ideas is through mental simulation or rehearsal. One general manager, for example, envisioned the consequences of a plan proposed by some of his staff members to announce a plant closing by calling a special meeting of the plant's managers: 'In my mind, I take all of my supervisors off the floor all of a sudden and ask them to come to a meeting. Now, everybody in the damn factory *sees* that, you know, and want to know, "What's going on?"' This manager's anticipatory thinking led him to devise a better plan: speaking with each supervisor individually. When the closing was announced to the workers, supervisors could respond fully and knowledgeably to their questions about the closing and its ramifications.

The ideas gathered by the manager form one aspect of his or her 'mental map': a rich, multidimensional set of associations among the myriad tasks, people, problems, issues, and goals the manager is dealing with at any one time (37). This map allows the manager to recognize and capitalize on new ideas that mesh with existing needs – an opportunity to generate more staff enthusiasm for a new product idea, say, or gain the support of community leaders, or recruit a new staff member.

One division manager, for example, hearing that a skilled, experienced personnel director would soon be leaving the division, realized that he could not fill her shoes quickly. He immediately redirected some of her tasks to other staff members, both in the division and at the corporate level. His mental map of the personnel director's role and the strengths of other staff members had enabled him to use 'chance' encounters during a visit to corporate headquarters to respond smoothly to the impending departure.

CREATING A VISION

The ideas that survive experimentation and testing eventually become building blocks of the manager's vision for the company. Much has been written about how a leader's vision inspires and motivates workers throughout an organization. What is just as important, as one senior executive explained, the vision helps top managers organize their own thoughts and actions: 'All of my actions are pieces of the same pattern. You can see that plan woven through everything. And so I'm trying to get the threads to interweave, to make sure that things are following roughly the same pattern.'

A manager's vision differs from a formal strategic plan. A strategic plan lists goals, which are usually objective, measurable, and time-bound. By contrast, a manager's vision of the company's future direction is often general, qualitative, difficult to articulate; it might entail such things as becoming the 'best' at a given function, the high-quality producer in an industry, or a lean, tough competitor (38).

Despite its apparent fuzziness, the manager's vision has very practical applications. It represents a great deal of information about numerous goals, compressed into a single overriding image that shapes the manager's day-to-day responses and guides decision making. A pharmaceutical executive put it this way: 'One rule of thumb that I've learned is to know, to the bottom of my soul, what it is I am trying to accomplish, so I can take advantage of opportunies when they come along.'

In other words, managers need not limit themselves to doing only those things that bear immediately and directly on long-term goals. Instead, guided by the vision, the manager can shape his or her immediate activities so that they all point in the same general direction.

SUMMARIZING

Even as managers create their visions, the business environment is always changing. There is an adage that says, when you're up to your ears in alligators, it's difficult to remember that your original objective was to drain the swamp. How then does the manager aiming, say, to create a new corporate culture achieve this goal when facing such 'alligators' as moving the department into new offices or dealing with the unexpected loss of an important contract?

The answer is, by climbing up on a hillside every now and then to take a look around: to assess accomplishments, to see how much work is left, even to make sure that draining the swamp is still important. For one CEO, the process works this way: 'When a topic is being discussed, I tend to say, "Is this relevant to the bigger problem we're talking about?" And I jot things like that down. Then someday I sit down, gather my notes from three or four different meetings, and I go over them and try to extract the things that tell the story; I look for a coherent pattern. Doing that helps jell my thinking.' Senior managers often engage in this summarizing activity – stopping to consolidate what they know and to define areas of confusion.

Summarizing has several benefits. Most obviously, it gives executives a way to revise their goals and ideas in light of new information. And, as in the CEO's case, it helps them build their mental map, which helps them interpret ambiguous events and ultimately act on them. Furthermore, by helping managers organize disparate data into a small number of 'packages', the summarizing process reduces their cognitive burden. People can think about only so many things at one time, and effective managers are adept at 'collapsing' the issues they face into categories. Finally, summarizing safeguards managers against losing the sense of direction that the vision sustains. Knowing that they will eventually be consolidating, summarizing, and sorting through ideas and information, managers can confidently give fuller rein to their creativity and innovativeness, which might otherwise pull them off course.

The patterns and categories managers identify when summarizing help them combine problems for economies of action – that is, they seize unexpected opportunities to make progress on multiple issues that they have mentally connected with each other. One manager told me how he took multiple advantage of a visit to a problematic branch: 'My ostensible purpose was to discuss budgetary concerns, but they were incidental. I used the opportunity to get into the issue of interpersonal conflict in the branch. The branch manager brought it up, and when that happened, I went with it. It might appear that I was jumping around, but to me it made sense; I was waiting for that window to open so I could get into what I wanted to discuss.'

Or consider the daily to-do list. Many managers quite naturally organize their tasks into mental categories, a practice that helps them remember the dozens of things they must accomplish each day. Indeed, the very process of making the to-do list illustrates a mini version of strategic opportunism: in listing immediate concerns, the manager is thinking opportunistically, and in relating these concerns to broad categories, the manager is taking stock and keeping the big picture in mind.

WAYS OF ACTING

One implication of this opportunistic modus operandi is that managers can be especially effective when they have overcrowded agendas. Managers usually carry a little extra work in their mental briefcases, work that they don't have to finish right away but that they are ready to deal with if the opportunity arises – if they recognize the opportunity. Part of the manager's mental map consists of these low-priority items: errands to run, questions to see people about, and so on.

The efficiency of carrying such crowded briefcases is obvious when two managers with rich agendas meet. Suppose the vice president of operations encounters the plant manager in the hallway; the VP learns how the new production-control specialist is working out, while the manager gets an informal reading on next month's production targets. Each walks away from the chance meeting with several lower priority tasks accomplished.

These kinds of interactions are 'inexpensive'; the only 'cost' to the manager is in keeping things straight. As one executive commented, 'You see someone, but it's not necessarily when it's on your mind, so you have to try to remember all that stuff.' But remembering things needn't be left to chance. Indeed, the habits of thinking that I have described – collecting ideas, creating a vision, summarizing – help managers remember all the things they have to do so that they can take advantage of all the chance meetings and openings that crop up in the course of a day.

PLANLESS BY DESIGN

It is impossible for managers to respond to unforeseen circumstances if their activities are planned too carefully or too far in advance. Recognizing that their company's situation is constantly changing, many managers have learned to leave strategic gaps in their plans – scheduled time-outs to reassess situations and reformulate actions, goals, or even mission statements. For the same reason, they often avoid formulating their long-term goals in excessive detail.

Some less experienced managers, by contrast, act as if they have to define all their goals first and next translate those goals into corresponding actions. Then and only then, they think, are they ready to implement the actions. But several facts of life undermine this textbook approach to planning. One is that business conditions change, and a goal that was appropriate just a few weeks ago may be inappropriate today.

Consider a six-step plan. Implementation of step one is based on all available current knowledge, but step six will be based only on earlier information, earlier assumptions about the future situation, and earlier projections about the effects of steps one through five.

Even if the business situation has not changed in the interim, the manager's perspective will surely be different. The manager's views on what goals are desirable and feasible may evolve; he or she might develop a better understanding of obstacles or acquire greater skill. As a result, frequent time-outs that allow executives to pause and reassess are an important component of managing in a changing environment.

Under some circumstances, managers may take this principle to an apparent extreme, taking action before committing themselves to any plan at all. This course can be a wise one, especially in situations characterized by high uncertainty.

A manager in a new high-technology industry decided to forgo any semblance of a formal business plan until he had some experience with the technology. His refusal to plan was not based on ignorance; he had assessed the technology and the markets as promising but thought there were so many unknowns that any multiyear plan would be an empty academic exercise. Perceiving the early risks as minor, he decided to enter the business incrementally – taking on one modest contract that could be handled easily, learning from that experience, and gradually building the company's technological knowledge and business experience until he could formulate sophisticated, realistic plans.

Several years ago, another company chose a similar course in adopting personal computers, with which it had no experience. Rather than conducting an extensive needs analysis, the company's CEO simply bought a dozen PCs and distributed them casually throughout the office. A few staff members received computer training and began experimenting with potential applications; within weeks, the computers were fully employed. The CEO's approach did lead to some confusion at first, but it gave the company the experience it needed to take a more systematic approach later in introducing personal computers in other parts of the operation.

The seeming simplicity of this deliberate lack of planning is, of course, deceptive. These managers' decisions were based on a sophisticated understanding of their businesses and on an equally sophisticated grasp of what they *didn't* know. It's one thing for a seasoned manager to say, 'We'll cross that bridge when we come to it,' and quite another for the novice. The skilled manager possesses the broad repertoire of analytical and intuitive skills needed to deal with the unexpected at each step of the plan – or of the nonplan, as the case may be.

BINDING TO GOALS

Many managers complain that short-term problems wreak havoc with their plans for tackling the 'truly important' management issues. Unfortunately, they too often blame themselves or their subordinates for poor planning skills. One reason, however, that urgent issues drive out important ones is a basic fact of human thinking: salient and vivid objects occupy a disproportionate amount of our attention and skew our thinking in the direction of what is noticed, not what is noteworthy.

So how do managers resolve timely and urgent matters while keeping in mind the larger issues – the tasks that have no immediate payoff but that in the long run are vital? To accomplish this, I found, many devise self-binding systems, tricks that force them to make progress toward important goals. To cite one simple example, they use tickler files to ensure that they eventually address issues that might otherwise get lost in the shuffle.

Another simple binding aid is the planning schedule. One division general manager, frustrated by his subordinates' poor planning, created a calendar listing all the division and corporate meetings that his managers had to prepare for throughout the year. The calendar represented a 'no excuses' philosophy; all the managers knew well in advance which meetings they had to attend and which ones they had to provide input for. The same manager used a calendar trick to force *himself*, as well as his executive committee, to tour the division's plants one day each month: 'If it weren't a regularly scheduled meeting, I wouldn't get off my ass and out into the plant, and neither would most of the other committee members. I have to do this to discipline myself.'

In other words, although executives attempt to retain as much flexibility as they can for managing the unexpected, they often balance this flexibility with rigid systems for managing their own limitations. Any mental device they can use to make the long term more immediate and tangible will help them focus on the noteworthy. This is why a vision – a vivid and compelling image of the company's future – is so important in linking short- and long-range concerns.

PIECING THE PUZZLE

Traditional theory suggests the management is a tightly structured, systematic, linear mental activity. Managers presumably formulate goals with painstaking precision, then undertake carefully prescribed actions. In reality, however, as one company president pointed out, managers never have enough information to make perfectly reasoned decisions: 'I think what you find when you get out into the cold, cruel world of business is that you never have all the information and there's always a bunch of facts missing. A manager is always faced with getting pieces of the puzzle, never really having all of the answers that you need, and yet being forced to make decisions.'

Therefore managers often begin the process of problem solving not by rigorously collecting hard data but by mulling over the incomplete information they already have, either in their memory or at their fingertips. 'I had to make judgments about things where I didn't have enough time to learn all the technology involved,' reported one general manager. 'So I had to start relying on other people's opinions. I learned that you can reach the point where you understand 75% or 80% fairly quickly; getting to 100% isn't worth the effort it takes. I've been involved in management long enough to know that there is no certainty.'

Effective management thus becomes an interactive process based on constant questioning, experimenting, reflecting, debugging, and retesting. Many senior managers have learned, for example, that the *order* in which they perform their most important thinking functions – formulating goals, developing understanding, devising plans, and taking action – is not that important. What really counts is that all of these functions are performed, that managers develop an understanding of the products and the markets, that over time they formulate goals that are clear enough to guide resource allocation but that they themselves can change, and that they take appropriate and timely action.

This unrelenting reflection by managers often takes the form of what cognitive scientists call 'reasoning plausibly,' or making logical guesses. Rather than waiting until they have all the facts, senior managers try to interpret new issues and problems as they arise. Why does the potential business partner seem to be turning cold? There's a message that the product expediter called – could there be a problem with delivery or price? Why are product returns up? And, as the president of a metal parts division wondered, what's on the boss's mind? 'The boss called to say he'll be dropping in tomorrow. I was thinking about why he's coming in and what approach he'll take. I guess he wants to make cuts; he'll insist that we have to be more profitable. He wants us to look good because it's easier to sell the company when it's profitable.'

Another example of reasoning plausibly can be seen in the ruminations of a branch general manager who for eight months could not fill a small order. The problem: another division of the company had not provided a necessary part. Said the general manager: 'This is aggravating because we need the business. Here we had an opportunity and we screwed it up – seven, eight months, and we can't deliver a part. I believe the product division has the part. What I think they're doing is allocating all of the product to one large customer. I'm going to have to ask the product manager to skim some from the large order and send me a trickle of that. Then I can get something to the customer now, and maybe buy a few more weeks to get the rest of the order out.'

Obviously, managers who rely exclusively on speculation run the risk of drawing false conclusions and taking inappropriate actions. But experienced managers have learned to combine inference with hard-nosed rationality. They are comfortable using hunches and guesses as a foundation for deciding whether a particular problem requires systematic analysis.

SINNING BRAVELY

The development of professional management education early in this century was an attempt to make managers more systematic, more 'scientific'. Recent criticism of strategic planning suggests that we management scholars may have overshot this goal. My research indicates that what managers need is a synthesis of rationality and entrepreneurial (or opportunistic) resourcefulness. Strategic opportunism is a way of approaching the complex, uncertain task of management both creatively and rigorously.

Several writers on management have recently pointed out what many practitioners have long known – descriptions of orderly management processes are unrealistic and misleading. Robert Hayes, for one, has argued that it is often more effective to develop resources, competencies, and strategies in an incremental, iterative way than to take the now traditional approach of developing goals, then strategies, then resources. Other writings on topics as diverse as product development and transfer pricing have also underscored the efficacy of taking a nonlinear, dynamic approach to management functions (39).

Thinking both strategically and opportunistically is clearly not easy. It requires a tolerance for ambiguity, intellectual intensity, mental hustle, and a vigilant eye for new ideas. It requires, in other words, a tough-minded approach to an inherently messy process, the ability to take action in the midst of uncertainty, to 'sin bravely'.

This approach to managing may at first anger some managers who struggle hard to think strategically themselves or harder yet to drive strategic discipline deep into their own corporate cultures. Yet there is nothing undisciplined or willy-nilly about strategic opportunism. Quite the opposite: it requires much intellectual courage to be open to new possibilities and to engage in reflective inquiry rather than rationalization.

And what purpose does rigidity serve? Managers who are afraid to choose opportunity over outmoded objectives are really afraid of themselves; deep inside they doubt their own ability to function under uncertainty, their own creativity and resourcefulness, their own resolve and willpower.

In its inherent disorderliness, strategic opportunism requires a great deal not only from the senior manager but also from the manager's subordinates, who must be able to tolerate working with a fluid set of agendas. Subordinates with a high need for clarity and control will find a strategic opportunist's continual experimentation frustrating rather than liberating.

Although a manager's tempest of day-to-day activities may appear aimless, the direction becomes clear in retrospect – two or three or five years later. One manager was reminded of an astronaut who was sent out to make repairs on a spacecraft: 'You watch that guy in his space suit, zooming back and forth on that little space gadget. You see the burst of energy, but you don't see a pattern. Afterward, you know, yes, he went up there and repaired something, but when he's in motion it's difficult to see the logic of what he's doing. The CEO has a vision that is semi-intuitive. He proceeds on several fronts simultaneously, pushing out his holistic vision. Gradually the blurring disappears.'

A fictional conversation between Dashiell Hammett's detective, Henry F. Neill, and his lady friend, Dinah Brand, captures the essence of strategic opportunism. Henry has sworn to rid a small town of its corruption, and Dinah has just asked him why he caused a battle between two rival factions in the town:

'That was only an experiment – just to see what would happen.'

'So that's the way you scientific detectives work. My God! For a fat, middle-aged, hard-boiled, pig-headed guy, you've got the vaguest way of doing things that I ever heard of.'

'Plans are all right sometimes,' I said, 'and sometimes just stirring things up is all right – if you're tough enough to survive, and keep your eyes open so you'll see what you want when it comes to the top.'

'That ought to be good for another drink.' (40)

Acknowledgment

I thank Bart Van Dissel and Marvin Mannheim for their comments on an earlier version of this article.

REFERENCES

1. Ansoff, H., Avner, J., Brandenberg, R. G., Portner, F. E. and Radosevich, R. (1970) 'Does planning pay? The effect of planning on success of acquisition in American firms', *Long Range Planning*, Vol. 3, no. 2, pp. 2–7.
2. Ansoff, H., Avner, J., Brandenberg, R. G., Portner, F. E. and Radosevich, R. (1977) 'The state of practice in planning systems', *Sloan Management Rev.*, 18, Winter, pp. 1–24.
3. Armstrong, J. S. (1978) 'Forecasting with econometric methods: folklore versus fact', *Jour. Business*, Vol. 51, no. 4, pp. 549–564.
4. Ascher, W. (1978) *Forecasting: An Appraisal for Policy Makers and Planners*, The Johns Hopkins University Press, Baltimore.
5. Brown, L. D. and Rozeff, M. S. (1978) 'The superiority of analyst forecasts as measures of expectations: evidence from earnings', *Jour. Finance*, Vol. 33, no. 1, pp. 1–16.
6. Dhalla, N. K. and Yuspeh, S. (1976) 'Forget the product life cycle concept', *Harvard Business Rev.*, Vol. 54, no. 1, pp. 102–112.
7. Emshoff, J. R. and Mitroff, I. I. (1978) 'Improving the effectiveness of corporate planning', *Business Horizons*, Vol. 21, no. 5, pp. 49–60.
8. Gold, B. (1976) 'The shaky foundations of capital budgeting', *California Management Rev.*, Vol. 19, no. 2, Winter, pp. 51–60.
9. Grinyer, P. H. and Norburn, D. (1975) 'Planning for existing markets: perceptions of executives and financial performance', *Jour. Roy. Statist. Soc. A*, 138, Part 1, pp. 70–98.
10. Guth, W. D. (1971) 'Formulating organizational objectives and strategy: a systematic approach', *Jour. Business Policy*, Fall, pp. 24–31.
11. Hayashi, K. K. (1978) 'Corporate planning practices in Japanese multinationals', *Acad. Management Jour.*, Vol. 21, no. 2, pp. 211–226.
12. Herold, D. M. (1972) 'Long range planning and organizational performance', *Acad. Management Jour.*, Vol. 15, no. 1, pp. 91–102.
13. Hogarth, R. M. (1975) 'Cognitive processes and the assessment of subjective probability distributions', *Jour. Amer. Statist. Assoc.*, Vol. 70, no. 350, pp. 271–289.
14. Hogarth, R. M. and Makridakis, S. (1979) 'Decision making in a dynamic, competitive environment: random strategies and causal attributions'. Unpublished manuscript, University of Chicago, Graduate School of Business, Center for Decision Research.
15. Kahneman, D. and Tversky, A. (1972) 'Subjective probability: a judgment of representativeness', *Cognitive Psychology*, Vol. 3, no. 3, pp. 430–454.
16. Karger, D. W. and Malik, Z. A. (1975) 'Long range planning and organizational performance', *Long Range Planning*, Vol. 8, no. 6, pp. 60–64.
17. Kudla, R. J. (1980) 'The effects of strategic planning on common stock returns', *Acad. Management Jour.*, Vol. 23, no. 1, pp. 5–20.

18. Langer, E. J. (1975) 'The illusion of control', *Jour. Personality and Social Psychology*, Vol. 32, no. 2, pp. 311–328.
19. Langer, E. J. and Roth, J. (1975) 'The effect of sequence of outcomes in a chance task on the illusion of control', *Jour. Personality and Social Psychology*, Vol. 32, no. 6, pp. 951–955.
20. Lichtenstein, S., Fischoff, B. and Phillips, L. D. (1977) 'Calibration of probabilities: the state of the art', in Jungermann, H. and de Zeeuw, G. (eds) *Decision Making and Change in Human Affairs*, Reidel, Dordrecht, Netherlands.
21. Lucado, W. E. (1974) 'Corporate planning – a current status report', *Management Planning*, Nov/Dec, pp. 27–34.
22. Makridakis, S. and Hibon, M. (1979) 'Accuracy of forecasting: an empirical investigation', *Jour. Roy, Statist. Soc. A.*, Vol. 142, Part 2, pp. 97–125.
23. McNees, S. K. (1979) 'Forecasting performance in the 1970s', *TIMS Studies in Management Sci.*, Vol. 12.
24. Oskamp, S. (1965) 'Overconfidence in case-study judgments', *Jour. Consulting Psychology*, Vol. 29, no. 3, pp. 261–265.
25. Perlmutter, L. C. and Monty, R. A. (1977) 'The importance of perceived control: fact or fantasy?', *Amer. Scientist*, Vol. 65, Nov/Dec, pp. 759–765.
26. Ringbakk, K. A. (1969) 'Organized planning in major US companies', *Long Range Planning*, Vol. 2, no. 2, pp. 46–57.
27. Russell, B. (1961) *History of Western Philosophy* (2nd edition), George Allen & Unwin, London.
28. Samuelson, P. (1974), quoted in *Business Week*, 21 Dec, p. 51.
29. Simon, H. A., Newell, A. and Sumner, R. K. (1968) 'Patterns in music', in Kleinmuntz, B. (ed) *Formal Representation of Human Judgment*, Wiley, New York.
30. Slovic, P. (1980) 'Toward understanding and improving decisions', in Howell, W. (ed) *Human Performance and Productivity*, Erlbaum, Hillsdale, New Jersey.
31. Stonich, P. J. (1975) 'Formal planning pitfalls and how to avoid them', *Management Rev.*, Vol. 64, no. 6, pp. 4–11.
32. Thune, S. S. and House, R. J. (1970) 'Where long-range planning pays off', *Business Horizons*, Vol. 13, no. 4, pp. 81–87.
33. Wildavsky, A. (1973) 'If planning is everything, maybe it's nothing' *Policy Sci.*, Vol. 4, no. 2, pp. 127–153.
34. Wood, D. R. Jr. and LaForce, R. L. (1979) 'The impact of comprehensive planning on financial performance', *Acad. Management Jour.*, Vol. 22, no. 3, pp. 516–526.
35. The term 'strategic opportunism' was first used in a different context by Barbara Hayes-Roth in 'A blackboard model of control,' *Heuristic Programming Project*, Report HPP-83-38, Stanford University Press, Stanford, Calif., 1983.
36. See Isenberg, D. J. (1986) 'Thinking and managing: a verbal protocol analysis of managerial problem solving', *Acad. Management Jour.*, Dec, p. 775; (1984) 'How senior managers think', *Harvard Business Rev.*, Nov/Dec, p. 80.
37. Streufert, S. and Swezey, R. (1986) *Complexity, Managers, and Organizations*, Academic Press, New York.
38. Quinn, J. B. (1977) 'Strategic goals: process and politics', *Sloan Management Rev.*, Fall, p. 21.
39. Hayes, R. H. (1985) 'Strategic planning – forward in reverse?', *Harvard Business Rev.*, Nov/Dec, p. 111; Takeuchi, H. and Nonaka, I. (1986) 'The new new product development game,' *Harvard Business Rev.*, Jan/Feb, p. 137; Bhide, A. (1986) 'Hustle as strategy,' *Harvard Business Rev.*, Sept/Oct, p. 59; Eccles, R. G. (1985) *The Transfer Pricing Problem: A Theory for Practice* Lexington Books, Lexington, Mass.
40. Hammett, D. (1929) *Red Harvest*, Alfred A. Knopf, New York, p. 79.

PART 3

CONCEPTS

'Concepts' can often mean jargon; clumsy and pretentious new words; elaborate and empty abstractions; obfuscations. But those that follow are different: they are intended to be practical and useful *tools for thought. This means, first, that they are not the tightly specified and fully operational terms beloved of social research; they are looser and more comfortable, meant to be used on a day-to-day basis, and relevant to everyday concerns. Secondly, they actually help; they can make things easier – or, at least, clearer. Because concepts are for helping us think. They highlight distinctions, clarify what we were half aware of, encapsulate aspects or relationships that we might otherwise overlook. Concepts are the creations and the bearers of different ways of seeing and thinking; and by using them to make sense of our experience, we learn those other ways of seeing and thinking.*

It may help to distinguish roughly between two different sorts of concepts presented in the selections that follow. First there are specific *concepts, those captured by a special term (or an ordinary term in a new use); these are usually distinctions, or some recurrent pattern, that is 'flagged' or captured by the term. Secondly, there are broader conceptual frameworks, or perspectives, that provide a particular way of looking at a subject, a distinctive 'angle' on it; such frameworks provide a set of related concepts, a sort of analytic tool-kit.*

The notion of concepts being tools for thought is also useful if it suggests that, as with other tools, mastering their proper use may take time: knowing about, *say, chisels, is very different from* knowing how *to use one. Or a better parallel may be with learning a foreign language: there is a great difference between someone who has recently learnt the basic grammar and a limited vocabulary and someone else who is a fluent speaker. The former thinks in his or her own native language, and laboriously works out the foreign equivalent. Conversations are so slow and difficult they are hardly worth the effort. The fluent speaker actually* thinks *in a foreign language – it's no effort at all (and there are any number of benefits to be gained). In learning concepts, there is a first, rather mechanical, stage of getting hold of the basic ideas: it may involve being able to remember definitions and recognize correct and incorrect uses of key terms. The second stage takes longer and is more problematic: it involves steadily greater familiarity with the ideas, being able to apply them more easily (and less self-consciously) to new situations and to everyday experience, until in due course they are taken for granted – part of the way one normally thinks about events of that sort.*

The implications should be clear: if you find initially that some of the concepts introduced in the selections that follow are strange and difficult, remember that until you have become fairly familiar with them you can't really assess their worth. But also, if the concepts seem sensible and straightforward, don't imagine that that means they will automatically be incorporated into your thinking. Frequent use is the only way to ensure that.

CHAPTER 12

Interpersonal Psychology

Interpersonal work relationships display the complete spectrum of possibilities: cooperative and competitive, loving and hateful, trustful and suspicious and so on. Most individuals would like to be able to improve some of their work relationships so as to make their job easier or more rewarding or more effective. The problem is that even though we can all recognize relationships that aren't right, only a very few know how to improve them. Often attempts to improve relationships are based on analyses of what the other person is doing wrong. Such an approach never works and usually makes things worse.

There are three requirements to improving relationships. The first is to have a well tried framework for thinking about and understanding what goes on in relationships – a theory. The second is to apply the theory to oneself so as to discover how one elicits the responses one gets and why these are unsatisfactory. The third is to use the theory and one's self-understanding to set about doing something different, i.e. relating to others in a different way. Experience in all sorts of management training, relating workshops, therapy groups, training groups and so on has demonstrated that such an approach can work; individuals who follow the above steps do find their relationships improving. One of the theoretical frameworks used in this sort of exercise in the 'transactional and structural analysis' developed by Eric Berne. The following article describes its main features and gives some examples of how relationships can be improved.

Personality Dynamics and Transactional Analysis (TA)

J. MARTIN

There are many *very* different approaches that have been devised for looking at human personality, and you should remember that we are only looking at one of them – Eric Berne's *transactional and structural analysis*, usually abbreviated as *TA*.

The way you describe a personality depends on your objectives in doing so. In TA the objectives of the description are:

1. that it should allow people to describe and understand their own and other people's normal interactions in a simple, clear and explicit way;

2. that the understanding so gained should allow people to exert more control over, and take more responsibility for, their own interactions with others.

In other words, this is a description of personality intended to be used in a practical setting, rather than being an academic description for a detached observer. As Berne puts it, it is 'a theory of personality and social action'.

The boundary is usually set around a very small group of people, usually two or three, and the *transactions* between them. A *transaction* in this sense is a single two-way communication exchange. If my dog puts her nose on my lap, and I push her away, that is a single transaction: dog to me, me back to dog.

The most basic transactions are those between infants and their parents; a simple touch or change of pressure responded to by another touch or change of pressure. Amongst animals and between people at their most intimate, these simple touch transactions remain very important throughout their lives; however, in most non-intimate adult human transactions touch is either formalized (shaking hands) or replaced completely by speech ('good morning!', 'what a beautiful design!') or reduced to gestures which can be as little as a momentary exchange of eye contact. Because touch is such a basic form of social exchange, Eric Berne talks of the two components of a basic two-way transaction as *strokes*. So if I walk into your room and say 'Isn't it a lovely day!' and you look up and grunt irritably at me, that is a two-stroke transaction: me to you, and you back to me.

It is quite possible that in a purely rational world inhabited solely by science fiction robots, transactions would occur only when communication was actually needed to carry out functionally necessary tasks (though even robots might find it necessary to inform one another of their presence and state of health!). Human transactions, particularly some verbal ones, do of course serve this rational function. But they also have other functions which have little to do with actual communication of practical information. Berne talks of *stimulus hunger* (the need for sensations of any sort) *recognition hunger* (the need for human, or at least animate, contact) and *structure hunger* (the need to have a framework that gives us something coherent to do). These are very powerful needs. Babies can quite literally die or suffer permanent psychological damage if these needs are not satisfied (and they can also be overwhelmed by inappropriate or excessive strokes), and solitary confinement has been a hated tool of punishment and torture for centuries.

This means that the simple *occurrence* of strokes of any kind can be almost as important as the practical information they carry. For instance, many of the transactions at a party are made purely for the pleasure of making them, rather than for the information they convey. In fact *even very unpleasant strokes are often much better than no strokes at all.* It may be much better to be kicked than to be ignored. In the words of the melancholy lyric to one of the songs by the rock group Cream:

> Born under a bad sign . . .
> If it wasn't for bad luck
> I wouldn't have no luck at all

Clearly we can distinguish between:

1. Direct symbol-free stroking by physical contact.
2. Indirect or symbolic stroking that carries rather little additional information, including non-verbal gestures, eye contact, voice inflexion, physical setting (such as a plushy restaurant), and the ritual statements such as 'hello'.
3. Indirect or symbolic stroking as a secondary function of speech whose primary function is to convey practically relevant information – such as in a committee that is trying to make an important decision.

As we grow and develop, the repertoire of strokes we can give and transactions we can take part in also develops. Obviously a new-born baby has a rather limited repertoire, but by the time a child is six or seven, and is very clearly a person in their own right, the major categories of transaction are largely developed, though they continue to evolve or change throughout life. It is often difficult for us to realize as adults just how much of our personality gets laid down in these very early years. Obviously we can change throughout our lives; for instance, we may well become richer or poorer, happier or sadder, more or less healthy, more or less successful, more or less entertaining or boring – there are always new possibilities that we can try out as we grow. But the deepest strategies we find ourselves adopting in our lives often go back a long way; for instance, how fundamentally private or sociable we are, or some of our deepest reactions to personal relationships and personal roles. It can be quite a thought-provoking experience to line up all the photos you can find of yourself at different ages, and see how early on you can begin to recognize the rudiments of some of your adult feelings and expressions. I can still identify quite closely with some aspects of an early photo of myself, aged three, even though some forty years have passed since then.

ADULT, PARENT AND CHILD

The central figure of TA is the observation that there seem to be three major *ego-states*, or sub-personalities, that can be involved when you interact with someone else. Berne calls them the Adult, the Parent and the Child, represented diagrammatically in Figure 12.1.

The *Adult* is the computer-like part of your behaviour that is concerned with external reality, collecting information about your environment, solving problems, making estimates and plausible guesses, devising and changing appropriate strategies, and so on. Some of this is conscious and explicitly worked out. Some of it is barely conscious and more or less automatic. Some of it can be argued logically, and some of it relies on intuitive judgement and pre-logical thought processes. It can use both current information and remembered information. Even when one of the other subsystems is taking the limelight, the Adult is usually still lurking in the corner, and able to retake control if necessary. Everyone has an Adult, even a small child, but obviously the Adult skills vary with age. The Adult of a five-year-old is struggling with problems such as how to get the crayons

Figure 12.1 The personality subsystem of TA

out of a box, while the Adult of a forty-year-old is working out how to pay the mortgage and also get the family to the Costa Brava for their holidays. The Adult is the part of you that 'grows up' as you get older, whereas in an important sense the Parent and Child do not – they develop very early on, and then stay with you largely unchanged.

The *Parent* is mainly laid down in the first three or four years of life, as a result of the young child copying the people in its environment that are most important to it – typically its parents. We may, of course continue throughout our lives to absorb cultural precepts by crude copying, but this early phase is the most important one because then we are at our most receptive, vulnerable and uncritical, so that it establishes the basic foundations that tend to direct the growth of our later value systems. The Parent is an important mechanism for passing on the parent role and the general value system of a particular culture from one generation to the next. But it can just as easily transmit *undesirable* behaviour patterns from generation to generation; and in a rapidly changing society, the useful practices of one generation may become the problems of the next. Therefore being a good parent is often very different from behaving as directed by your Parent subsystem.

When a child is developing its Parent subsystem it often looks quite comic – long words, exaggerated social conventions copied from adults it knows, elaborate caring or controlling, all addressed to a doll or a pet. You can often see a clear continuity, with this behaviour leading to caring for or controlling younger children at home, then at school, and eventually in adult life, where it may become part of successful leadership or parenting, or, if it misfires, of overbearing, smothering or rigidly traditional behaviour.

The *Child* is the basic biologically given subsystem and at birth it is the only subsystem operating. Do not be misled by its title into dismissing it as something you ought to grow out of. Not only does it stay with you all your life, but it is by far the most important subsystem, because it provides all the basic drives, emotions, feelings and energy.

It is the cause of all pleasure, sadness, excitement, destructiveness, curiosity and fun. The Child is very much the biological core of what you are, and the other two sub-personalities are merely its agents or tools – the Parent keeping it on the rails culturally, and the Adult trying to solve its problems and satisfy its needs.

The Child subsystem has virtually all its basic components at birth, though they do adjust and rearrange themselves under various pressures over the first few years. Like the Parent subsystem, a fairly stable configuration has usually emerged by the age of four or five, and the only further major event is the emergence of adult sexuality at puberty.

One useful way of distinguishing these three subsystems is to remember that the key phrase of the Adult is 'I think I could do *X*', the key phrase of the Parent is 'I ought to do *X*', and the key phrase of the Child is 'I want *X*'.

Because the Parent and Child subsystems are both established so early, the transactional viewpoint is essentially to ask 'What would a one-, two- or three-year-old child do that would correspond to this grown-up's behaviour?'

SUBDIVISIONS WITHIN PARENT, ADULT AND CHILD

While there are only three basic subsystems, it is possible to subdivide each in various ways, giving the elaborated structure shown in Figure 12.2. The Parent, for instance, could be divided up according to the different individuals the child did actually copy (typically its mother and its father). More usefully, it can be divided into the two main functions parents have to

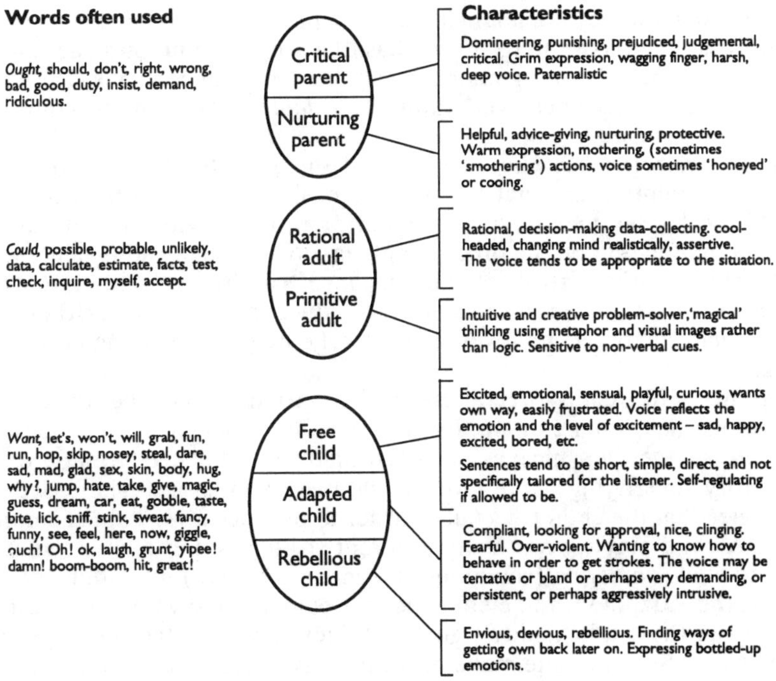

Figure 12.2 Characteristics of the TA sub-personalities

exercise – the *Nurturing Parent* who cuddles, supports and forgives, and the *Critical Parent* who makes demands, sets standards and gives reprimands.

The Adult is not usually subdivided in TA, but it will be useful to distinguish the two main types of computation that we seem to be capable of as the *Primitive Adult*, and the *Rational Adult*. The Primitive Adult tends to rely on complex imagery and on pre-logical or 'magical' relationships such as analogy and metaphor. It may use empathy and marked sensitivity to non-verbal cues as the basis for interacting with others. It may have great difficulty in explaining in words why particular activities seemed right. It is the most primitive form of problem-solving mechanism, quite close to the way an inarticulate animal solves problems. It is the most important part of the Adult in young children who have not yet developed their Rational Adults and is probably the basis for the uncanny ability children often show at picking up emotions that adults are trying to conceal. The Rational Adult evolves from the Primitive Adult as the child's linguistic and conceptual skills increase, and includes the logical, convergent, analytical behaviour we normally think of as problem-solving. In our culture it often tends to *replace* rather than *add onto* the Primitive Adult in adolescence. It can be very important in creative thought for this not to happen, and for the two to develop side by side.

The Child starts off at birth as the *Natural* or *Free Child*, expressing direct, uncomplicated and immediate needs that switch rapidly into frustration and anger if they are not met. Since simple self-regulation on this basis is rarely acceptable for long, it soon has to learn to compromise, accepting substitute or delayed satisfaction instead of its original demands. The Free Child therefore becomes overlaid by the *Adapted Child*, and its converse the *Rebellious Child*.

In children, the key characteristics of the Adapted Child/Rebellious Child combination are that the behaviour always tends to be a bit 'too much', perhaps rather obviously good, or rather obviously bad, and it tends to be focused on the other people involved, usually adults, in a way that gets attention (strokes). For instance, children can get attention *passively* either by demure niceness or seductive prettiness, or they can get it *actively* by being over-supportively helpful or antagonistically naughty.

Parents will readily recognize many variants, and the concealed kickbacks they often contain; for instance, fear underlying dependence, bitchiness underlying niceness, jealousy underlying the need for approval, insecurity underlying aggressive naughtiness, and so on. These are all strategies that the child tries out in order to produce a workable compromise. A child may try out many different strategies, but one or two will tend to stick, surviving (sometimes much transformed) into adult life. In adults, the Adapted Child element is very evident in, say the ultra-dutiful employee, the adult 'daddy's girl' or 'mummy's boy', the 'nice' person who never seems to quite make it, the abrasive person who always seems to pick unnecessary fights, the alcoholic who drinks in order to get sympathy, and so on. We all show Adapted Child behaviour of one sort or another.

SIMPLE TRANSACTIONS

A stroke always arises from one particular subsystem in you and is directed towards one particular subsystem in the other person. The reply likewise comes from one of the other person's subsystems, and is directed towards one or other of yours. Transactions should ideally be viewed holistically, with the particular words or gestures that make up the central parts of the strokes seen merely as the focal points of complete behavioural units involving context, posture, feelings and so on. In a text like this, all I can give you to practise on are transcripts of the verbal elements of the stroke, and that is obviously far from ideal.

Imagine that you have spent all morning at a difficult meeting in which plans for improving your section's output were discussed. The divisional manager, in collaboration with staff from Finance, want to restructure the way your section works. You have an alternative plan that you've worked out in conjunction with Charlie Barnes, the head of production. However Charlie didn't turn up at the meeting and you spent all your time trying to defend your plan and resist having the Finance plan imposed on you. You come back to your office where you meet Ken, who shares responsibility for part of the section.

You: 'I feel lousy. I have a terrible headache – *that meeting*, it went on all morning! I could kill Charlie – he never showed up!'

Here are seven replies that you might get from Ken:

A. I warned you to be better prepared for that meeting. You knew Charlie's unreliable, you should have arranged for someone else to support you. One of these days you'll learn.

B. You poor sod! You have had a rough time. Sit and read the paper while I get you a cup of coffee. I've got some aspirins for your headache if you want.

C. Yes, long meetings can be very stressful. If you want some peace and quiet I can make sure you're not disturbed for a while.

D. What's up? Sounds as if things went badly. Was it serious?

E. Didn't show up at all? Those meetings are such a pain. Hey, come on! Let's go to the golf course this afternoon to get a breath of fresh air.

F. Oh I am sorry. Would you like a cup of tea or a drink? I had thought to talk to you about budgets this afternoon, but if you're not well I wouldn't dream of it. Shall I get you some aspirin, or would you prefer something else? Do you want to rest or go straight off to lunch?

G. Serves you right for being in such a bloody awful mood this morning. *You* can sort out the problem on the Nicoll's contract this afternoon, I'm going out.

Compare these seven replies with the sub-personalities and their components and see if you can work out which goes with which, and why. The next few sections look at some of the ways in which transactions can go wrong, leading to apparently irrational behaviour.

CROSSED AND COMPLEMENTARY TRANSACTIONS

It looks from the replies above as if you were directing your comment at either the listener's Free Child or their Nurturing Parent, though it is hard

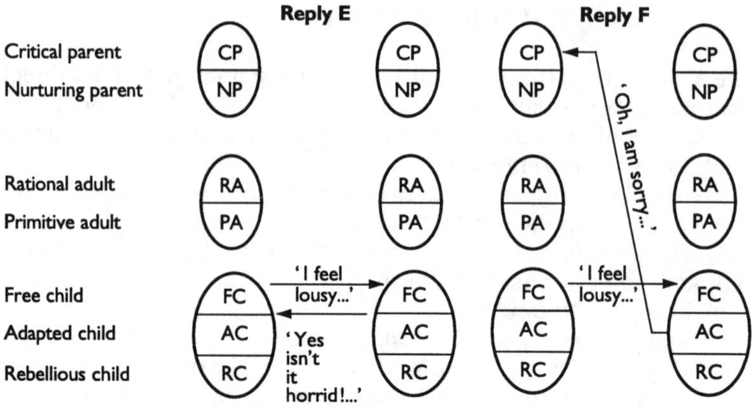

Figure 12.3 Parallel and crossed transactions

to be sure without actually hearing and seeing you. Let us say you wanted a Free Child response. Then you will be happiest with reply E (Free Child). Replies B (Nurturing Parent), C (Rational Adult) or D (Primitive Adult) suggest that the other person is not going to match your mood, but is at least responding positively. If you get replies A (Critical Parent), F (Adapted Child) or G (Rebellious Child) something is obviously very wrong; clearly you're not seeing eye to eye! Figure 12.3 illustrates what happens for replies E and F.

If a transaction is to work, there must be agreement about which sub-personality is talking to which. If someone is feeling pathetic and inadequate, as in the example, they may want you to be strong and supportive; that is, their Child is trying to talk to your Parent, and wants your Parent to talk back to their Child. If this works, you have a smoothly running *complementary* or *parallel* transaction in which each side plays its role 'correctly'.

However, if two people involved do *not* agree about the roles they are supposed to play, you get a *crossed transaction*. Perhaps I am feeling that I would like a nice, Parental, reassuring gossip about how much better things used to be in the old days, and yet you insist on replying with serious Adult statistics, comparing now and then objectively. Or I am trying to talk to you in an Adult way because I want us to work out how to make our money last till the end of the week, but you reply with some generalized Parental clichés about thrift and good management. In the example in Figure 12.3, the Adapted Child response (reply F) was a *crossed* transaction because it was treating you as a powerful Parent figure to be placated and asked to make decisions, when in fact you were not feeling remotely able to cope with the Parent role, and wanted to be Parented yourself. Crossed transactions do not always result in crossed lines on the diagram, but they often do.

In a smoothly running dialogue, a single crossed transaction may simply signal that one of the participants wishes to change role, starting a new sequence of parallel transactions of a different type – P–C, P–C, P–A, A–

A, A–A, and so on, where P–A indicates the transition point. But when crossed transactions do not result in a smooth transition, the result is at very least a sense of embarrassment or irritation, which easily grows to frustration, anger or a disturbing sense of being unable to make contact or see eye to eye. This is why crossed transactions are a major source of apparently irrational behaviour.

You can see that even if you only consider the three main personality subsystems, there are nine different complementary transactions: P–P, P–A, P–C, A–P, A–A, A–C, C–P, C–A and C–C. Berne argues that a stable, rich relationship between two people is often connected with the ability to relate well transactionally over most of the possible complementary combinations without generating many crossed transactions.

DOUBLE MESSAGES

As well as getting your messages crossed, you can also create confusion by giving double (or even treble) messages. Typically there is an explicit, spoken message forming one level of transaction, and a second tacit level communicated by non-verbal means, called the *ulterior* transaction.

For instance, suppose that as a junior member of your organization you are called into a senior manager's office. He asks you an Adult to Adult question, but his gestures and manner unconsciously convey an ulterior Parent and Child stroke as well because of the way he regards your junior status. If you reply at Adult level only, the Adult to Adult complementary transaction is satisfied, but the expected Child to Parent response to his stroke is not and he is going to feel uncomfortable. Since he is unaware of his ulterior stroke, he may interpret his discomfort as you being pushy or over-confident.

Sometimes, of course, we may be fully aware of both levels. The apparently Adult to Adult transaction 'Why not come and see my new flat?', 'Oh yes, I'd love to!' illustrated in Figure 12.4 may well have unmistakable Child to Child undertones that both people fully recognize!

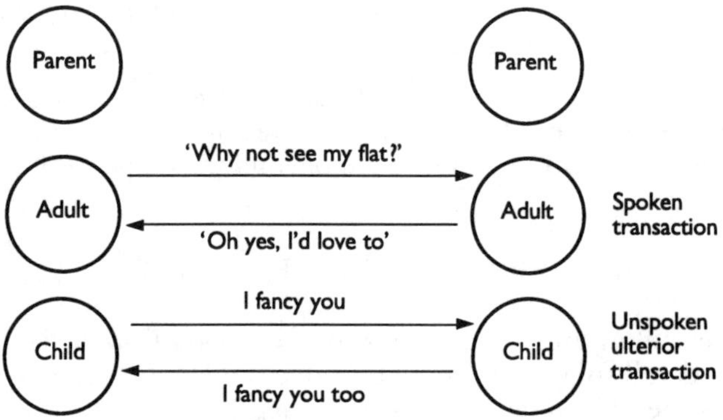

Figure 12.4 Two-level transactions

LONGER SEQUENCES: THE STRUCTURING OF TIME

As we saw earlier, one of the purposes of transactions is to structure time. Berne suggests that there are six levels of structuring activity that permit progressively richer and richer supplies of strokes, but also leave you more open and vulnerable. These are:

A Periods of privacy or withdrawal with no strokes at all. You can have too many strokes, and everyone needs periods of privacy to recuperate.

B Rituals. These are totally stereotyped conventional activities. Each side knows exactly what will happen. The commonest example is a greeting (smile, shake hands, 'Good morning', 'How are you?', 'Lovely day, isn't it?').

C Pastimes. These form the superficial conversation that follows ritual greetings, before people have begun to relax. They tend to be a little like multiple-choice questions, with a very limited range of possible answers. They are a safe way of probing to see if it is worth going further.

D Activity or work, including job, sports, hobbies, and so on. The practical requirements of the activity structure the way time is spent and generate strokes as a by-product.

E Games. We all have our own special patterns of 'stroking' we need, often established back in childhood (for instance, as part of our Adapted Child). We therefore have to find a reliable and safe way of getting them. One solution is to develop a repertoire of situations we set up (often quite unconsciously) that allow us to manoeuvre someone else into providing the needed strokes. If the partner is compatible, they will get their secret supply of strokes out of it also. Some examples of games are given in the next section.

F Intimacy or openness. This is the state in which all or most of the nine combinations of transactions can function easily and appropriately. Since the defensive barriers that normally restrict transactions are reduced in this state, intimacy provides the greatest potential for getting and giving positive strokes, since you can simply ask for them or offer them; but being open in this way also involves sensitivity to being rejected and hurt.

In addition to these relatively brief structures, Berne has also explored what he calls *scripts* – very long-term structures that may take a complete lifetime to work out. However, these are beyond the scope of this article.

SOME EXAMPLES OF GAMES

Two examples below are adapted from Berne's book *Games People Play*, which lists in detail some forty common games and mentions many others. In both cases the behaviour appears *irrational* if you set the boundary of analysis at the public, social, level. In *Why don't you . . . Yes, but . . .* White never gets a reasonable answer; in *Now I've got you, you son of a bitch*

White's response is out of all proportion to the degree to which he is provoked. This behaviour becomes understandable when the boundary of analysis is extended to include the psychological level, with various *invisible* pay-offs arising from ulterior, private and often unconscious, fears or needs in White.

Why don't you . . . Yes, but . . .

A typical exchange illustrating this game runs as follows. Mr White enters the office of his boss, Mr Black, looking flustered and upset. Hardly waiting for Black to look up he starts . . .

White 'We have lost the file on the Noble contract. This is the third time this week a file has been lost. I'm fed up with wasting my time chasing lost files.'

Black 'Why don't you get the secretaries from next door to help?'

White 'Yes, but they're busy typing the Annual Report, it's got to go off tomorrow.'

Black 'How about Pam and Judy from downstairs?'

White 'Yes, but Pam's not in today and Judy can't leave the office unattended.'

Black 'Why don't you get security to chase it up?'

White 'Yes, but they get annoyed at chasing trivial things, after all it's not a confidential file – thank goodness.'

Black 'Why don't you find out who last had it?'

White 'Yes, but half the department are out today and none of the people in can remember using it.'

Such an exchange is typically followed by a silence.

Since the solutions are, with rare exceptions, rejected, it is apparent that this game must serve some ulterior purpose. It is not played for its ostensible purpose (an Adult quest for information or solutions), but to reassure and gratify the Child. A bare transcript may sound Adult, but in the living tissue it can be observed that White presents himself as a Child inadequate to meet the situation, whereupon Black becomes transformed into a sage Parent anxious to dispense his wisdom for White's benefit.

This is illustrated in Figure 12.5. The game can proceed because at the social level both stimulus and response are Adult to Adult, and at the psychological level they are also complementary, with Parent to Child stimulus ('Why don't you . . .') eliciting Child to Parent response ('Yes, but . . .'). The psychological level is usually unconscious on both sides, but the shifts in ego state (Adult to 'inadequate' Child on White's part, Adult to 'wise' Parent by Black) can often be detected by an alert observer from changes in posture, muscular tone, voice and vocabulary. The basic principle is that no suggestion is ever accepted, the Parent is never successful. The motto of the game is 'Don't get panicky, the Parent never succeeds'.

In summary, then, while each move is amusing, so to speak, to White, and brings its own little pleasure in rejecting the suggestion, the real payoff is the silence or masked silence which ensues when the other has racked his brains and grown tired of trying to think of acceptable solutions. This

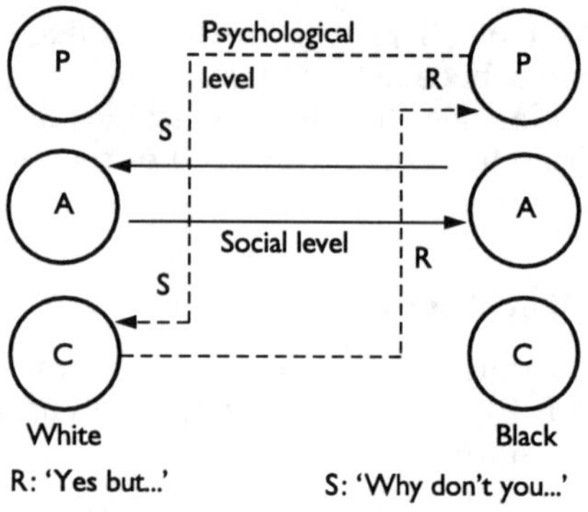

Figure 12.5 Why don't you . . . Yes, but . . .

signifies to both that White has won by demonstrating it is Black who is inadequate. If the silence is not masked, it may persist for several minutes.

If the opening is of the form 'What do you do if . . .' (*WYDI*), a suggested response (to prevent the game) is: 'That is a difficult problem. What are you going to do about it?' If it is of the form '*X* didn't work out properly,' the response then should be 'That is too bad'. Both of these are polite enough to leave White at a loss, or at least to elicit a crossed transaction, so that his frustration becomes manifest and can then be explored.

Now I've got you, you son of a bitch

White needed some plumbing fixtures installed, and he reviewed the costs very carefully with the plumber before giving him a go-ahead. The price was set and it was agreed that there would be no extras. When the plumber submitted his bill, he included a few dollars extra for an unexpected valve that had to be installed – about four dollars on a four-hundred-dollar job. White became infuriated, called the plumber on the phone and demanded an explanation. The plumber would not back down. White wrote him a long letter criticizing his integrity and ethics and refused to pay the bill until the extra charge was withdrawn. The plumber finally gave in.

It soon became obvious that both White and the plumber were playing games. In the course of their negotiations, they had recognized each other's potentials. The plumber made his provocative move when he submitted his bill. Since White had the plumber's word, the plumber was clearly in the wrong. White now felt justified in venting almost unlimited rage against him. Instead of merely negotiating in a dignified way that befitted the Adult standards he set for himself, perhaps with a little innocent annoyance, White took the opportunity to make extensive criticisms of the plumber's whole way of living. On the surface their argument was Adult to Adult, a legitimate business dispute over a stated sum of money. At the psychological level it was Parent to Adult; White was exploiting his trivial but socially defensible objection to vent the pent-up furies of many years on his cozening opponent, just as his mother might have done in a similar situation. In discussing the incident later, he quickly recognized his underlying attitude and realized how secretly delighted he had been at the plumber's provocation. He then recalled that ever since early childhood he had looked for similar injustices, received them with delight and exploited them with the same vigour. In many of the cases he recounted, he had forgotten the actual provocation, but remembered in great detail the course of the ensuing battle.

The best antithesis is correct behaviour. The contractual structure of a relationship with a player of this game should be explicitly stated in detail at the first opportunity, and the rules strictly adhered to. In everyday life, business dealings with them are always calculated risks. The wife of such a person should be treated with polite correctness, and even the mildest flirtations, gallantries or slights should be avoided, especially if the husband himself seems to encourage them.

Clearly 'games' are recurring patterns of complex behaviour that do not seem to be wholly (or even partially) explainable in terms of some sort of externally visible objective, so that they appear irrational to the onlooker (though not usually to the participants).

The particular explanation given by Berne (derived from the types of explanation originally developed by Sigmund Freud) describes these activities as re-enactments of childhood patterns (often from the Adapted Child subsystem) in order to satisfy anxieties and needs that were real in childhood, but are now maintained only as powerful emotional memories. On this theory, the source of the game lies within the individuals, in the concealed childhood memory that continues to 'fuel' the game; if the force of this memory can be discharged in some way, the game should dissolve completely, since its concealed pay-offs no longer function. Therefore for Berne the real key to change lies in recovering and disentangling the individual's memories. He does also recognize that you can intervene in the communications pattern if you want to avoid getting into someone else's game, in the ways he recommends in the two games quoted above. But he sees this purely as a temporary expedient, not a 'cure'.

Bateson, and the other writers who have explored the same idea, suggested that you can often reverse the emphasis characteristic of Berne and other post-Freudians. They argue that while there probably was some pattern of events in childhood that started it all going, it would be largely irrelevant for practical purposes if its effect had been maintained into adulthood not by *internal* memories but by *external* communication systems. In such cases the splits created around the original events have been exaggerated by positive feedback and then 'frozen' by very stable networks of feedback loops within the family system. In other words, we have a homeostatic system whose target state is suboptimal (and sometimes pathological) from the point of view of some or all of the people caught up in it.

On this type of theory, the best way to dissolve the game playing is not to poke around in early memories but to try to understand the current self-maintaining mechanisms. In this way you can work out how to block or modify some of the key feedback channels so as to break the homeostatic grip they hold over the system, so that it can re-establish a different target state that is less stressful to the individual system components.

This piece has necessarily been an introduction intended to convey the nature of the approach and provide some usable ideas; in no way is it a full exposition. Anyone interested in learning more about TA should consult one of the following books:

Berne, E. (1963) *The Structure and Dynamics of Organizations and Groups*, Grove Press, New York.
Berne, E. (1964) *Games People Play*, Grove Press, New York.
Novey, T. B. (1964) *T.A. for Management*, Jalmar Press, California.

CHAPTER 13

Goals and Decision-making

An enormous amount of management teaching proclaims the virtues of what is basically an engineering model of rational choice. This model uses clear and explicit goals to evaluate rival options. But how much do these formal statements of organizational purpose actually tell us about what is going on? When organizational decision-making occurs in quite other ways (as it often does), is this necessarily wrong? And since there are other bases for rational choice, is greater clarity over goals always important? These are the questions addressed by the three pieces in this section. The first draws a simple distinction that is as relevant today as when the famous article from which it was taken first appeared thirty-five years ago. Indeed, it attracts the ultimate accolade of being 'common sense' – an easily overlooked commodity. The second piece is a succinct summary of a very different, but perfectly reasonable, view of how decisions are made, and often should be made. Finally, the third piece is an authoritative survey of different views of decision-making. The piece starts with the rational view and considers the problems posed for it by uncertainty and ambiguity. It then discusses alternative conceptions of decision-making in terms of conflict, rules, disorder and symbolic action. In each case, it points to the implications of these views for a practical understanding of decision processes. These alternative views do not make the rational view irrelevant but they do support a more sympathetic attitude to the common vagaries of decision-making. These views reveal how deviations from the rational model may yet be wise in their own way.

13A
The Analysis of Goals in Complex Organizations

C. PERROW

THE OVER-RATIONALISTIC VIEW

Most studies of the internal operation of complex organizations, if they mention goals at all, have taken official statements of goals at face value. This may be justified if only a limited problem is being investigated, but even then it contributes to the view that goals are not problematical. In this view, goals have no effect upon activities other than in the grossest terms; or it can be taken for granted that the only problem is to adjust means to given and stable ends. This reflects a distinctive 'model' of organizational behavior, which Gouldner has characterized as the rational model.[1] Its proponents see the managerial elite as using rational and logical means to pursue clear and discrete ends set forth in official statements of goals, while the worker is seen as governed by nonrationalistic, traditionalistic orientations. If goals are unambiguous and achievement evaluated by cost-accounting procedures, the only turmoil of organizational life lies below the surface with workers or, at best, with middle management maneuvering for status and power. Actually, however, nonrational orientations exist at all levels, including the elite who are responsible for setting goals[2] and assessing the degree to which they are achieved.

One reason for treating goals as static fixtures of organizational life is that goals have not been given adequate conceptualization, though the elements of this are in easy reach. If making a profit or serving customers is to be taken as a sufficient statement of goals, then all means to this end might appear to be based on rational decisions because the analyst is not alerted to the countless policy decisions involved. If goals are given a more elaborate conceptualization, we are forced to see many more things as problematic.

OFFICIAL AND OPERATIVE GOALS

Two major categories of goals will be discussed here, official and 'operative' goals.[3] Official goals are the general purposes of the organization as put forth in the charter, annual reports, public statements by key executives, and other authoritative pronouncements. For example, the goal of an employment agency may be to place job seekers in contact with firms seeking workers. The official goal of a hospital may be to promote the health of the community through curing the ill, and sometimes through preventing illness, teaching, and conducting research. Similar organizations may emphasize different publicly acceptable goals. A business corporation, for example, may state that its goal is to make a profit or adequate return on investment, or provide a customer service, or produce goods.

This level of analysis is inadequate in itself for a full understanding of organizational behavior. Official goals are purposely vague and general and do not indicate two major factors which influence organizational behavior: the host of decisions that must be made among alternative ways of achieving official goals and the priority of multiple goals, and the many unofficial goals pursued by groups within the organization. The concept of 'operative goals'[4] will be used to cover these aspects. Operative goals designate the ends sought through the actual operating policies of the organization; they tell us what the organization actually is trying to do, regardless of what the official goals say are the aims.

Where operative goals provide the specific content of official goals they reflect choices among competing values. They may be justified on the basis of an official goal, even though they may subvert another official goal. In one sense they are means to official goals, but since the latter are vague or of high abstraction, the 'means' become ends in themselves when the organization is the object of analysis. For example, where profit-making is the announced goal, operative goals will specify whether quality or quantity is to be emphasized, whether profits are to be short run and risky or long run and stable, and will indicate the relative priority of diverse and somewhat conflicting ends of customer service, employee morale, competitive pricing, diversification, or liquidity. Decisions on all these factors influence the nature of the organization, and distinguish it from another with an identical official goal. An employment agency must decide whom to serve, what characteristics they favour among clients, and whether a high turnover of clients or a long-run relationship is desired. In the voluntary general hospital, where the official goals are patient care, teaching, and research, the relative priority of these must be decided, as well as which group in the community is to be given priority in service, and are these services to emphasize, say, technical excellence or warmth and 'hand-holding'.

Unofficial operative goals, on the other hand, are tied more directly to group interests and while they may support, be irrelevant to, or subvert official goals, they bear no necessary connection with them. An interest in a major supplier may dictate the policies of a corporation executive. The prestige that attaches to utilizing elaborate high-speed computers may dictate the reorganization of inventory and accounting departments. Racial prejudice may influence the selection procedures of an employment agency. The personal ambition of a hospital administrator may lead to community alliances and activities which bind the organization without enhancing its goal achievement. On the other hand, while the use of interns and residents as 'cheap labor' may subvert the official goal of medical education, it may substantially further the official goal of providing a high quality of patient care.

The discernment of operative goals is, of course, difficult and subject to error. The researcher may have to determine from analysis of a series of apparently minor decisions regarding the lack of competitive bidding and quality control that an unofficial goal of a group of key executives is to maximize their individual investments in a major supplier. This unofficial goal may affect profits, quality, market position, and morale of key skill groups. The executive of a correctional institution may argue that the goal of the organization is treatment, and only the lack of resources creates an apparent emphasis upon custody or deprivation. The researcher may find, however, that decisions in many areas establish the priority of custody or punishment as a goal. For example, few efforts may be made to obtain more treatment personnel; those hired are misused and mistrusted; and clients are viewed as responding only to deprivations. The president of a junior college may deny the function of the institution is to deal with the latent terminal student, but careful analysis such as Clark has made of operating policies, personnel practices, recruitment procedures, organizational alliances, and personal characteristics of elites will demonstrate this to be the operative goal.[5]

13B
Lindblom on Policy Making

A. O. HIRSCHMAN AND C. E. LINDBLOM

Lindblom's point of departure is a denial of the general validity of two assumptions implicit in most of the literature on policy making. The first is that public policy problems can best be solved by attempting to understand them; the second is that there exists sufficient agreement to provide adequate criteria for choosing among possible alternative policies. Although the first is widely accepted – in many circles almost treated as a self-evident truth – it is often false. The second is more often questioned in contemporary social science; yet many of the most common prescriptions for rational problem solving follow only if it is true.

Conventional descriptions of rational decision making identify the following aspects: (a) clarification of objectives or values, (b) survey of alternative means of reaching objectives, (c) identification of consequences, including side effects or by-products, of each alternative means, and (d) evaluation of each set of consequences in light of the objectives. However, Lindblom notes, for a number of reasons such a *synoptic* or comprehensive attempt at problem solving is not possible to the degree that clarification of objectives founders on social conflict, that required information is either not available or available only at prohibitive cost, or that the problem is simply too complex for man's finite intellectual capacities. Its complexity may stem from an impossibly large number of alternative policies and their possible repercussions, from imponderables in the delineation of objectives even in the absence of social disagreement on them, from a supply of information too large to process in the mind, or from still other causes.

It does not logically follow, Lindblom argues, that when synoptic decision making is extremely difficult it should nevertheless be pursued as far as possible. And he consequently suggests that in many circumstances substantial departures from comprehensive understanding are both inevitable and on specific grounds desirable. For the most part, these departures are familiar; and his exposition of them serves therefore to formalize our perceptions of certain useful problem-solving strategies often mistakenly dismissed as aberrations in rational problem solving.

These strategies, which we shall call 'disjointed incrementalism', are the following:

1. Attempts at understanding are limited to policies that differ only incrementally from existing policy.
2. Instead of simply adjusting means to ends, ends are chosen that are appropriate to available or nearly available means.
3. A relatively small number of means (alternative possible policies) is considered, as follows from 1.
4. Instead of comparing alternative means or policies in the light of postulated ends or objectives, alternative ends or objectives are also com-

pared in the light of postulated means or policies and their consequences.
5. Ends and means are chosen simultaneously; the choice of means does not follow the choice of ends.
6. Ends are indefinitely explored, reconsidered, discovered, rather than relatively fixed.
7. At any given analytical point ('point' refers to any one individual, group, agency, or institution), analysis and policy making are serial or successive; that is, problems are not 'solved' but are repeatedly attacked.
8. Analysis and policy making are remedial – they move *away* from ills rather than *toward* known objectives.
9. At any one analytical point, the analysis of consequences is quite incomplete.
10. Analysis and policy making are socially fragmented; they go on at a very large number of separate points simultaneously.

The most striking characteristic of disjointed incrementalism is (as indicated in 9) that no attempt at comprehensiveness is made; on the contrary, unquestionably important consequences of alternative policies are simply ignored at any given analytical or policy-making point. But Lindblom goes on to argue that through various specific types of partisan mutual adjustment among the large number of individuals and groups among which analysis and policy making is fragmented (see 10), what is ignored at one point in policy making becomes central at another point. Hence, it will often be possible to find a tolerable level of rationality in decision making when the process is viewed as a whole in its social or political context, even if at each individual policy-making point or center analysis remains incomplete. Similarly, errors that would attend overambitious attempts at comprehensive understanding are often avoided by the remedial and incremental character of problem solving. And those not avoided can be mopped up or attended to as they appear, because analysis and policy making are serial or successive (as in 7).

While we cannot here review the entire argument, Lindblom tries to show how the specific characteristics of disjointed incrementalism, taken in conjunction with mechanisms for partisan mutual adjustment, meet each of the characteristic difficulties that beset synoptic policy making: value conflicts, information inadequacies, and general complexity beyond man's intellectual capacities. His line of argument shows the influence of pluralist thinkers on political theory, but he departs from their interest in the control of power and rather focuses on the level of rationality required or appropriate for decision making.

13c
Theories of Choice and Making Decisions

J. G. MARCH

Actual decision making, particularly in organizations, often contrasts with the visions of decision making implicit in theories of choice. Because our theoretical ideas about choice are partly inconsistent with what we know about human processes of decision, we sometimes fail to understand what is going on in decision making, and consequently sometimes offer less than perfect counsel to decision makers. Behavioral research on how decisions are made does not lead to precise prescriptions for the management of choice. It will not tell the president of the United States, the president of Mitsubishi, or the reigning mafioso how to make decisions. Nor will it tell a headmistress of a private academy what she should do as she decides what new programs to offer, whom to hire, what kinds of staff development to authorize, what uniforms to prescribe, what new rooms to build, what kinds of disciplinary procedures to implement, and what kinds of promises to make to what kinds of patrons. However, the research results may contain a few observations that might – when combined with a headmistress's own knowledge and imagination – provide clues of how to think about decision making. In that spirit, this article attempts to summarize some recent work on how decisions are made in organizations. It draws heavily on work I have done jointly with Michael Cohen, Martha Feldman, Johan Olsen, Guje Sevón, and Zur Shapira.

RATIONAL CHOICE

Standard theories of choice view decision making as intentional, consequential action based on four things:

- A knowledge of alternatives. Decision makers have a set of alternatives for action. These alternatives are defined by the situation and known unambiguously.
- A knowledge of consequences. Decision makers know the consequences of alternative actions, at least up to a probability distribution.
- A consistent preference ordering. Decision makers have objective functions by which alternative consequences of action can be compared in terms of their subjective value.
- A decision rule. Decision makers have rules by which to select a single alternative of action on the basis of its consequences for the preferences.

In the most familiar form of the model, we assume that all alternatives, the probability distribution of consequences conditional on each alternative, and the subjective value of each possible consequence are known, and we assume a choice is made by selecting the alternative with the highest expected value.

The durability of the structure has been impressive. It is also understandable. Simple choice models capture some truth. Demand curves for consumer products generally have negative slopes, and labor unions usually are more resistant to wage cuts than to wage increases. Moreover, the core ideas are flexible. When the model seems not to fit, it is often possible to reinterpret preferences or knowledge and preserve the axioms. Finally, choice is a faith as well as a theory; it is linked to the ideologies of the Enlightenment. The prevalence of willful choice models of behavior in economics, political science, psychology, sociology, linguistics, and anthropology attests to the attractiveness of choice as a vision of human behavior.

The attraction extends to ordinary discourse and journalism. A reading of the leading newspapers or journals of any Western country will show that the primary interpretive model used by individuals in these societies is one of willful choice. The standard explanation provided for the actions of individuals or institutions involves two assertions: Someone decided to have it happen. They decided to have it happen because it was in their self-interest to do so. In cases involving multiple actors, a third assertion may be added. Different people, in their own self-interest, wanted different things and the people with power got what they wanted. Ideas of willful, rational choice are the standard terms of discourse for answering the generic questions: Why did it happen? Why did you do it?

The same basic structure underlies modern decision engineering. Operations analysis, management science, decision theory, and the various other analytical approaches to improving choices are variations on a theme of rational choice, as are standard ideas for determining the value of information and the design of information systems. These efforts at improving the decisions of individuals and organizations have been helpful. Systematic rational analyses of choice alternatives have improved the blending of aviation fuel, the location of warehouses, the choice of energy sources, and the arrangement of bank queues, as well as providing the solutions to many other decision problems. And although it is also possible to cite examples in which the consequences of decision analysis have been less benign, a balanced judgment must conclude that these modern technologies of choice have done more good than harm.

Within such a framework, the advice we give to a headmistress is straightforward: Determine precisely what your alternatives are. Define clearly what your preferences are. Estimate the possible consequences stemming from each alternative and the likelihood of occurrence. Select the alternative that will maximize the expected value.

This basic theory of choice has been considerably elaborated over the past thirty years with the discovery of computational procedures for solving problems and the development of various more specific models within the general frame. At the same time, empirical research on the ways in which decisions are actually made by individuals and organizations has identified some problems in fitting the standard theory of choice to observed decision behavior.

UNCERTAINTY AND AMBIGUITY

Theories of choice presume two improbably precise guesses about the future: a guess about the future consequences of current actions and a guess about future sentiments with respect to those consequences. Actual decision situations often seem to make both guesses problematic.

The first guess – about the uncertain future consequences of current action – has attracted attention from both students of decision making and choice theorists. In fact, some of the earliest efforts to relate studies of decision making and theories of choice raised questions about the informational assumptions of the theories. Even if decisions are made in a way generally consistent with choice theories – that is, that estimates of the consequences of alternative actions are formed and that action is *intendedly* rational – there are informational and computational limits on human choice. There are limits on the number of alternatives that can be considered, and limits on the amount and accuracy of information that is available. Such a set of ideas leads to the conception of limited rationality for which Herbert Simon received the Nobel Prize in 1978.

The core ideas are elementary and by now familiar. Rather than all alternatives or all information about consequences being known, information has to be discovered through search. Search is stimulated by a failure to achieve a goal, and continues until it reveals an alternative that is good enough to satisfy existing, evoked goals. New alternatives are sought in the neighborhood of old ones. Failure focuses search on the problem of attaining goals that have been violated, success allows search resources to move to other domains. The key scarce resource is attention: and theories of limited rationality are, for the most part, theories of the allocation of attention.

They are also theories of slack – that is, unexploited opportunities, undiscovered economies, waste, etc. As long as performance exceeds the goal, search for new alternatives is modest, slack accumulates, and aspirations increase. When performance falls below the goal, search is stimulated, slack is decreased, and aspirations decrease. This classic control system does two things to keep performance and goals close. First, it adapts goals to performance; that is, decision makers learn what they should expect. At the same time, it adapts performance to goals by increasing search and decreasing slack in the face of failure, by decreasing search and increasing slack when faced with success. To the familiar pattern of fire alarm management are added the dynamics of changes in aspirations and slack buffers.

These ideas have been used to explore some features of adaptation to a changing environment. Decision makers appear often to be able to discover new efficiencies in their operations under conditions of adversity. If we assume that decision makers optimize, it is not immediately obvious why new economies can be discovered under conditions of adversity if they could not be discovered during good times. The explanation is natural in the slack version of adaptation. During favorable times, slack accumulates. Such slack becomes a reservoir of search opportunities during subsequent periods of trouble. As a result, environmental fluctuations are dampened by the decision process. Such a description seems to provide a partial understanding of the resilience of human institutions in the face of adversity.

Thus, in the case of our headmistress, we would expect that so long as the academy prospered, slack would accumulate. Control over the pursuit of private pleasures by staff members would be relaxed; search for improvements in existing programs would be lackadaisical; discipline would decline. If, on the other hand, a major patron were dissatisfied, or demand for the product weakened, or a loss in quality recorded, then discipline and control would be tightened and search for refinements in existing techniques would be stimulated. As a result, we would probably expect that refinements of existing techniques in the academy, or more energetic performances, would be more likely during times of adversity, but that, because of the extra slack, experiments with unusual new techniques would be more common during time of success.

Partly as a result of such observations by students of decision making, theories of choice have placed considerable emphasis on ideas of search, attention, and information costs in recent years, and these efforts in combination with concern for the problems of incomplete information and transaction costs have turned substantial parts of recent theories of choice into theories of information and attention – tributes to the proposition that information gathering, information processing, and decision making impose heavy demands on the finite capacity of the human organism. Aspiration levels, incrementalism, slack, and satisfaction have been described as sensible under fairly general circumstances.

The second guess – about the uncertain future preferences for the consequences of current actions – has been less considered, yet poses, if anything, greater difficulties. Consider the following properties of preferences as they appear in standard theories of choice:

- Preferences are *absolute*. Theories of choice assume action in terms of preferences; but they recognize neither discriminations among alternative preferences, nor the possibility that a person reasonably might view his own preferences and action based on them as morally distressing.
- Preferences are *stable*. In theories of choice, current action is taken in terms of current preferences. The implicit assumption is that preferences will be unchanged when the outcomes of current actions are realized.
- Preferences are *consistent* and *precise*. Theories of choice allow inconsistency or ambiguity in preferences only insofar as they do not affect choice (i.e., only insofar as they are made irrelevant by scarcity or the specification of tradeoffs).
- Preferences are *exogenous*. Theories of choice presume that preferences, by whatever process they may be created, are not themselves affected by the choices they control.

Each of these features of preference seems inconsistent with observations of choice behavior among individuals and social institutions: not always, but often enough to be troublesome. Individuals commonly find it possible to express both a preference for something and a recognition that the preference is repugnant to moral standards they accept. Choices are often made without much regard for preferences. Human decision makers routinely ignore their own, fully conscious preferences in making decisions. They follow rules, traditions, hunches, and the advice or actions of others. Preferences change over time in such a way that predicting future preferences is often difficult. Preferences are inconsistent. Individuals and organizations are aware of the extent to which some of their preferences conflict with others: yet they do little to resolve those inconsistencies. Many preferences are stated in forms that lack precision. And while preferences are used to choose among actions, it is also often true that actions and experience with their consequences affect preferences.

Such differences between preferences as they are portrayed in theories of choice and preferences as they appear in decision making can be interpreted as reflecting some ordinary behavioral wisdom that is not always well accommodated within the theory. Human beings seem to recognize in their behavior that there are limits to personal and institutional integration in tastes. As a result they engage in activities designed to manage preferences. These activities make little sense from the point of view of a theory that assumes decision makers know what they want and will want, or a theory that assumes wants are morally equivalent. But ordinary human actors sense that they might come to want something that they should not, or that they might make unwise choices under the influence of fleeting but powerful desires if they do not act to control the development of unfortunate preferences or to buffer actions from preferences. Like Ulysses, they know the advantages of having their hands tied.

Human beings seem to believe that the theory of choice considerably exaggerates the relative power of a choice based on two guesses compared with a choice that is itself a guess. As observers of the process by which their beliefs have been formed and are consulted, ordinary human beings seem to endorse the good sense in perceptual and moral modesty.

They seem to recognize the extent to which preferences are constructed, or developed, through a confrontation between preferences and actions that are inconsistent with them, and among conflicting preferences. Though they seek some consistency, they appear to see inconsistency as a normal and necessary aspect of the development and clarification of preferences. They sometimes do something for no better reason than that they must, or that someone else is doing it.

Human beings act as though some aspects of their beliefs are important to life without necessarily being consistent with actions, and important to the long-run quality of decision making without controlling it completely in the short run. They accept a degree of personal and social wisdom in simple hypocrisy.

They seem to recognize the political nature of argumentation more clearly and more personally than the theory of choice does. They are unwilling to gamble that God made those people who are good at rational argument uniquely virtuous. They protect themselves from cleverness, in themselves as well as in others, by obscuring the nature of their preferences.

What are the implications for our headmistress? Uncertainty about future consequences (the first guess) and human limitations in dealing with them lead decision makers, intelligently, to techniques of limited rationality. But what can a sensible decision maker learn from observations of preference ambiguity, beyond a reiteration of the importance of clarifying goals and an appreciation of possible human limits in achieving preference orderliness? Considerations of these complications in preferences, in fact, lead to a set of implications for the management of academies and other organizations, as well as for human choice more generally.

To begin with, we need to re-examine the function of decision. One of the primary ways in which individuals and organizations develop goals is by interpreting the actions they take, and one feature of good action is that it leads to the development of new preferences. As a result, decisions should not be seen as flowing directly or strictly from prior objectives. A headmistress might well view the making of decisions somewhat less as a process of deduction, and somewhat more as a process of gently upsetting preconceptions of what she is doing.

In addition, we need a modified view of planning. Planning has many virtues, but a plan can often be more effective as an interpretation of past decisions than as a blueprint for future ones. It can be used as part of our efforts to develop a new, somewhat consistent theory of ourselves that incorporates our recent actions into some moderately comprehensive structure of goals. A headmistress needs to be tolerant of the idea that the meaning of yesterday's action will be discovered in the experiences and interpretations of today.

Finally, we need to accept playfulness in action. Intelligent choice probably needs a dialectic between reason and foolishness, between doing things for no 'good' reason and discovering the reasons. Since the theory and ideology of choice are primarily concerned with strengthening reason, a headmistress is likely to overlook the importance of play.

CONFLICT

[. . .] Political perspectives on organizations emphasize the problems of using self-interested individuals as agents for other self-interested individuals. It is a set of problems familiar to studies of legislators, lawyers, and bureaucrats. If we assume that agents act in their own self-interest, then ensuring that the self-interest of agents coincides with the self-interest of principals becomes a central concern. This has led to extensive discussions of incentive and contractual schemes designed to assure such a coincidence, and to the development of theories of agency. It is clear, however, that principals are not always successful in assuring the reliability of agents. Agents are bribed or coopted. As a result, politics often emphasizes trust and loyalty, in parallel with a widespread belief that they are hard to find. The temptations to revise contracts unilaterally are frequently substantial, and promises of uncertain future support are easily made worthless in the absence of some network of favor giving.

Such complications lead to problems in controlling the implementation of decisions. Decisions unfold through a series of interrelated actions. If all conflicts of interest were settled by the employment contract, the unfolding would present only problems of information and coordination, but such problems are confounded by the complications of unresolved conflict. For example, one complication in control is that the procedures developed to measure performance in compliance with directives involve measures that can be manipulated. Any system of controls involves a system of accounts, and any system of accounts is a roadmap to cheating on them. As a result, control systems can be seen as an infinite game between controllers and the controlled in which advantage lies with relatively full-time players having direct personal interest in the outcomes.

Such features of organizations arise from one very simple modification of classical theories of choice: seeing decisions as being based on unreconciled preferences. It seems hard to avoid the obvious fact that such a description comes closer to the truth in many situations than does one in which we assume a consistent preference function. Somewhat more problematic is the second feature of much of the behavioral study of decision making – the tendency for the political aspects of decision making to be interminable. If it were possible to imagine a two-step decision process in which first we established (through side-payments and formation of coalitions) a set of joint preferences acceptable to a winning coalition and *then* we acted, we could treat the first stage as 'politics' and the second as 'economics'. Such a division has often been tempting (e.g. the distinction between policy making and administration), but it has rarely been satisfactory as a description of decision making. The decisions we observe seem to be infused with strategic actions and politics at every level and at every point.

An academy, like a business firm or government agency, is a political system of partly conflicting interests in which decisions are made through bargaining, power, and coalition formation. In general, there appear to be a few elementary rules for operating in a political system. Power comes from a favorable position for trading favors. Thus it comes from the possession of resources and the idiosyncrasy of preferences, from valuing things that others do not and having things that others value. If you have valued resources, display them. If you don't have them, get them – even if you don't value them yourself. Grab a hostage. Power comes from a reputation for power. Thus it comes from appearing to get what you want, from the trappings of power, and from the interpretations people make of ambiguous historical events. [. . .]

RULES

Theories of choice underestimate both the pervasiveness and sensibility of an alternative decision logic – the logic of obligation, duty, and rules. Actual decisions seem often to involve finding the 'appropriate' rule as much as they do evaluating consequences in terms of preferences.

Much of the decision-making behavior we observe reflects the routine way in which people do what they are supposed to do. For example, most of the time, most people in organizations follow rules even when it is not obviously in their self-interest to do so. The behavior can be viewed as contractual, an implicit agreement to act appropriately in return for being treated appropriately, and to some extent there certainly is such a 'contract'. But socialization into rules and their appropriateness is ordinarily not a case of willful entering into an explicit contract. It is a set of understandings of the nature of things, of self-conceptions, and of images of proper behavior. It is possible, of course, to treat the word *rule* so broadly as to include any regularity in behavior, and sometimes that is a temptation too great to be resisted. But for the most part, we mean something considerably narrower. We mean regular operating procedures, not necessarily written but certainly standardized, known and understood with sufficient clarity to allow discourse about them and action based on them.

The proposition that organizations follow rules – that much of the behavior in an organization is specified by standard operating procedures – is a common one in the bureaucratic and organizational literature. To describe behavior as driven by rules is to see action as a matching of behavior with a position or situation. The criterion is appropriateness. The terminology is one of duties and roles rather than anticipatory decision making. The contrast can be characterized by comparing the conventional litanies for individual behavior.

Consequential action:
1. What are my alternatives?
2. What are my values?
3. What are the consequences of my alternatives for my values?
4. Choose the alternative that has the best consequences.

Obligatory action:
1. What kind of situation is this?
2. What kind of person am I?
3. What is appropriate for me in a situation like this?
4. Do it.

Research on obligatory action emphasizes understanding the kinds of rules that are evoked and used, the ways in which they fit together, and the processes by which they change.

The existence and persistence of rules, combined with their relative independence of idiosyncratic concerns of individuals, make it possible for societies and organizations to function reasonably reliably and reasonably consistently. Current rules store information generated by previous experience and analysis, even though the information cannot easily be retrieved in a form amenable to systematic current evaluation.

[. . .] Insofar as action can be viewed as rule-following, decision making is not willful in the normal sense. It does not stem from the pursuit of interests and the calculation of future consequences of current choices. Rather it comes from matching a changing set of contingent rules to a changing set of situations. The intelligence of the process arises from the way rules store information gained through learning, selection, and contagion, and from the reliability with which rules are followed. The broader intelligence of the adaptation of rules depends on a fairly subtle intermeshing of rates of change, consistency, and foolishness. Sensibility is not guaranteed. At the least, it seems to require occasional deviation from the rules, some general consistency between adaptation rates and environmental rates of change, and a reasonable likelihood that networks of imitation are organized in a manner that allows intelligent action to be diffused somewhat more rapidly and more extensively than silliness.

In these terms, decision making in our headmistress's academy involves a logic of appropriateness. The issue is not what the costs and benefits are of an innovative new idea, but what a good headmistress does in a situation like this. The headmistress's role, like other roles, is filled with rules of behavior that have evolved through a history of experience, new year's resolutions, and imitation. There are rules about dress and decorum, rules about the treatment of staff members and guests, rules about dealing with grievances, rules about the kinds of equipment that should be provided and how it should be used. People in the organization follow rules: professional rules, social rules, and standard operating procedures. In such a world, some of the most effective ways of influencing decision outcomes involve the relatively dull business of understanding standard operating procedures and systems of accounting and control and intervening unobtrusively to make a particular decision a routine consequence of following standard rules.

DISORDER

Theories of choice underestimate the confusion and complexity surrounding actual decision making. Many things are happening at once: technologies are changing and poorly understood; alliances, preferences, and perceptions are changing; problems, solutions, opportunities, ideas, people, and outcomes are mixed together in a way that makes their interpretation uncertain and their connections unclear.

Decision making ordinarily presumes an ordering of the confusions of life. The classic ideas of order in organizations involve two closely related concepts. The first is that events and activities can be arranged in chains of ends and means. We associate action with its consequences; we participate in making decisions in order to produce intended outcomes. Thus, consequential relevance arranges the relation between solutions and problems and the participation of decision makers. The second is that organizations are hierarchies in which higher levels control lower levels, and policies control implementation. Observations of actual organizations suggest a more confusing picture. Actions in one part of an organization appear to be only loosely coupled to actions in another. Solutions seem to have only a modest connection to problems. Policies are not implemented. Decision makers seem to wander in and out of decision arenas. In *Ambiguity and Choice in Organizations*, Pierre Romelaer and I described the whole process as a funny soccer game: 'Consider a round, sloped, multi-goal soccer field on which individuals play soccer. Many different people (but not everyone) can join in the game (or leave it) at different times. Some people can throw balls into the game or remove them. Individuals while they are in the game try to kick whatever ball comes near them in the direction of goals they like and away from goals they wish to avoid.'

The disorderliness of many things that are observed in decision making has led some people to argue that there is very little order to it, that it is best described as bedlam. A more conservative position, however, is that the ways in which organizations bring order to disorder is less hierarchical and less a collection of means–ends chains than is anticipated by conventional theories. There is order, but it is not the conventional order. In particular, it is argued that any decision process involves a collection of individuals and groups who are simultaneously involved in other things. Understanding decisions in one arena requires an understanding of how those decisions fit into the lives of participants.

From this point of view, the loose coupling that is observed in a specific decision situation is a consequence of a shifting intermeshing of the demands on the attention and lives of the whole array of actors. It is possible to examine any particular decision as the seemingly fortuitous consequence of combining different moments of different lives, and some efforts have been made to describe organizations in something like that cross-sectional detail. A more limited version of the same fundamental idea focuses on the allocation of attention. The idea is simple. Individuals attend to some things, and thus do not attend to others. The attention devoted to a particular decision by a particular potential participant depends on the attributes of the decision and alternative claims on attention. Since those alternative claims are not homogeneous across participants and change over time, the attention any particular decision receives can be both quite unstable and remarkably independent of the properties of the decision. The same decision will attract much attention, or little, depending on the other things that possible participants might be doing. The apparently erratic character of attention is made somewhat more explicable by placing it in the context of multiple, changing claims on attention.

Such ideas have been generalized to deal with flows of solutions and problems, as well as participants. In a garbage-can decision process it is assumed that there are exogenous, time-dependent arrivals of choice problems, solutions and decision makers. Problems and solutions are attached to choices, and thus to each other, not because of their inherent connection in a means–end sense, but in terms of their temporal proximity. The collection of decision makers, problems, and solutions that come to be associated with a particular choice opportunity is orderly – but the logic of the ordering is temporal rather than hierarchical or consequential. At the limit, for example, almost any solution can be associated with almost any problem – provided they are contemporaries.

The strategies for a headmistress that can be derived from this feature of decision making are not complicated. First, persist. The disorderliness of decision processes and implementation means that there is no essential consistency between what happens at one time or place and what happens at another, or between policies and actions. Decisions happen as a result of a series of loosely connected episodes involving different people in different settings, and they may be unmade or modified by subsequent episodes. Second, have a rich agenda. There are innumerable ways in which disorderly processes will confound the cleverest behavior with respect to any one proposal, however important or imaginative. What such processes cannot do is frustrate large numbers of projects. Third, provide opportunities for garbage-can decisions. One of the complications in accomplishing things in a disorderly process is the tendency for any particular project to become intertwined with other issues simply by virtue of their simultaneity. The appropriate response is to provide irrelevant choice opportunities for problems and issues; for example, discussions of long-run plans or goals.

SYMBOLS

Theories of choice assume that the primary reason for decision making is to make choices. They ignore the extent to which decision making is a ritual activity closely linked to central Western ideologies of rationality. In actual decision situations, symbolic and ritual aspects are often a major factor.

Most theories of choice assume that a decision process is to be understood in terms of its outcome, that decision makers enter the process in order to affect outcomes, and that the point of life is choice. The emphasis is instrumental: the central conceit is the notion of decision significance. Studies of decision arenas, on the other hand, seem often to describe a set of processes that make little sense in such terms. Information that is ostensibly gathered for a decision is often ignored. Individuals fight for the right to participate in a decision process, but then do not exercise the right. Studies of managerial time persistently indicate very little time spent in making decisions. Rather, managers seem to spend time meeting people and executing managerial performances. Contentiousness over the policies of an organization is often followed by apparent indifference about their implementation.

These anomalous observations appear to reflect, at least in part, the extent to which decision processes are only partly – and often almost incidentally – concerned with making decisions. A choice process provides an occasion:

- for defining virtue and truth, during which decision makers discover or interpret what has happened to them, what they have been doing, what they are going to do, and what justifies their actions.
- for distributing glory or blame for what has happened; and thus an occasion for exercising, challenging, or reaffirming friendship or trust relationships, antagonisms, power, or status relationships.
- for socialization, for educating the young.
- for having a good time, for enjoying the pleasures connected with taking part in a choice situation.

In short, decision making is an arena for symbolic action, for developing and enjoying an interpretation of life and one's position in it. The rituals of choice infuse participants with an appreciation of the sensibility of life's arrangements. They tie routine events to beliefs about the nature of things. The rituals give meaning, and meaning controls life. From this point of view, understanding decision making involves recognizing that decision outcomes may often be less significant than the ways in which the process provides meaning in an ambiguous world. The meanings involved may be as grand as the central ideology of a society committed to reason and participation. They may be as local as the ego needs of specific individuals or groups.

Some treatments of symbols in decision making portray them as perversions of decision processes. They are presented as ways in which the gullible are misled into acquiescence. In such a portrayal, the witch doctors of symbols use their tricks to confuse the innocent, and the symbolic features of choice are opiates. Although there is no question that symbols are often used strategically, effective decision making depends critically on the legitimacy of the processes of choice and their outcomes, and such legitimacy is problematic in a confusing, ambiguous world. It is hard to imagine a society with modern ideology that would not exhibit a well elaborated and reinforced myth of choice, both to sustain social orderliness and meaning and to facilitate change.

The orchestration of choice needs to assure an audience of two essential things: first, that the choice has been made intelligently, that it reflects planning, thinking, analysis, and the systematic use of information; second, that the choice is sensitive to the concerns of relevant people, that the right people have had a word in the process. For example, part of the drama of organizational decision making is used to reinforce the idea that managers (and managerial decisions) affect the performance of organizations. Such a belief is, in fact, difficult to confirm using the kinds of data routinely generated in a confusing world. But the belief is important to the functioning of a hierarchical system. Executive compensation schemes and the ritual trappings of executive advancement reassure managers (and others) that an organization is controlled by its leadership, and appropriately so.

Thus, by most reasonable measures, the symbolic consequences of decision processes are as important as the outcome consequences; and we are led to a perspective that challenges the first premise of many theories of choice, the premise that life is choice. Rather, we might observe that life is not primarily choice; it is interpretation. Outcomes are generally less significant – both behaviorally and ethically – than process. It is the process that gives meaning to life, and meaning is the core of life. The reason that people involved in decision making devote so much time to symbols, myths, and rituals is that we (appropriately) care more about them. From this point of view, choice is a construction that finds its justification primarily in its elegance, and organizational decision making can be understood and described in approximately the same way we would understand and describe a painting by Picasso or a poem by T. S. Eliot.

As a result, a headmistress probably needs to see her activities as somewhat more dedicated to elaborating the processes of choice (as opposed to controlling their outcomes), to developing the ritual beauties of decision making in a way that symbolizes the kind of institution her academy might come to be. Just as educational institutions have libraries and archives of manuscripts to symbolize a commitment to scholarship and ideas, so also they have decision processes that express critical values. For example, if an important value of an organization is client satisfaction, then the decision process should be one that displays the eagerness of management to accept and implement client proposals, and one that symbolizes the dedication of staff to principles of availability and service.

INFORMATION AND IMPLICATIONS

These observations on decision making and theories of choice are not surprising to experienced decision makers. But they have some implications, one set of which can be illustrated by examining a classical problem: the design of an information system in an organization. In the case of our headmistress, there are issues of what information to gather and store, which archives to keep and which to burn, what information to provide to potential contributors, and how to organize the records so they are easily accessible to those who need them.

In most discussions of the design of information systems in organizations, the value of information is ordinarily linked to managerial decision making in a simple way. The value of an information source depends on the decisions to be made, the precision and reliability of the information, and the availability of alternative sources. Although calculating the relevant expected costs and returns is rarely trivial, the framework suggests some very useful rules of thumb. Don't pay for information about something that cannot affect choices you are making. Don't pay for information if the same information will be freely available anyway before you have to make a decision for which it is relevant. Don't pay for information that confirms something you already know. In general, we are led to an entirely plausible stress on the proposition that allocation of resources to information gathering or to information systems should depend on a clear idea of how potential information might affect decisions.

A notable feature of the actual investment in information and information sources that we observe is that they appear to deviate considerably from these conventional canons of information management. Decision makers and organizations gather information and do not use it; ask for more, and ignore it; make decisions first, and look for the relevant information afterwards. In fact, organizations seem to gather a great deal of information that has little or no relevance to decisions. It is, from a decision theory point of view, simply gossip. Were one to ask why organizations treat information in these ways, it would be possible to reply that they are poorly designed, badly managed, or ill-informed. To some extent, many certainly are. But the pervasiveness of the phenomenon suggests that perhaps it is not the decision makers who are inadequate, but our conceptions of information. There are several sensible reasons why decision makers deal with information the way they do.

Decision makers operate in a surveillance mode more than they do in a problem-solving mode. In contrast to a theory of information that assumes that information is gathered to resolve a choice among alternatives, decision makers scan their environments for surprises and solutions. They monitor what is going on. Such scanning calls for gathering a great deal of information that appears to be irrelevant to 'decisions'. Moreover, insofar as decision makers deal with problems, their procedures are different from those anticipated in standard decision theory. They characteristically do not 'solve' problems; they apply rules and copy solutions from others. Indeed, they often do not recognize a 'problem' until they have a 'solution'.

Decision makers seem to know, or at least sense, that most information is tainted by the process by which it is generated. It is typically quite hard to disaggregate social belief, including expert judgment, into its bases. The social process by which confidence in judgment is developed and shared is not overly sensitive to the quality of judgment. Moreover, most information is subject to strategic misrepresentation. It is likely to be presented by someone who is, for personal or subgroup reasons, trying to persuade a decision maker to do something. Our theories of information-based decision making (e.g. statistical decision theory) are, for the most part, theories of decision making with innocent information. Decision information, on the other hand, is rarely innocent, and thus rarely as reliable as an innocent would expect.

Highly regarded advice is often bad advice. It is easy to look at decision making and find instances in which good advice and good information were ignored. It is a common occurrence. Consequently, we sometimes see decision making as perversely resistant to advice and information. In fact, much highly regarded advice and much generally accepted information is misleading. Even where conflict of interest between advice givers and advice takers is a minor problem, advice givers typically exaggerate the quality of their advice; and information providers typically exaggerate the quality of their information. It would be remarkable if they did not. Decision makers seem to act in a way that recognizes the limitations of 'good' advice and 'reliable' information.

Information is a signal and symbol of competence in decision making. Gathering and presenting information symbolizes (and demonstrates) the ability and legitimacy of decision makers. A good decision maker is one who makes decisions in a proper way, who exhibits expertise and uses generally accepted information. The competition for reputations among decision makers stimulates the overproduction of information.

As a result of such considerations, information plays both a smaller and a larger role than is anticipated in decision theory-related theories of information. It is smaller in the sense that the information used in decision making is less reliable and more strategic than is conventionally assumed, and is treated as less important for decision making. It is larger in the sense that it contributes not only to the making of decisions but to the execution of other managerial tasks and to the broad symbolic activities of the individual and organization.

If it is possible to imagine that life is not only choice but also interpretation, that they are heavily intertwined, and that the management of life and organizations is probably as much the latter as the former, it is possible to sketch some elements of the requirements for the design of useful management information systems.

We require some notion of the value of alternative information sources that is less tied to a prior specification of a decision (or class of decisions) than to a wide spectrum of possible decisions impossible to anticipate in the absence of the information; less likely to show the consequences of known alternatives for existing goals than to suggest new alternatives and new objectives; less likely to test old ideas than to provide new ones; less pointed toward anticipating uncertain futures than toward interpreting ambiguous pasts. [. . .]

More generally, research on how organizations make decisions leads us to a perspective on choice different from that provided by standard theories of choice, and may even provide some hints for an academy headmistress. The ideas are incomplete; the hints are rough. They point toward a vision of decision making that embraces the axioms of choice but acknowledges their limitations; that combines a passion for the technology of choice with an appreciation of its complexities and the beauties of its confusions; and that sees a headmistress as often constrained by sensibility and rules, but sometimes bouncing around a soccer field.

NOTES

1. Gouldner, A. (1959) 'Organizational analysis', in Merton, R., Broom, L. and Cottrell, L. S. Jnr. (eds) *Sociology Today*, Basic Books, New York, p. 407.
2. A strong argument for considering changes in goals is made by Thompson, J. D. and McEwen, W. J. (1958) 'Organizational goals and environments; goals-setting as an interaction process', *Amer. Sociological Rev.*, 23, February, pp. 23–31.
3. A third may be distinguished: social system goals, which refer to those contributions an organization makes to the functioning of a social system in which it is nested. In Parsons' terminology, organizations may serve adaptive, integrative, or pattern-maintenance functions. See Parsons, T. (1956) 'Sociological approach to the theory of organizations,' *Administrative Science Quarterly*, 1, June–September, pp. 63–86, 225–240. This alone, however, will tell us little about individual organizations, although Scott, in a suggestive article applying this scheme to prisons and mental hospitals, implies that organizations serving integrative functions for society will place particular importance upon integrative functions within the organization. See Scott, F. G. (1959) 'Action theory and research in social organizations', *Amer. Jour. of Sociology*, 64, January, pp. 386–395. Parsons asserts that each of the four functions mentioned above also must be performed within organizations if they are to survive. It is possible to see a parallel between these four functions and the four tasks discussed below, but his are, it is felt, too general and ambiguous to provide tools for analysis.
4. The concept of 'operational goals' or 'sub-goals' put forth by March and Simon bears a resemblance to this but does not include certain complexities which we will discuss, nor is it defined systematically. See March, J. G. and Simon, H. A. (1958) *Organizations*, Wiley, New York, pp. 156–157.
5. Clark, B. (1960) *The Open Door College*, McGraw-Hill, New York.

CHAPTER 14

Control

Sir Geoffrey Vickers is often described as the 'father of systems thinking'. Scientific management had made extensive use of metaphors derived from mechanical systems. One of Vickers' most notable achievements in this field was to show that these metaphors could, and should, be extended and enriched to include values and 'appreciation'. This piece gives a quick but comprehensive sketch of Vickers' contribution and shows how the mechanical view of control is both a 'tool for thought' and the starting-point for a much deeper conception of the messy complexities of organizational control.

Sir Geoffrey Vickers

D. S. PUGH, D. J. HICKSON AND C. R. HININGS

Sir Geoffrey Vickers (1894–1982) served in the First World War, and was awarded the Victoria Cross for bravery. He worked as a solicitor and then took charge during the Second World War of British economic intelligence. He was knighted in 1946 and then became the member of the National Coal Board in charge of manpower, education, health and welfare. It was in the last twenty years or so of his life that he developed, systematized and recorded his ideas about institutions, organizations and policy-making. At his death in his eighty-eighth year, he was visiting Professor of Systems at the University of Lancaster and still engaged on fresh work.

The processes of policy-making, decision-making and control are at the centre of Vickers's analysis. All of these processes take place within an organized setting – a group, an organization, an institution or a society. They are the key to understanding how organizations actually work.

Much of Vickers's extensive writing derives from his principal concern with the idea of *regulation*. Regulation is essentially the process of ensuring that any system follows the path that has been set for it. It is a concept that derives from information theory, systems theory, cybernetics and the control of machines. Vickers used ideas deriving primarily from technological contexts as a basis for developing a whole range of analytical concepts about policy-making and management.

If one is to ensure that an organization is to carry out the functions and activities specified by its controllers, a number of activities have to happen which, taken together, constitute the regulation of a system. First, it is necessary for the controllers (the managers) to establish what the state of the system is, to find out what is happening. For Vickers this involves making what he calls *reality judgements*, establishing the facts. But facts do not have an independent meaning; their significance has to be judged. This involves the second part of the process of regulation, namely, making a *value judgement*. This can only be done by comparing the actual state of an organization with a standard which acts as a norm. The third part of the process involves devising the means to reduce any disparity between the norm and actuality. Taken together these three elements make up the regulative process of information, valuation and action.

It may initially sound as though regulation is a mechanical process, but this would be far from the truth. While the basic ideas come from machine systems Vickers is very clear that adaptations and additions are necessary when it comes to the management of organizations and other human systems. The making of judgements is a uniquely human function which he describes as an art (see *The Art of Judgement*). Central to making judgements is the process of *appreciation* because judgements involve the selection of information, the application of values and the choice of action. None of these processes is self-evident or straightforward. Any manager facing a situation has to make an appreciation of it. This is true not just of arriving at standards, but also of collecting information. Appreciation involves the manager in making choices and selections; deciding what indicators to use to describe the state of the organizations; choosing what standards to set and what courses of action to follow. Appreciation requires the specifically human capacity of a readiness to see and value objects and situations in one way rather than another.

There is a very important relationship between regulation and appreciation. To regulate (control), the regulator (manager) has to deal with a series of variables, elements of a situation which establish how well a system (organization) is performing. But a manager can only deal with a limited number of such variables. Which variables are chosen for the purpose of regulation is a function of a manager's appreciative system. Like Herbert Simon on whose work he draws, Vickers points out that there are cognitive limits to what an individual can handle, the amount that he can usefully watch and regulate. A manager is also limited by his interests in the selection of variables to attend to. Cognition and interests are elements in his appreciative system.

Appreciation has a major role to play in organizational and institutional management because it steers the judgements that controllers make by setting the system. Because it is through his appreciative system that a manager makes both his reality and value judgements, such a system sets the limits to what are to be regarded as choices and what as constraining. This steering function establishes what is enabling, what is limiting and what is crucial. The basic policy choice in any organization is what to regard as regulatable, and the choice made lays down what the key relations and central norms of the system are to be.

Having established the central and analytical constructs of regulation and appreciation and their relationship to one another, much of Vickers's work is then concerned with integrating a psychologically based approach to control, emphasizing individual characteristics, with further analysis which places the controller in a collective setting. Managers have to operate with and through others; the process of regulation is not machine-like for human systems. This means that choice and action have to be organized and operated on a collective basis. For this to happen there has to be a set of shared understandings, an agreed set of norms.

The manager, through his organizational position and appreciative system, has a key role in both building up the general appreciative setting of his organization through which organizational members establish common ways of operating, and also in setting up communication systems to deal with disparities that arise. It is a central issue for a manager to cope with the fact that shared norms, shared understandings and shared communication cannot be taken for granted. Indeed, Vickers suggests that control and regulation in organizations and insitutions are becoming more problematic precisely because of the difficulty of maintaining agreement. This is because, on the one hand, there is a continuing escalation of expectations and organizations which reflect this attempt to try and regulate more and more relations. On the other hand, the capacity of individuals for accepting regulation is steadily being eroded with the evaporation of loyalty to organizations and the growing emphasis on *individual* self-realization (of which Vickers is highly critical). Together these produce a paradox for the contemporary manager, dealing with employees and clients who are at one and the same time highly *dependent* and very *alienated.*

Attempting to deal with this paradox brings the wheel full circle to the importance of the appreciative system of the manager. This is because it is his appreciative system which determines how the issues will be seen and defined and what action will be taken. The manager is involved in making choices which are problematic because they are multi-valued. Choices are not simple and straightforward, they require the assessment of a number of dimensions which can be valued in a variety of ways. To regulate this involves the ability to predict possible outcomes and to learn about the relationship between action and outcomes.

The ability to deal with the paradox and so to regulate an organizational and institutional system is limited by the nature of what is changing. The rate and predictability of regulatable change sets limits to what is regulatable. To regulate an organization, the variables which the appreciative system regards as key in evaluating performance have to be predicted over time. Indeed, such variables need to be predicted over a time period at least as long as the time needed to make an effective response. Part of the reason for the breakdown of confidence in institutions derives from the fact that rates of change are high, shared understandings of what they mean and why they occur are difficult to establish, the prediction of future action is extremely problematic.

In the end, it is the manager with his appreciative system operating in a particular setting who carries out control and regulation. He helps to set, and is affected by, what are regarded as standards of success, what scope of discretion is allowed and what is the extent of power. Crucial to the operation is what is regarded as possible. It is necessary for those responsible for control to constantly examine how they appreciate the world, to test the limits of their logic and skill and to always be open to new ideas. Learning is control because of the role of appreciation in regulation.

BIBLIOGRAPHY

Vickers, Sir G., *The Art of Judgement*, Paul Chapman, 1983.
Vickers, Sir G., *Towards a Sociology of Management*, Chapman & Hall, 1967.
Vickers, Sir G., *Value Systems and Social Process*, Tavistock Publications, 1968.
Vickers, Sir G., *Making Institutions Work*, Associated Business Programmes, 1973.

CHAPTER 15

Organizational structure

Questions about organizational structures have fascinated writers on organizations as much as they have baffled senior managers and administrators. Why do organizations come to arrange and coordinate their activities in such different ways? How should they do it? Indeed, this aspect of organizations may have attracted more attention than any other – the corpus of literature is enormous. The special offering of the piece that follows is its broad overview of organizational structure. It offers a plausible and simple explanation for the diversity of forms; and it highlights the areas of choice in the structure of organizational activities and relationships – first, which of the basic options will be adopted; and secondly, what are appropriate ways of implementing that option? The condensed and somewhat abstract style of the piece may make it less easy to read (no one could accuse Galbraith of being longwinded) but the basic ideas are straightforward and very rewarding.

Organization Design: An Information Processing View

J. R. GALBRAITH

THE INFORMATION PROCESSING MODEL

A basic proposition is that the greater the uncertainty of the task, the greater the amount of information that has to be processed between decision makers during the execution of the task. If the task is well understood prior to performing it, much of the activity can be preplanned. If it is not understood, then during the actual task execution more knowledge is acquired which leads to changes in resource allocations, schedules, and priorities. All these changes require information processing *during* task performance. Therefore *the greater the task uncertainty, the greater the amount of information that must be processed among decision makers during task execution in order to achieve a given level of performance.* The basic effect of uncertainty is to limit the ability of the organization to preplan or to make decisions about activities in advance of their execution. Therefore it is hypothesized that the observed variations in organizational forms are variations in the strategies of organizations to (1) increase their ability to preplan, (2) increase their flexibility to adapt their inability to preplan, or, (3) to decrease the level of performance required for continued viability. Which strategy is chosen depends on the relative costs of the strategies. The function of the framework is to identify these strategies and their costs.

THE MECHANISTIC MODEL

This framework is best developed by keeping in mind a hypothetical organization. Assume it is large and employs a number of specialist groups and resources in providing the output. After the task has been divided into specialist subtasks, the problem is to integrate the subtasks around the completion of the global task. This is the problem of organization design. The behaviors that occur in one subtask cannot be judged as good or bad *per se*. The behaviors are more effective or ineffective depending upon the behaviors of the other subtask performers. There is a design problem because the executors of the behaviors cannot communicate with all the roles with whom they are interdependent. Therefore the design problem is to create mechanisms that permit coordinated action across large numbers of interdependent roles. Each of these mechanisms, however, has a limited range over which it is effective at handling the information requirements necessary to coordinate the interdependent roles. As the amount of uncertainty increases, and therefore information processing increases, the organization must adopt integrating mechanisms which increase its information processing capabilities.

1 Coordination by rules or programs

For routine predictable tasks March and Simon have identified the use of rules or programs to coordinate behavior between interdependent subtasks (March and Simon 1958, Chap. 6). To the extent that job related situations can be predicted in advance, and behaviors specified for these situations, programs allow an interdependent set of activities to be performed without the need for inter-unit communication. Each role occupant simply executes the behavior which is appropriate for the task related situation with which he is faced.

2 Hierarchy

As the organization faces greater uncertainty its participants face situations for which they have no rules. At this point the hierarchy is employed on an exception basis. The recurring job situations are programmed with rules while infrequent situations are referred to that level in the hierarchy where a global perspective exists for all affected subunits. However, the hierarchy also has a limited range. As uncertainty increases the number of exceptions increases until the hierarchy becomes overloaded.

3 Coordination by targets or goals

As the uncertainty of the organization's task increases, coordination increasingly takes place by specifying outputs, goals or targets (March and

Simon 1958, p. 145). Instead of specifying specific behaviors to be enacted, the organization undertakes processes to set goals to be achieved and the employees select the behaviors which lead to goal accomplishment. Planning reduces the amount of information processing in the hierarchy by increasing the amount of discretion exercised at lower levels. Like the use of rules, planning achieves integrated action and also eliminates the need for continuous communication among interdependent subunits as long as task performance stays within the planned task specifications, budget limits, and within targeted completion dates. If it does not, the hierarchy is again employed on an exception basis.

The ability of an organization to coordinate interdependent tasks depends on its ability to compute meaningful subgoals to guide subunit action. When uncertainty increases because of introducing new products, entering new markets, or employing new technologies these subgoals are incorrect. The result is more exceptions, more information processing, and an overloaded hierarchy.

DESIGN STRATEGIES

The ability of an organization to successfully utilize coordination by goal setting, hierarchy, and rules depends on the combination of the frequency of exceptions and the capacity of the hierarchy to handle them. As the task uncertainty increases the organization must again take organization design action. It can proceed in either of two general ways. First, it can act in two ways to reduce the amount of information that is processed. And second, the organization can act in two ways to increase its capacity to handle more information. The two methods for reducing the need for information and the two methods for increasing processing capacity are shown schematically in Figure 15.1. The effect of all these actions is to reduce the number of exceptional cases referred upward into the organization through hierarchical channels. The assumption is that the critical limiting factor of an organizational form is its ability to handle the non-routine, consequential events that cannot be anticipated and planned for in advance. The nonprogrammed events place the greatest communication load on the organization.

1 Creation of slack resources

As the number of exceptions begin to overload the hierarchy, one response is to increase the planning targets so that fewer exceptions occur. For example, completion dates can be extended until the number of exceptions that occur are within the existing information processing capacity of the organization. This has been the practice in solving job shop scheduling problems (Pounds 1963). Job shops quote delivery times that are long enough to keep the scheduling problem within the computational and information processing limits of the organization. Since every job shop has the same problem standard lead times evolve in the industry. Similarly budget targets could be raised, buffer inventories employed, etc. The

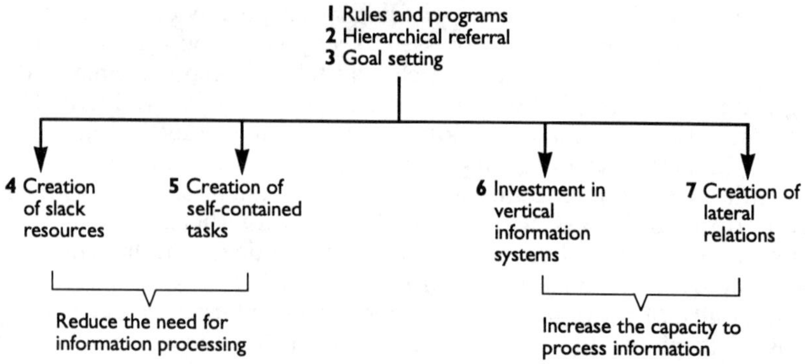

Figure 15.1 Organizing design strategies

greater the uncertainty, the greater the magnitude of the inventory, lead time or budget needed to reduce an overload.

All of these examples have a similar effect. They represent the use of slack resources to reduce the amount of interdependence between subunits (March and Simon 1958, Cyert and March 1963). This keeps the required amount of information within the capacity of the organization to process it. Information processing is reduced because an exception is less likely to occur and reduced interdependence means that fewer factors need to be considered simultaneously when an exception does occur.

The strategy of using slack resources has its costs. Relaxing budget targets has the obvious cost of requiring more budget. Increasing the time to completion date has the effect of delaying the customer. Inventories require the investment of capital funds which could be used elsewhere. Reduction of design optimization reduces the performance of the article being designed. Whether slack resources are used to reduce information or not depends on the relative cost of the other alternatives.

The design choices are: (1) among which factors to change (lead time, overtime, machine utilization, etc.) to create the slack, and (2) by what amount should the factor be changed. Many operations research models are useful in choosing factors and amounts. The time-cost trade off problem in project networks is a good example.

2 *Creation of self-contained tasks*

The second method of reducing the amount of information processed is to change the subtask groupings from source (input) based to output based categories and give each group the resources it needs to supply the output. For example, the functional organization could be changed to product groups. Each group would have its own product engineers, process engineers, fabricating and assembly operations, and marketing activities. In other situations, groups can be created around product lines, geographical areas, projects, client groups, markets, etc., each of which would contain the input resources necessary for creation of the output.

The strategy of self-containment shifts the basis of the authority structure from one based on input, resource, skill, or occupational categories to one based on output or geographical categories. The shift reduces the amount of information processing through several mechanisms. First, it reduces the amount of output diversity faced by a single collection of resources. For example, a professional organization with multiple skill specialities providing service to three different client groups must schedule the use of these specialities across three demands for their services and determine priorities when conflicts occur. But, if the organization changed to three groups, one for each client category, each with its own full complement of specialities, the schedule conflicts across client groups disappears and there is no need to process information to determine priorities.

The second source of information reduction occurs through a reduced division of labor. The functional or resource specialized structure pools the demand for skills across all output categories. In the example above each client generates approximately one-third of the demand for each skill. Since the division of labor is limited by the extent of the market, the division of labor must decrease as the demand decreases. In the professional organization, each client group may have generated a need for one-third of a computer programmer. The functional organization would have hired one programmer and shared him across the groups. In the self-contained structure there is insufficient demand in each group for a programmer so the professionals must do their own programming. Specialization is reduced but there is no problem of scheduling the programmer's time across the three possible uses for it.

The cost of the self-containment strategy is the loss of resource specialization. In the example, the organization forgoes the benefit of a specialist in computer programming. If there is physical equipment, there is a loss of economies of scale. The professional organization would require three machines in the self-contained form but only a large time-shared machine in the functional form. But those resources which have large economies of scale or for which specialization is necessary may remain centralized. Thus, it is the degree of self-containment that is the variable. The greater the degree of uncertainty, other things equal, the greater the degree of self-containment.

The design choices are the basis for the self-containment structure and the number of resources to be contained in the groups. No groups are completely self-contained or they would not be part of the same organization. But one product divisionalized firm may have eight or fifteen functions in the division while another may have 12 or 15 in the divisions. Usually accounting, finance and legal services are centralized and shared. Those functions which have economies of scale, require specialization, or are necessary for control remain centralized and not part of the self-contained group.

The first two strategies reduced the amount of information by lower performance standards and creating small autonomous groups to provide the output. Information is reduced because an exception is less likely to occur and fewer factors need to be considered when an exception does occur. The next two strategies accept the performance standards and division of labor as given and adapt the organization so as to process the new information which is created during task performance.

3 Investment in vertical information systems

The organization can invest in mechanisms which allow it to process information acquired during task performance without overloading the hierarchical communication channels. The investment occurs according to the following logic. After the organization has created its plan or set of targets for inventories, labor utilization, budgets, and schedules, unanticipated events occur which generate exceptions requiring adjustments to the original plan. At some point when the number of exceptions becomes substantial, it is preferable to generate a new plan rather than make incremental changes with each exception. The issue is then how frequently should plans be revised – yearly, quarterly, or monthly? The greater the frequency of replanning the greater the resources, such as clerks, computer time, input-output devices, etc., required to process information about relevant factors.

The cost of information processing resources can be minimized if the language is formalized. Formalization of a decision-making language simply means that more information is transmitted with the same number of symbols. It is assumed that information processing resources are consumed in proportion to the number of symbols transmitted. The accounting system is an example of formalized language.

Providing more information, more often, may simply overload the decision maker. Investment may be required to increase the capacity of the decision maker by employing computers, various man-machine combinations, assistants-to, etc. The cost of this strategy is the cost of the information processing resources consumed in transmitting and processing the data.

The design variables of this strategy are the decision frequency, the degree of formalization of language, and the type of decision mechanism which will make the choice. This strategy is usually operationalized by creating redundant information channels which transmit data from the point of origination upward in the hierarchy where the point of decision rests. If data is formalized and quantifiable, this strategy is effective. If the relevant data are qualitative and ambiguous, then it may prove easier to bring the decisions down to where the information exists.

4 Creation of lateral relationships

The last strategy is to employ selectively joint decision processes which cut across lines of authority. This strategy moves the level of decision making down in the organization to where the information exists but does so within reorganizing around self-contained groups. There are several types of lateral decision processes. Some processes are usually referred to as the informal organization. However, these informal processes do not always arise spontaneously out of the needs of the task. This is particularly true in multi-national organizations in which participants are separated by physical barriers, language differences, and cultural differences. Under these circumstances lateral processes need to be designed. The lateral processes evolve as follows with increases in uncertainty.

4.1 *Direct contact* between managers who share a problem. If a problem arises on the shop floor, the foreman can simply call the design engineer, and they can jointly agree upon a solution. From an information processing view, the joint decision prevents an upward referral and unloads the hierarchy.

4.2 *Liaison roles.* When the volume of contacts between any two departments grows, it becomes economical to set up a specialized role to handle this communication. Liaison men are typical examples of specialized roles designed to facilitate communication between two interdependent departments and to bypass the long lines of communication involved in upward referral. Liaison roles arise at lower and middle levels of management.

4.3 *Task forces.* Direct contact and liaison roles, like the integration mechanism before them, have a limited range of usefulness. They work when two managers or functions are involved. When problems arise involving seven or eight departments, the decision making capacity of direct contacts is exceeded. Then these problems must be referred upward. For uncertain, interdependent tasks such situations arise frequently. Task forces are a form of horizontal contact which is designed for problems of multiple departments.

The task force is made up of representatives from each of the affected departments. Some are full-time members, others may be part-time. The task force is a temporary group. It exists only as long as the problem remains. When a solution is reached, each participant returns to his normal tasks.

To the extent that they are successful, task forces remove problems from higher levels of the hierarchy. The decisions are made at lower levels in the organization. In order to guarantee integration, a group problem solving approach is taken. Each affected subunit contributes a member and therefore provides the information necessary to judge the impact on all units.

4.4 *Teams.* The next extension is to incorporate the group decision process into the permanent decision processes, that is, as certain decisions consistently arise, the task forces become permanent. These groups are labeled teams. There are many design issues concerned in team decision making such as at what level do they operate, who participates, etc. (Galbraith 1973, Chapters 6 and 7). One design decision is particularly critical. This is the choice of leadership. Sometimes a problem exists largely in one department so that the department manager is the leader. Sometimes the leadership passes from one manager to another. As a new product moves to the market place, the leader of the new product team is first the technical manager followed by the production and then the marketing manager. The result is that if the team cannot reach a consensus decision and the leader decides, the goals of the leader are consistent with the goals of the organization for the decision in question. But quite often obvious leaders cannot be found. Another mechanism must be introduced.

4.5 *Integrating roles.* The leadership issue is solved by creating a new role – an integrating role (Lawrence and Lorsch 1967, Chapter 3). These roles carry the labels of product managers, program managers, project managers, unit managers (hospitals), materials managers, etc. After the role is created, the design problem is to create enough power in the role to influence the decision process. These roles have power even when no one reports directly to them. They have some power because they report to the general manager. But if they are selected so as to be unbiased with respect to the groups they integrate and to have technical competence, they have expert power. They collect information and equalize power differences due to preferential access to knowledge and information. The power equalization increases trust and the quality of the joint decision process. But power equalization occurs only if the integrating role is staffed with someone who can exercise expert power in the form of persuasion and informal influences rather than exert the power of rank or authority.

4.6 *Managerial linking roles.* As tasks become more uncertain, it is more difficult to exercise expert power. The role must get more power of the formal authority type in order to be effective at coordinating the joint decisions which occur at lower levels of the organization. This position power changes the nature of the role which for lack of a better name is labeled a managerial linking role. It is not like the integrating role because it possesses formal position power but is different from line managerial roles in that participants do not report to the linking manager. The power is added by the following successive changes:

(a) The integrator receives approval power of budgets formulated in the departments to be integrated.
(b) The planning and budgeting process starts with the integrator making his initiation in budgeting legitimate.
(c) Linking manager receives the budget for the area of responsibility and buys resources from the specialist groups.

These mechanisms permit the manager to exercise influence even though no one works directly for him. The role is concerned with integration but exercises power through the formal power of the position. If this power is insufficient to integrate the subtasks and creation of self-contained groups is not feasible, there is one last step.

4.7 *Matrix organization.* The last step is to create the dual authority relationship and the matrix organization (Galbraith 1971). At some point in the organization some roles have two superiors. The design issue is to select the locus of these roles. The result is a balance of power between the managerial linking roles and the normal line organization roles. Figure 15.2 depicts the pure matrix design.

The work of Lawrence and Lorsch is highly consistent with the assertions concerning lateral relations (Lawrence and Lorsch 1967, Lorsch and Lawrence 1968). They compared the types of lateral relations undertaken by the most successful firm in three different industries. Their data are summarized in Table 15.1. The plastics firm has the greatest rate of new product introduction (uncertainty) and the greatest utilization of lateral processes. The container firm was also very successful but utilized only standard practices because its information processing task is much less formidable. Thus, the greater the uncertainty the lower the level of decision making and the integration is maintained by lateral relations.

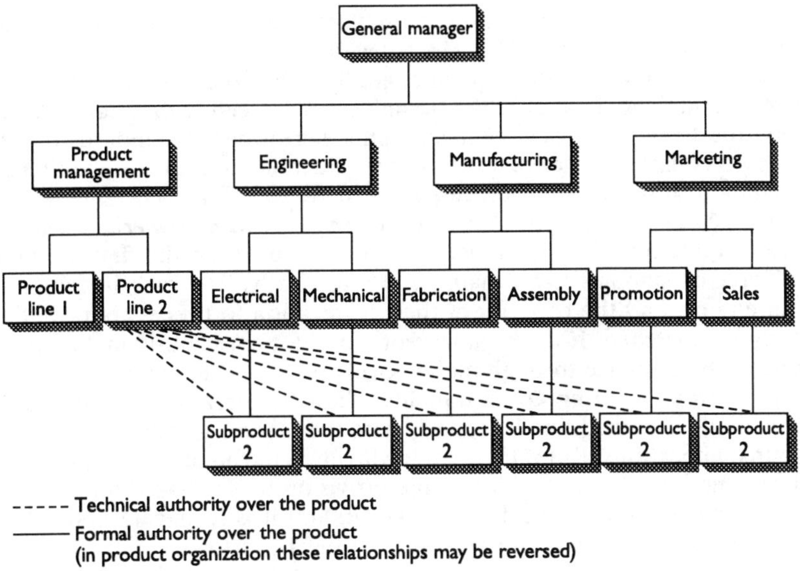

Figure 15.2 A pure matrix organization

TABLE 15.1

	PLASTICS	FOOD	CONTAINER
% new products in last ten years	35%	20%	0%
Integrating devices	Rules Hierarchy Planning Direct contact Teams at 3 levels Integrating dept.	Rules Hierarchy Planning Direct contact Task forces Integrators	Rules Hierarchy Planning Direct contact
% Integrators/ managers	22%	17%	0%

Adapted from Lawrence and Lorsch 1967, pp. 86–138 and Lorsch and Lawrence 1968.

Table 15.1 points out the cost of using lateral relations. The plastics firm has 22 per cent of its managers in integration roles. Thus, the greater the use of lateral relations the greater the managerial intensity. This cost must be balanced against the cost of slack resources, self-contained groups, and information systems.

CHOICE OF STRATEGY

Each of the four strategies has been briefly presented. The organization can follow one or some combination of several if it chooses. It will choose that strategy which has the least cost in its environmental context. (For an example, see Galbraith 1970.) However, what may be lost in all of the explanations is that the four strategies are hypothesized to be an exhaustive set of alternatives. That is, if the organization is faced with greater uncertainty due to technological change, higher performance standards due to increased competition, or diversifies its product line to reduce dependence, the amount of information processing is increased. *The organization must adopt at least one of the four strategies when faced with greater uncertainty.* If it does not consciously choose one of the four, then the first, reduced performance standards, will happen automatically. The task information requirements and the capacity of the organization to process information are always matched. If the organization does not consciously match them, reduced performance through budget overruns and schedule overruns will occur in order to bring about equality. Thus the organization should be planned and designed simultaneously with the planning of the strategy and resource allocations. But if the strategy involves introducing new products, entering new markets, etc., then some provision for increased information must be made. Not to decide is to decide, and it is to decide upon slack resources as the strategy to remove hierarchical overload.

There is probably a fifth strategy which is not articulated here. Instead of changing the organization in response to task uncertainty, the organization can operate on its environment to reduce uncertainty. The organization through strategic decisions, long term contracts, coalitions, etc., can control its environment. But these maneuvers have costs also. They should be compared with costs of the four design strategies presented above.

SUMMARY

The purpose of this paper has been to explain why task uncertainty is related to organizational form. In so doing the cognitive limits theory of Herbert Simon was the guiding influence. As the consequences of cognitive limits were traced through the framework various organization design strategies were articulated. The framework provides a basis for integrating organizational interventions, such as information systems and group problem solving, which have been treated separately before.

REFERENCES

Cyert, R. and March, J. (1963) *The Behavioral Theory of the Firm*, Prentice-Hall, Englewood Cliffs, New Jersey.

Galbraith, J. (1970) 'Environmental and technological determinants of organization design: a case study', in Lawrence, P. and Lorsch, J. (eds) *Studies in Organization Design*, Richard D. Irwin Inc., Homewood, Illinois.

Galbraith, J. (1971) 'Designing matrix organizations', *Business Horizons*, February, pp. 29–40.

Galbraith, J. (1973) *Organization Design*, Addison-Wesley, Reading, Mass.

Lawrence, P. and Lorsch, J. (1967) *Organization and Environment*, Division of Research, Harvard Business School, Boston, Mass.
Lorsch, J. and Lawrence, P. (1968) 'Environmental factors and organization integration'. Paper read at the Annual Meeting of the American Sociological Association, 27 August, Boston, Mass.
March, J. and Simon, H. (1958) *Organizations*, John Wiley & Sons, New York.
Pounds, W. (1963) 'The scheduling environment', in Muth and Thompson (eds) *Industrial Scheduling*, Prentice-Hall, Englewood Cliffs, New Jersey.
Simon, H. (1957) *Models of Man*, John Wiley & Sons, New York.

CHAPTER 16

Power in Organizations

In recent years the analysis of organizations as political systems has received greatly increased attention. It is a perspective that makes good sense to many managers and administrators whose day-to-day experience involves a considerable amount of lobbying and manoeuvring to promote or deflect particular initiatives. But central to any such analysis must be a treatment of topics like power, influence, authority and interests; phenomena which are notoriously slippery – and contentious. The following piece aims to provide a workable simplification of this difficult terrain.

Powers Visible and Invisible

R. PATON

POWERS VISIBLE . . .

Anyone who must regularly attempt to get things done with and through other people has the problem of generating agreement, or perhaps just consent, or at least compliance, with regard to what will be done, how, when and on what terms. Characteristically, opinions will differ on the importance of the different goals and on what is an appropriate, or fair, basis to proceed. Such disagreements may be more or less significant and far reaching and conducted in a style ranging from the polite and circumspect to the openly threatening and coercive. But however it is done each side is attempting to influence the conduct of the other. And in doing so they will make use of whatever resources or means are available, and seem appropriate. Hence, to understand or anticipate the course of a particular conflict and its outcome requires an appreciation of the different sorts of resources that those involved may use, or attempt to use. What follows is a brief catalogue of these different resources and the areas in which they may be used, starting with the more obvious ones that are regularly employed in relation to conflicts and disagreements that have 'surfaced' in the decision-making processes of the organization – that's to say, both sides know what's going on, even if it is not treated explicitly and is amicably handled and resolved. These more obvious 'visible' power resources provide a fairly straightforward way into a difficult topic. But it is worth emphasizing from the start that the power of individuals and groups in organizations will vary over different issues. A safety officer may be able to bring the entire plant to a halt on a matter concerning safety or manning levels, but this doesn't mean he or she can influence the decision to purchase a subsidiary or enter a new overseas market. So you shouldn't think of these different sorts of power as something that people can carry around to use whenever it suits them. The distribution of power is always *issue specific*.

Position power

The most obvious source of power in organizations is that which stems from a person's formal position. In the first place, roles carry the right to make particular decisions. The head of a department may be entitled to say 'This is the way we're going to do it'; the issue – and any conflict associated with it – is closed (bar the grumblings, of course). Related to this formal authority is the status and respect often attributed to those in 'high' organizational positions. Someone from headquarters, for example, may be trusted and believed when the local manager is not: 'he or she must be in a position to know the full picture', 'someone of that calibre wouldn't do this unless it were absolutely necessary', and so on. Hence the prestige of a particular post may enable the incumbent to persuade and influence others even in areas that are not strictly within that person's authority.

Next, those in positions of authority can control the rewards of those they supervise – the foreman who allocates overtime, or the departmental head who can recommend promotions, salary increases, training courses and the like. This is sometimes called *reward power*.

Expert power

Organizations use specialist knowledge to cope with task and environmental uncertainty. This means that on certain issues they must rely on and accept the judgement of those who possess that knowledge. Experts – or rather, those who are seen as experts – thus possess a power resource which is more or less independent of their formal position in the organization. The middle-ranking research chemist who calmly says 'it just can't be done' can stop the marketing director of a chemical firm dead in his or her tracks. If the director is unwise enough to press the point he or she simply invites a lecture on, say, some finer points of polymer chemistry, whereupon – whether he or she pretends to understand and agree, or instead admits to not understanding and refuses to agree – the point is irretrievably lost.

The problem, essentially, is that no one can be an expert in all the activities of a complex organization. So some individuals will be formally superior to those whose expertise they cannot emulate. Hence, when the general manager disagrees with the head of one of his or her specialist departments it may be a straight tussle between position and expert power.

Such conflicts are now a distinctive characteristic of large-scale organizations of all sorts, including government ministries. Nevertheless, it remains very difficult to say with whom the advantage lies, unless one has very detailed knowledge of the particular case in question. To a large extent the expert's power will depend on the importance to the organization of the uncertainty on which the expert pronounces. Thereafter it is up to the expert to make the *best use* of such power.

Dependence power

When people join organizations it is because they want something from (or through) the organization and they are willing to contribute so long as they get what they want. Likewise, when recruiting employees or soliciting members, organizations offer inducements of one sort or another in order to gain what they want. So whatever else it represents, membership of an organization involves a straightforward *exchange*; *inducements* are offered in return for *contributions*. However, since each side wants what the other is offering, this exchange may also involve a measure of *dependence*.

The extent to which one side depends on the other is affected by a number of factors: How important is it to have what the other offers? Can it be obtained elsewhere? Are substitutes available? If the answers to these questions are 'very', 'no' and 'no', then the party concerned is very dependent indeed on the other party – *and need not be similarly dependent on the first party*. The final step is to point out that if someone depends on you for something then, for you, this is a source of power. Unless they do what you want, you may withhold what they want so badly.

So, starting from the basic and very general idea of an *exchange*, one can specify conditions for unequal exchanges and *dependence*, which itself is indicative of a *power relationship*, whether or not that power is actually used. Such power is illustrated in strikes and other forms of industrial action. Workers withhold their labour, upon which management depends. The classic case is given by sequentially interdependent production operations in which a small group of employees can bring an entire plant, or perhaps several plants, to a standstill. However, this depends on other workers refusing to 'cover' jobs; on there being no alternative source of the components, or whatever; and on the strikers having an alternative source of income sufficient for the duration of the strike.

Although most common in industrial relations, dependence power may be used at other organizational levels: there have been occasions when a number of senior managers have blocked particular proposals by threatening to resign *en bloc*! The important point is that those in subordinate positions can, under certain conditions, possess *very considerable power indeed*. So *dependence power* is the power of subordinates or peers arising from a dependence, not on their expertise or the rights of their position, but on their *willing cooperation*. It's worth pointing out, however, that the term can be applied much more generally – including, for example, expert power as the dependence of organizations on specialist knowledge. But a broad definition of dependence power would cover such a wide range of situations that one would immediately have to break it down into subcategories. So it is simpler to use it in a restricted sense as defined.

This sort of power has also been called 'negative power', but the term 'dependence' relates it to the idea of exchanges. This has advantages when some of its more subtle manifestations are considered later.

Personal power

The attributes of many organizational roles – such as outward confidence, decisiveness and an authoritative tone – are often mistakenly seen as personal qualities. The new head of department may start off pretending to be 'just one of the team' but it won't last long; in no time he or she will be adopting the style and mannerisms expected of someone in that position. There may be nothing about it in the job description, but it's an almost inescapable part of the job none the less. A doctor's 'bed-side manner' is a classic example – calm, sympathetic, reassuring, but serious and authoritative – these look like personal qualities but they are clearly the learnt patterns expected of someone in that role.

Personal power does not refer to these apparently personal qualities that more or less 'come with the job'. Nor to those reputations for dynamism and charisma that tell us little about the person concerned, but a great deal about the public relations business. It refers to those abilities and qualities which enable some people to make the most of whatever other power resources they have. Charm, intelligence and a silver tongue are obviously useful in many situations. Likewise sensitivity to the progress of a meeting can mean success for a well timed proposal that would have been rejected if it had been made at the start. Similarly, the ability to 'take the role of the other' and anticipate the reactions of potential opponents is characteristic of successful negotiators. This form of power also overlaps a bit with expert power – one can be trained in negotiation and interpersonal skills. Nevertheless, some people have these capacities, without training, far more than others who have been trained.

To start with, then, four forms of 'visible' power have been loosely distinguished. The first, position power, involves several elements (formal authority, status and control of rewards) that may be associated with particular, and especially the more senior, positions in a hierarchy. The second, expert power, referred to the use of appeals to expertise to influence others. The third, dependence power, draws attention to the fact that those who lack other forms of power may still be able to influence peers or superiors by suspending or threatening to suspend, an exchange those others have come to depend on. Finally, the term personal power was used to cover those personal qualities (or leadership and the like) which make some individuals far more influential than others with otherwise comparable power resources. So far, so good; but this much is only the beginning.

. . . AND INVISIBLE

The preceding discussion considered the various forms of power that may be employed when a contentious issue appears on the agenda of organizational decision-making. They concern *whose solution will be accepted* to resolve a given problem. But there are three other ways in which power may be exercised. In the first place, how an issue is presented can affect the way it is treated; secondly, many organizational practices develop informally and are not dealt with in an explicit decision-making process; thirdly, if power is exercised when a group ensures, against opposition, that its preferred option is selected, then power is also exercised if that group ensures that an option detrimental to its interests is *not even considered* by the parties to a conflict. These three less obvious arenas for the exercise of power are considered in turn and reveal important additional dimensions of position and dependence power in particular.

The following quotation provides a clear example of how an issue can be presented in a way that favours a particular outcome:

> The marketing manager of an insurance company was on the brink of launching a large product development campaign. At the next management meeting, it had been decided to discuss poor profit performance in the previous two quarters. At issue was whether to deploy resources to expand sales or to cutting costs by increasing automation (via electronic data processing). He knew that if this issue were to be raised at the meeting, he would be outvoted by a small majority of peers who leaned toward investing the funds in automation. However, he was convinced that automation didn't sell insurance! Therefore, he needed to find an issue that would rearrange the coalition structure currently against him. He realized that the key issue that he would prefer to have discussed was market share and not profits, so he did three things. First, he sent a report to all the management committee members that showed how losses in market share could be regained by his proposal. Second, he sent to all members of the management committee a memo asking them to consider ways in which his proposed product development program could be carried out effectively and at a lower cost. Third, he persuaded the chief executive to place his project proposal first on the agenda. When the meeting started, the issue was not whether the product launch should take place or not, but what funds would be required to launch the product; the automation proposal was postponed, because some marginal members of the automation coalition had become committed to the marketshare issue.[1]

In this case the marketing manager's efforts were directed at focusing attention on certain questions at the expense of others. Although he did not decide the agenda for the meeting himself, he recognized its importance and was able to influence the chief executive. In general, position power – through control of information and agendas – also allows a person to affect the terms on which an issue will be discussed. But as this example shows, those who hold position power may themselves be influenced (in this case, presumably by the marketing manager's expert and personal power). The meeting before the meeting is often the one that matters. Hence the apparent paradox of a chairperson who is immensely influential, and yet scrupulously impartial in the conduct of meetings.

These aspects of position power are also relevant to clashes or tensions between 'experts' and 'generalists' (the latter relying primarily on position power). Even if the uncertainty on which the expert's power is based is considerable, the generalist still has a number of cards to play. In the first place because he or she usually holds a higher position in the organization, the generalist can often determine the areas in which the expert will operate, the questions they must answer and the assumptions they will make. Moreover, the generalist may be able to break down the various specialist tasks into smaller units which only he or she can coordinate. If need be, one expert can then be played off against another. Finally, the generalist may actually be able to choose the expert concerned; since experts often disagree, this can allow the appointment to the job of a 'sympathetic' expert. Hence it may very well be the case that experts only possess power on issues which directly and substantially concern them, while on more general matters *they exist as a resource to be tapped by others*. Certainly, many operations research practitioners have claimed that when their reports are used it is often only to provide a convenient 'scientific' rationale for what the generalist wanted to do anyway.

The second domain in which power may be exercised 'invisibly' is that of the gradual, informal evolution of working practices and arrangements. The idea of 'dependence power' was introduced earlier with the example of strikes, and related forms of industrial action.

The power in such cases derives from the employer's dependence on what is primarily an economic exchange with employees – cash in return for time and effort. But other sorts of exchange pervade organizational life: they are largely informal *social* exchanges, typically an exchange of *favours* of one sort or another. It is worth quoting from the classic analysis of the way in which social exchanges can be a power resource in shaping organizational practices:

> Thus dependence together with the manipulation of the dependency relationship is the key to the power of lower participants.
>
> A number of examples can be cited which illustrate the preceding point. Scheff, for example, reports on the failure of a state mental hospital to bring about intended reform because of the opposition of hospital attendants. He noted that the power of hospital attendants was largely a result of the dependence of ward physicians on attendants. This dependence resulted from the physician's short tenure, his lack of interest in administration, and the large amount of administrative responsibility he had to assume. An implicit trading agreement developed between physicians and attendants, whereby attendants would take on some of the responsibilities and obligations of the ward physician in return for increased power in decision-making processes concerning patients. Failure of the ward physician to honor his part of the agreement resulted in information being withheld, disobedience, lack of cooperation, and unwillingness of the attendants to serve as a barrier between the physician and a ward full of patients demanding attention and recognition. When the attendant withheld cooperation, the physician had difficulty in making a graceful entrance and departure from the ward, in handling necessary paper work (officially his responsibility), and in obtaining information needed to deal adequately with daily treatment and behavior problems. When attendants opposed change, they could wield influence by refusing to assume responsibilities officially assigned to the physician.

> Similarly, Sykes describes the dependence of prison guards on inmates and the power obtained by inmates over guards. He suggests that although guards could report inmates for disobedience, frequent reports would give prison officials the impression that the guard was unable to command obedience. The guard, therefore, had some stake in ensuring the good behavior of prisoners without use of formal sanctions against them. The result was a trading agreement whereby the guard allowed violations of certain rules in return for cooperative behavior. A similar situation is found in respect to officers in the Armed Services or foremen in industry. To the extent that they require formal sanctions to bring about cooperation, they are usually perceived by their superiors as less valuable to the organization. For a good leader is expected to command obedience, at least, if not commitment.[2]

Dependence power is thus a pervasive feature of organizations and it can be a formidable resource. It sets the limits on position power so that every organization represents a negotiated order. Such negotiation is usually tacit or even unspoken, but most bosses recognize that it will do them no good at all to push too hard. Not cooperating can make another person's life very difficult.

The third way in which power can be exercised is by *preventing* particular issues or conflicts of interest from being considered. In other words, power is exercised not only in relation to matters that have become the subject of disagreement and dispute; it may also be exercised in relation to what does *not* become an issue. This can happen in a number of ways considered briefly below; but it should be emphasized that this is a contentious area. It raises some difficult questions concerning, for example, the notion of 'real interests' (are people sometimes unaware of what is in their own interests?). In fact, most people do seem prepared to say that certain others (though not themselves, of course) are mistaken about what is in their interests as a result of propaganda or 'social conditioning'. But where there is disagreement is over which groups are mistaken, and what the 'real interests' really are. In short, this, more than any other, is an area where social and political ideology can colour organizational analysis, but a thorough treatment of these topics is well beyond the scope of this article.

The first way in which issues can be suppressed is by latent intimidation: for example, a belief that certain proposals are completely unacceptable and would provoke outright, unrestrained opposition, may be enough to ensure that demands are well tailored within a range that is 'acceptable'. In authoritarian organizations, as in totalitarian countries, certain matters are not worth discussing, indeed even to raise such issues (for example, concerning one's own inability to carry through a task; but at management level questioning a particular policy commitment) may be a recklessly deviant act. Note, too, that such a state of affairs does not require explicit and frequent threats or demonstrations of determination by those in power: a belief that some form of punishment or coercion would follow may derive from past conflicts, may be maintained by very occasional and implicit threats, and may be sufficient to prevent it having to be used.

Thus, the fact that in the normal course of disagreements superiors do not threaten to dismiss a number of subordinates does not mean that the power to do so is irrelevant – as cabinet ministers have sometimes found. Of course, the most colourfully ruthless examples of determined coercion are associated with employers' use of the fear of unemployment. The American South, even in quite recent years, has seen some spectacular conflicts in which physical intimidation and outside agencies (the police, the courts and the local press) have been used to break strikes or prevent unionization – events which also highlight the extent to which controllers of an organization may be particularly well placed to enlist the support of elements in the organization's environment for support in a conflict. However, the point of such cases is that, although they are exceptional, their impact may live on in shaping people's beliefs about what is 'realistic'. So the earlier discussion of 'visible power' has to be seen in a much wider context if it is not to be seriously limited and naive. For example, it was suggested in discussing dependence power that every organization can be seen as representing a 'negotiated order', and there will always be some measure of give and take, of mutual accommodation, simply because it is patently provocative and self-defeating to trample roughshod over subordinates and 'lower participants' in organizations. But it should now be clear that this tacit 'negotiation' and mutual accommodation occurs within very definite limits, and in normal times those in power may only have to use a small fraction of the resources they have at their disposal.

However, this is still a long way from being the full story. The fact that employees *pragmatically* accept – because they see no realistic alternative – a regime that they do not consider fair or legitimate provides a somewhat fragile basis for organizational order. Given a reservoir of grievances and resentment, even a comparatively small incident can be the trigger for a fierce dispute – as many paternalistically autocratic family businesses have discovered (similar eruptions occur in totalitarian regimes and, in both cases, the angry but puzzled response of the power holders is to credit a few 'dissidents' and 'trouble-makers' with an astonishing talent for organization and persuasion). A much more stable order exists where there is a *normative* acceptance by subordinates and employees of the organizational arrangements – that's to say, they are seen as fair and legitimate. This suggests another area of 'invisible' power: the use of an organization's resources deliberately to promote values and beliefs that legitimize particular practices and policies can reduce the areas of disagreement to the point where only marginal adjustments are at issue.

In promoting such attitudes and beliefs the organization's controllers may be able to appeal to, or take advantage of, ideas and values that are dominant in the wider society – and which indeed they may also have been well placed to promote. But arguably the resources and scope for subordinates to do so is more limited; for, as the following passage makes plain, this conflict of meanings and perspectives is not conducted solely through rival announcements and newsheets. It was extracted from an internal document of a major British company:

> The core of the approach is the *work group* structure. This is both a fundamental and radical concept – our basic answer to a whole range of (at present wholly intractable) problems ranging from genuine participation without an-

archy to increased employee productivity. Essentially, and we should recognize this, it is not an industrial concept at all, but a socio-political one, applied in the industrial context. It represents, in fact, a capitalist version of the Marxist 'cell' structure . . .

The full development of so radical a concept will necessarily be long and difficult. Certain immediate steps, however, can already be identified under each of the elements of the personnel plan.

Under *redeployment*, intensive efforts must be made to identify the *natural* work group leaders for subsequent training and indoctrination, and to retrain the new supervisors and superintendents . . .

Under *retraining and development*, we therefore need to put a heavy emphasis on the development of work group leaders on the one hand and the new supervision on the other, so that these two classes become, in fact, capitalist equivalents to the Marxist 'cadres'. We should not be frightened to admit that this means specifically the exploitation of training and development schemes for *indoctrination* as well as technical training.

Under *pay*, we must provide the group with a monetary system of group penalties and rewards which means, in fact, that the group itself will lean on any of its members who fall short because they will lose solid cash for the group as a whole, that is, *group self-discipline*.

Under *organization structure*, the key work unit should be pushed down as close as possible to the shop floor (away from abstractions like 'the company' or 'the union') – starting first with the unit and then proceeding down to the basic work group. The basic unit of organization should thus be based on the *natural* work unit (a common group organized around a common task).

Under *organization style*, the attempt must be made to withdraw *exterior* discipline to those areas where it will be recognized by the group as legitimate (targeting, criteria and group sanctions and, to substitute for this within the group, 'group self-discipline'). British tradition is still so firmly based on the 'warders and convicts' syndrome that, at this stage, extending the right to consultation on the appointment of the work group leader to the group as a whole will be seen as a genuine management concession to industrial democracy . . .

The new 'consultation' structure must be progressed in step with the development of the work group concept so as to provide a new system of worker representation as an alternative to the union system.

Apart from the promotion of 'congenial' values and beliefs, this extract also points to another aspect of 'invisible' power: in the longer term, the controllers of an organization may have the opportunities to structure the work or relationships among the workforce in ways that will minimize the likelihood of effective opposition. 'Divide and rule' is the most familiar way this can be done and there are numerous instances where it has been suggested that managers have been able to play on divisions within a workforce (for example, between skilled and unskilled workers, between office and manual workers, between separate plants) in order to prevent concerted opposition emerging. Also under this same general heading are such decisions as the automation of particular jobs – among the reasons for which may be a concern to reduce dependence on particular skilled and well organized workers. Or decisions to transfer production of particular items to another country. Such decisions reflect in part a strategic concern to preserve or enhance control over the workforce by shaping the context of and terms on which any future conflicts will be played out.

Finally, invisible power also appears in the form of what has been called 'institutional bias'. The point is that organizations provide individuals and groups with scope for the pursuit of certain sorts of goals, and they restrict the scope for pursuing others. For example, as numerous writers on production practices have pointed out, an unfocused frustration with, say, repetitive machine-paced work is not something one can easily negotiate about. Negotiations, by their nature, end in a bargained compromise; and that means the sorts of things that can be dealt with must be quantitative: wage rates, hours of work, days of holiday and so on. If people did want autonomy and variety in their jobs, or better working relationships, it's hard to see these goals being attained by incremental changes achieved in annual negotiations. Industrial relations practices, therefore, have an inherent bias towards the resolution of certain sorts of demands, while others are, in effect, screened out. Comparable 'biases' occur in other organizations: secondary and tertiary education and biased towards certain sorts of teaching and learning – crudely, that which can be readily assessed – while other sorts and styles of learning are restricted, or even denied altogether. Such 'biases' can be considered an aspect of 'invisible power' because they may benefit some of the 'stakeholders' in an organization far more than others, namely, those whose interests are well served through the existing arrangements. Normally, such groups will be the dominant groups, but this is not always nor necessarily the case, since on occasions they may be the ones who are attempting to promote changes. On such occasions the biases and inertia of particular institutional arrangements may be a significant obstacle; expectations, motivational patterns, beliefs, identities and loyalties may be affected gradually by the sorts of deliberate methods already described, but in no way can they be reconstructed at will. Militants and radicals are not the only people who bemoan the difficulties of inducing systemic changes.

In summary, the idea of 'invisible power' is a general one that has been used to refer to the indirect or informal exercise of power that occurs outside of the accepted decision-making process, and which may not be recognized by some of those concerned. It was suggested that invisible power can be exercised in three domins:

- First, through the scope for shaping the terms on which a contentious matter will be dealt with; typically, the control of information and agendas, associated with particular positions, is important.
- Secondly, through the scope for the informal development (or corruption) of working practices to suit those involved; typically, this reflects the dependence power of subordinates that can arise from social exchanges, as when cooperation over some matters is given in return for autonomy over others.
- Thirdly, through the scope for preventing potential conflicts from emerging.

This last area is the most difficult but it was suggested that potential conflicts could be suppressed, obscured, avoided or screened out in the following ways:

- By latent intimidation.
- By promoting values and beliefs to legitimize arrangements that may otherwise be contested.
- By structuring work and relationships so as to prevent, avoid or divide any significant opposition.
- As a result of 'institutional biases' whereby those whose concerns can be met through existing arrangements are at an enormous advantage compared to those whose concerns can only be met by changing the arrangements.

Overall, the aim has been to catalogue the principal resources that may allow people to exercise power, and to indicate the different areas and ways in which they may exercise it.

It should be clear that there may be a great deal more to the conflicts and struggles for control that occur in organizations than appears on the surface. And while many of the examples have been drawn from the area of industrial relations which is well documented, it would be naive to pretend that ruthlessness and a concern for strategic advantage in relation to others do not also occur at all levels in organizations, including the boardroom.

REFERENCES

1. MacMillan, I. C. (1978) *Strategy Formulation: Political Concepts*, St. Paul, MN, West Publishing, pp. 61–62.
2. Mechanic, D. (1962) 'Sources of power of lower participants in complex organizations', *Administrative Science Quarterly*, 7, December.

CHAPTER 17

Leadership

Leadership is a multifaceted thing which has a strong influence on organizational culture. In hierarchical organizations, the entire 'flavour' of organizational activity can be determined by a single individual. Other organizations have more distributed leadership with different individuals supplying different facets of the leadership role. The following readings illustrate different leadership styles. Few people could, or would perhaps wish to, emulate Harold Geneen's style of leadership, but it led to phenomenal success for ITT. Avoidance of the confrontation can be just as uncomfortable as illustrated by the experience of one American insurance company. Lao Tzu, writing two and a half thousand years ago in Chinese, offers timeless wisdom. The Wise Leader leads invisibly and everything in the organization appears to happen naturally – what Handy calls the 'Aha Effect' – the interaction between a vision and the people it inspires. Finally, Starhawk, writing from her experience of community living, uses traditional Native American and mythological European metaphors to describe the distributed leadership roles that allow a non-hierarchical organization to function effectively.

17A
Harold Geneen at ITT

GARETH MORGAN

At International Telephone & Telegraph (ITT) under the tough and uncompromising leadership of Harold Geneen we find an example of [a particular] kind of corporate culture. The story here is one of success built on a ruthless style of management that converted a medium-sized communications business with sales of $765 million in 1959 into one of the world's largest and most powerful and diversified conglomerates, operating in over ninety countries, with revenues of almost $12 billion in 1978. Under Geneen's twenty-year reign, the company established a reputation as one of the fastest-growing and most profitable American companies – and, following its role in overseas bribery and the down-fall of the Allende government in Chile, as one of the most corrupt and controversial.

Geneen's managerial style was simple and straightforward. He sought to keep his staff on top of their work by creating an intensely competitive atmosphere based on confrontation and intimidation. The foundation of his approach rested in his quest for what were known as 'unshakable facts'. He insisted that all managerial reports, decisions, and business plans be based on irrefutable premises, and developed a complete information system, a network of special task forces, and a method of cross-examination that allowed him to check virtually every statement put forward. Geneen possessed an extraordinary memory and an ability to absorb vast amounts of information in a relatively short time. This made it possible for him to keep his executives on their toes by demonstrating that he knew their situations as well as, if not better than, they did. His interrogation sessions at policy review meetings have become legendary. These meetings, which have been described as 'show trials', were held around an enormous table capable of seating over fifty people, each executive being provided with a microphone into which to speak. It is reported that Geneen's approach was to pose a question to a specific executive, or to sit back listening to the reports being offered while specially appointed staff people cross-examined what was being said. As soon as the executive being questioned showed evasiveness or lack of certainty, Geneen would move in to probe the weakness. In complete command of the facts, and equipped with a razor-sharp ability to cut to the center of an issue, he would invariably also cut the floundering executive and his argument to shreds. It is said that these experiences were so grueling that many executives were known to break down and cry under the pressure.

Geneen's approach motivated people through fear. If an executive was making a presentation there was every incentive to stay up preparing throughout the night to ensure that all possible questions and angles were covered. This intimidating style was set by Geneen from the very beginning of his tenure. For example, it is reported that early in his career with ITT he would call executives at all hours, perhaps in the middle of the night, to inquire about the validity of some fact or obscure point in a written report. The message was clear: ITT executives are expected to be company men and women on top of their jobs at all times. The idea that loyalty to the goals of the organization should take precedence over loyalty to colleagues or other points of reference was established as a key principle.

ITT under Geneen was a successful corporate jungle. High executive performance was undoubtedly achieved, but at considerable cost in terms of staff stress and in terms of the kind of actions that this sometimes produced, such as the company's notorious activities in Chile. The pressure on ITT executives was above all to perform and deliver the goods they had promised. Their corporate necks were always on the line. Geneen's approach typifies the managerial style that psychoanalyst Michael Maccoby has characterized as that of the 'jungle fighter': the power-hungry manager who experiences life and work as a jungle where it is eat or be eaten, and where winners destroy losers. The jungle fighter tends to see his peers as accomplices or enemies, and subordinates as objects to be utilized. The 'lions' among these fighters are conquerors who, like Geneen, build empires. More foxlike jungle fighters move ahead with more stealth and politicking. Interestingly, the actions of both types help to *create* the dog-eat-dog world that is implied in their basic philosophy of action. [. . .]

17B

The American Insurance Company

GARETH MORGAN

[. . .] Linda Smircich [. . .] studied the top executive group of an American insurance company. The company was a division of a much larger organization serving agriculture, and offered a broad range of insurance services to agriculture and to the general public. Sustained observation of day-to-day management generated two key impressions. First, the company seemed to emphasize cooperative values and an identity rooted in the world of agriculture rather than in that of competitive business. The staff were polite and gracious and always seemed prepared to give help and assistance wherever it was needed. This ethos was reflected in one of the company mottoes: 'We grow friends.' However, coexisting with this surface of friendly cooperation was a second dimension of organizational culture that suggested that the cooperative ethos was at best superficial. Meetings and other public forums always seemed dominated by polite yet disinterested exchange. Staff rarely got involved in any real debate and seemed to take very little in-depth interest in what was being said. For example, hardly anyone took any notes, and the meetings were in effect treated as ritual occasions. This superficiality was confirmed by observed differences between the public and private faces of the organization. Whereas in public the ethos of harmony and cooperation ruled, in private people often expressed considerable anger and dissatisfaction with various staff members and with the organization in general.

Many organizations have fragmented cultures of this kind, where people say one thing and do another. One of the interesting features of Linda Smircich's study was that she was able to identify the precise circumstances that had produced the fragmentation within the company, and was able to show why it continued to operate in its somewhat schizophrenic fashion. Ten years earlier, when the organization was just four years old, it had passed through a particularly 'traumatic' period that witnessed the demotion of its president, the hiring and firing of his successor, and the appointment of a group of professionals from the insurance industry at large. These events led to the development of separate subcultures. The first of these was represented by the original staff, or the 'inside group' as they came to be known; the second by the new professionals – 'the outside group'. Most of the outside group had been recruited from the same rival insurance company and brought with them very strong beliefs as to what was needed in their new organization. 'This was how we did it at . . .'

became a frequent stance taken in discussion. They wanted to model the new organization on the old.

The new president, appointed after the firing of the second, was a kind and peace-loving man. He set out to create a team atmosphere that would bind the organization together. However, rather than encourage a situation where organizational members could explore and resolve their differences in an open manner, he adopted a style of management that really required organizational members to put aside or repress their differences. The desire for harmony was communicated in a variety of ways, particularly through use of specific rituals. For example, at special management meetings the staff became an Indian tribe. Each member was given an Indian name and a headband with a feather. The aim was to forge unity between inside and outside groups. During this ritual, the practice of levying a fifty-cent fine on anyone who mentioned the name of the rival insurance firm was introduced.

In both subtle and more obvious ways, the president continued to send messages about the need for harmony. He introduced regular staff meetings to review operations at which calm, polite cooperation quickly established itself as a norm. As some staff members reported,

> We sit in the same seats, like cows always go to the same stall.
>
> It's a real waste of time. It's a situation where you can say just about anything and no one will refute it.
>
> People are very hesitant to speak up, afraid to say too much. They say what everyone else wants to hear.

Harmony and teamwork were also sought through the use of imagery to define the desired company spirit – for example, the slogan 'wheeling together'. The logo of a wagon wheel was spread through the company. The idea of 'putting one's shoulder to the wheel' or 'wheeling together' featured in many discussions and documents. And an actual wagon wheel, mounted on a flat base, was moved from department to department.

The effect of this leadership style was to create a superficial appearance of harmony while driving conflict underground. This created the divergence between the public and private faces of the organization observed by Smircich, and led to a situation where the organization became increasingly unable to deal with real problems. Since the identification of problems or concerns about company operation frequently created controversy which the organization didn't really want to handle, the staff tended to confine their discussion of these issues to private places. In public, the impression that all was well gained the upper hand. When problematic issues were identified, they were always presented in the form of 'challenges' to minimize the possibility of upsetting anyone. Driven underground by a style of management that effectively prevented the discussion of differences, genuine concerns were not given the attention they deserved. Not surprisingly, the organization no longer exists as a separate entity; the parent group eventually decided to reabsorb the insurance division into the main company. [. . .]

17C
Tao Te Ching: The Way of Subtle Influence
LAO TZU (TRANSLATED BY R. L. WING)

Superior leaders are those whose existence is merely known;
    The next best are loved and honored;
The next are respected;
    And the next are ridiculed.

Those who lack belief
Will not in turn be believed.
But when the command comes from afar
And the work is done, the goal achieved,
The people say, 'We did it naturally.'

17D
The Language of Leadership
CHARLES B. HANDY

The new organizations need to be run in new ways. As we have seen, these new ways need a new language to describe them, a language of federations and networks, of alliances and influences, as well as of shamrocks and do'nuts. The language, and the philosophy which it describes, requires us to learn new ways and new habits, to live with more uncertainty but more trust, less control but more creativity. To those of us reared in another tradition it can be a strange and a frightening language but I think that we have to recognize that it is the *right* language. No one, after all, has ever liked being managed, even if they didn't mind being the manager, for anyone who has tried to run an organization has always known that it was more like running a small country than a machine. It was only the theorists who tried to apply the hard rules of number and logic and mechanics to an essentially soft system. Maybe we were instinctively right to pay little heed to them until people like Peters and Waterman first started talking the new language in their *In Search of Excellence*, a book which obviously touched some chord.

As a result, leadership is now fashionable and the language of leadership increasingly important but, as Warren Bennis says in his book on *Leaders*, it remains the most studied and least understood topic in all the social sciences. Like beauty, or love, we know it when we see it but cannot easily define or produce it on demand. Again, like beauty and love, the writings on it are fun, sexy even, with their pictures of heroes and stories that can be our private fantasies. To read MacGregor Burns, Maccoby, Alistair Mant,

Warren Bennis, Cary Cooper or Peters and Waterman themselves is to escape into a private world of might-have-beens.

They may even do a disservice, these fun books, with their tales of heroes and their myths of the mighty, by suggesting that leadership is only for the new and the special. The significance of the new language is, I believe, that leadership has to be endemic in organizations, the fashion not the exception. Everyone with pretensions to be anyone must begin to think and act like a leader. Some will find it comes naturally and will blossom, some will not enjoy it at all, but unless you try, and are allowed to try, no one will ever know, for leadership is hard if not impossible to detect in embryo – it has to be seen in action to be recognized by oneself as much as by others.

So what is this mysterious thing and how does one acquire it? The studies agree on very little but what they do agree on is probably at the heart of things. It is this: 'A leader shapes and shares a vision which gives point to the work of others.' Would that it were as easy to do as to say! Think on these aspects of that short sentence:

– The vision must be different. A plan or a strategy which is a projection of the present or a replica of what everyone else is doing is not a vision. A vision has to 're-frame' the known scene, to re-conceptualize the obvious, connect the previously unconnected dream. Alistair Mant talks of the leader as 'builder' working with others towards a 'third corner', a goal. Those who are interested only in power or achievement for its own sake he calls 'raiders' or mere 'binary' people. MacGregor Burns talks of the 'transforming' leader as opposed to the mere 'transactional' one, the busy fixer.
– The vision must make sense to others. Ideally it should create the 'Aha Effect', as when everyone says 'Aha – of course, now I see it', like wit perhaps – what often was thought but ne'er so well expressed. To make sense it must stretch people's imaginations but still be within the bounds of possibility. To give point to the work of others it must be related to their work and not to some grand design in which they feel they have no point. If 'vision' is too grand a word, try 'goal' or even 'manifesto'.
– The vision must be understandable. No one can communicate a vision that takes two pages to read, or is too full of numbers and jargon. It has to be a vision that sticks in the head. Metaphor and analogy can be keys because they provide us with vivid images with room for interpretation – low definition concepts as opposed to the more precise high definition words of engineering and management.
– The leader must live the vision. He, or she, must not only believe in it but must be seen to believe in it. It is tempting credulity to proclaim a crusade for the impoverished from a luxury apartment. Effective leaders, we are told, exude energy. Energy comes easily if you love your cause. Effective leaders, again, have integrity. Integrity, being true to yourself, comes naturally if you live for your vision. In other words, the vision cannot be something thought up in the drawing office, to be real it has to come from the deepest parts of you, from an inner system of belief. The total pragmatist cannot be a transforming leader.
– The leader must remember that it is the work of others. The vision remains a dream without that work of others. A leader with no followers is a voice in

the wilderness. Leaders like to choose their teams but most inherit them and must then make them their own. Trust in others is repaid by trust from them. If it is to be *their* vision too, then their ideas should be heeded.

These six principles sound simple, obvious even, but in practice they are hard to deliver. Old-fashioned management is easier than the new leadership. Yet, if the new organizations are going to succeed, and they must succeed, our managers must think like leaders. If it happens, and in places it is happening, it will mark yet one more important discontinuity turned to advantage. [. . .]

17E
Leadership Roles

STARHAWK

In every group, certain tasks need to be done and roles need to be filled if the group is to function. If we think of a group as an entity, a being in and of itself, it needs a mind, a heart, and a spirit; it runs on energy and generates emotion. These are the roles leadership must fulfill.

In hierarchical groups, all roles are filled by one person or a small elite, who are rewarded more highly than others. The leader, the 'king', may be the brains, the mouthpiece, the drive, of a group. The various aspects of the King are aspects of hierarchical leadership: the Orderer determines the group's plans, the Judge makes decisions and establishes rules, the Conqueror defines the group's boundaries and establishes who its allies and enemies are, the Censor speaks for the group, and the Master of Servants demands that the other members of the group play a respectful, subservient role. Such leadership is bolstered by all the trappings and symbols of status and rank.

Nonhierarchical groups also have roles and functions that need to be fulfilled. In a group in which everyone has immanent value, fulfilling certain roles does not set one apart from the group or establish anyone as being intrinsically more valuable than others. The role we fill may be valuable and vital, and we may be appreciated for performing it well. But our inherent value does not depend on the performance of our role, and our leadership does not diminish anyone else's value.

The four directions and four elements [Figure 17.1] are a useful framework for thinking about the roles and tasks of leadership. None of these roles are exclusive, and although they can be formalized when appropriate, they are not necessarily assigned to different people. Rather, they are aspects of power we each might assume at different times. The names I provide here are aids in helping us identify the powers that are needed if a group is to survive and grow. [. . .]

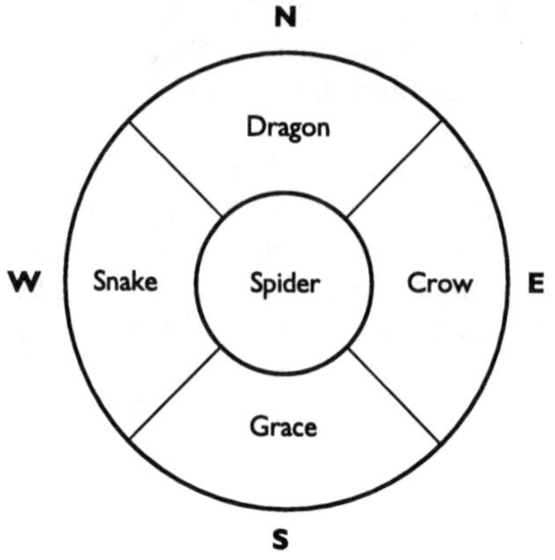

Figure 17.1

Responsive leadership is exercised less by providing the group with answers than by posing questions for the group itself to consider. I will describe each leadership role more fully and provide examples of questions.

CROWS

Crows fly high and see far, from above. They take the long view, see the long-term vision, keep in focus the group's goals. They suggest new directions, make plans and develop strategies, and look ahead to anticipate problems and needs.

Questions for Crows

1. What is our primary purpose?
2. Are we accomplishing it? Moving toward it?
3. What stage are we in?
4. Where are we going?
5. How do we get there – and by what steps, and with what timing?
6. What are our strengths and resources?
7. What are our weaknesses?
8. Is our structure working? How might it serve us better?
9. Who is with us and who against us?
10. Who are our potential allies? Opposition?
11. Whom are we reaching? Whom failing to reach?
12. What are the broader needs of the community around us? Are we, should we be meeting them? How?
13. What future needs can we anticipate? How can we provide for them?
14. What future problems can we foresee? How can we plan for them?
15. What details need to be taken care of?
16. What is falling through the cracks?
17. What can we learn from past mistakes? Successes?

The function of Crow is the one most closely resembling the role of hierarchical leadership. Crows often develop a lot of influence in a group. If one or two people are thinking about long-range plans, others may be likely to agree to them simply because they haven't come up with anything different. The group may benefit by considering together the Crow questions.

GRACES

Fire is the element of energy. Graces are continually aware of the group's energy, helping to raise it when it flags, and to direct and channel it when it is strong. Graces provide the group with fire: enthusiasm, raw energy, ability to expand. They make people feel good, generate enthusiasm about the group, welcome newcomers, bring people in. They furnish inspiration and generate new ideas.

Questions for Graces

1. What does the group get excited about?
2. What inspired each of us to join the group?
3. What/who made us feel welcome? Unwelcome?
4. In what directions might we expand?
5. How do we bring new people in?
6. How do we help new people catch up on the information, skills, experience, gossip, and so on the group has developed?
7. Who is interested in joining the group? Why?
8. How do we appear to outsiders?
9. How do we interact with people outside the group? How can we help them feel welcome?
10. What resources in the larger community might we share? What needs might we help fill?
11. Where do we direct the group's energy?
12. Whom do we want to reach out to – and how?

The role of Grace tends to make one well liked, but Graces must temper their enthusiasm with some of the grounding qualities of Dragons. Women are trained early to be good Graces. The role has been described as 'what ladies do at parties': welcoming people, starting conversations, making introductions, being charming. But no one should be expected to be charming all of the time, and everyone can benefit by taking on the role some of the time. Again, the group as a whole might consider these questions, and take care that many share the role of Grace.

SNAKES

Water is identified with feelings and emotions, and also fertility and renewal. The snake is the ancient symbol of the Goddess and of life's renewal, for the snake sheds its skin and is continually reborn. Snakes cultivate an awareness of how people are feeling. The snake glides through the water, sees from below the surface, or burrows into the ground and brings up the dirt. Effective Snakes keep current with the group's gossip. They become aware early of conflict, and bring it into the open, where they may help to mediate or resolve problems.

Questions for Snakes

1. How are people feeling?
2. What are people feeling that they aren't saying?
3. Who really likes and dislikes each other in the group?
4. What personal histories – known or secret – do people have? What sexual entanglements?
5. What secrets exist in the group?
6. What are the unspoken rules in the group?
7. What conflicts are people avoiding?
8. What do people grumble about privately and not say openly?
9. What do the smokers talk about when they congregate outside the door of the meeting? (Perhaps this phenomenon is peculiar to California, where smoking inside a meeting is frowned upon. Often the conversation among the smokers expresses a very different and more negative perspective than what is openly expressed in the meeting. Does smoking lead to cynicism, or do cynics tend to become smokers? Whichever, the bitching going on outside the door is sometimes the most important interchange happening.)
10. What's the latest gossip?
11. What hidden agendas are operating?
12. Who's alienated? Why?
13. What conflicts are brewing? Unresolved?

Snakes violate the Censor, speak the unspeakable, bring out into the open what others may not see or prefer to keep hidden. The role of Snake can be an extremely uncomfortable one – and Snakes may become heartily disliked, but theirs is a vital role and the one that perhaps does most to undermine the King's attempts to gain control of the group. The mouth is the greatest organ of resistance. A group cannot function by avoiding conflict and not acknowledging feelings. The role of bringing conflict into the open is vital and valuable.

Snakes can minimize how much they are disliked if they remember to bring *questions* to the group, not analyses. An effective Snake might say, for example: 'I feel tension in the room. What are other people feeling?' Rather than: 'I know you really hate Mary and can't deal with powerful women, John, so why don't you admit it!' Being the Snake is no excuse for sliding into the Judge's role or playing group therapist.

If the Snake is truly aware of how others are feeling, she or he can help mediate conflicts by asking the questions that improve communication. It is also important to rotate this role. Someone who continually brings up conflicts may lose influence and eventually come to be considered a crank. A wise Snake occasionally turns enthusiastic or visionary.

DRAGONS

Earth is the element of nurturing, grounding, of the practicalities that assure our sustenance. Dragons keep the group grounded, in touch with the practical, the realistic. Dragons also live on the boundaries of the wild, guarding hordes of treasure with their claws and fiery breath. The Dragon in the group guards its resources and its boundaries and articulates its limitations.

Questions for Dragons

1. Is our work sustainable?
2. Are our resources being replenished?
3. Are people burning out? Why?
4. How can we better nurture each other?
5. What concrete skills and resources do we have? How can they be augmented? Passed on?
6. What concrete limitations do we have? Are we acknowledging them? Planning for them?
7. How much time can each of us really commit?
8. How much money do we have? Need? Can we really afford this?
9. Can we really take this project on, and do it well?
10. How many new people can we realistically absorb? In what time frame?
11. What boundaries do we need and want? How do we establish them? How do we protect ourselves from intrusion? Invasion? Distraction? From having our energies drained?
12. Who is in the group and who is out?
13. How do people leave the group?
14. How do we end relationships with people we no longer want to work with?
15. What practical tasks need to be done?
16. What are we going to eat? Who is going to shop, cook, clean up, and so on?
17. How can we better provide for our physical safety? Needs? Comforts?

Dragons establish boundaries that give the group a sense of safety, and limits that keep the group's service sustainable. They may be perceived as throwing a wet blanket on the fires of fresh enthusiasm, but they may win great appreciation from those in the group who are feeling overwhelmed and can't buck the driving force of the Crows and Graces. Nurturing Dragons may sustain the group for a time, but again, unless the role rotates even the Dragons will be drained.

SPIDERS

The spider spins a web that connects points across a stretch of empty space. Every circle needs a center, a way in which people feel connected. A group's center may be a spiritual heart, a common goal or vision, or it may manifest in a person. In hierarchical spirituality, the teacher or guru sits metaphorically at the center of the web. Each member of the group is connected to the teacher and through her or him to each other.

In nonhierarchical groups, one person may be perceived as being central: having information others need, being a point of connection for others. A person may volunteer for this task; or a group itself may serve as Spider for a larger community. [. . .]

In a group, when the task of Spider is not consciously assigned, the role may fall on someone who becomes the person everybody calls when they've misplaced the address of the meeting, the person people complain to and confide in. A Spider is most effective, however, not by monopolizing communication but by asking the questions that can create and strengthen a true and complex web of interactions.

Questions for Spiders

1. Who in this group communicates with whom?
2. How can we strengthen and expand those networks?
3. Why don't you talk to——directly? Have you said that to her/him? Why not?
4. What is our common heart?
5. What can we do to bond more closely? To have more fun? To see each other more often?
6. What formal lines of communication would serve us?
7. What informal networks of communication do we have? Need?
8. What would serve to put them in place? A physical space? Time? Consciousness that we need them?

The Spider's role can be flattering, but can also lead to burnout. To be the one who receives everyone's complaints, the one whose phone is constantly ringing, is to be a form of group servant. Groups do better to create systems of communication that encourage shared responsibility and clear ways to transmit information. For the group's own security, important information should never become the property of only one person. And new people must have ways to find out information and learn history. The person with information is often perceived as the person in charge. The Spider will hear everyone's suggestions, complaints, fears, and questions, and needs support from the group and a way to bring problems and suggestions back to a body that can make decisions.

OTHER ROLES

Other, more formal roles exist in groups. Ideally, in a nonhierarchical group, they also are shared and rotated. The group may choose a representative to speak for it. In a nonhierarchical group, in which decision-making power extends throughout, the representative must know the answers to the following questions.

Questions for group representatives

1. Which decisions am I empowered to make independently?
2. Which decisions should I bring back to the group?
3. How do I bring them back to the group?
4. Who is my backup person? With whom do I share information?

The group should not expect to establish rules to cover every possible contingency, but discussing these questions ahead of time will help the group's representative develop an intuitive sense of the boundaries of her or his mandate. [. . .]

CHAPTER 18

Organizational Learning

The last few years have seen an explosion of literature on 'the learning organization'. This piece is just four sections of a chapter which explores the metaphor of the organization as a brain. This metaphor is but one of the images explored in Morgan's imaginative book, but it captures both the liveliness and power of the metaphor and the spirit of what a learning organization might be.

Can Organizations Learn to Learn?

GARETH MORGAN

[. . .] Are our organizations able to learn in an ongoing way? Is this learning single-loop or double-loop? What are the main barriers to learning? Are they intrinsic to the nature of human organization, or can they be overcome?

Clearly, it is difficult to answer these questions in an abstract way, because learning capacities vary from one organization to another. But certain general conclusions can be drawn.

For example, many organizations have become proficient at a single-loop learning, developing an ability to scan the environment, to set objectives, and to monitor the general performance of the system in relation to these objectives. This basic skill is often institutionalized in the form of information systems designed to keep the organization 'on course'. For example, budgets often maintain single-loop learning by monitoring expenditures, sales, profits, and other indications of performance to ensure that organizational activities remain within the limits established through the budgeting process. Advances in computing have done much to foster the use of this kind of single-loop control. Through the use of 'exception reports', which highlight critical deviations, managers and employees are often able to zero in on potential problems. Interestingly, a memory function is also often built into these single-loop controls, previous levels of achievement being used as standards to control current levels.

However, the ability to achieve proficiency at double-loop learning often proves more elusive. While some organizations have been successful in institutionalizing systems that review and challenge basic norms, policies, and operating procedures in relation to changes occurring in their environment – e.g., by encouraging ongoing debate and innovation – many fail to do so. This failure is especially true of bureaucratic organizations, since their fundamental organizing principles often operate in a way that actually *obstructs* the learning process. Three of these obstructions are worthy of special attention, and are often found in nonbureaucratic organizations as well.

First there is the general problem that bureaucratic approaches to organization impose fragmented structures of thought on their members and do not really encourage employees to think for themselves. Organizational goals, objectives, structures, and roles create clearly defined patterns of attention and responsibility, fragmenting interest in and knowledge of what the organization is doing. Where hierarchical and horizontal divisions within the organization are particularly powerful, information and knowledge rarely flow in a free manner, so that different sectors of the organization often operate on the basis of different pictures of the total situation, and can pursue subunit goals almost as ends in themselves, unaware of or disinterested in the way they fit the wider picture. The existence of such divisions tends to emphasize the distinctions between different elements of the organization, and foster the development of political systems that place yet further barriers in the way of learning. The bounded rationality inherent in organizational design thus actually *creates* boundaries! Moreover, employees are usually encouraged to occupy and keep a predefined place within the whole, and are rewarded for doing so. Situations in which policies and operating standards are challenged thus tend to be exceptional rather than the rule. For example, a person in a business firm challenging the relevance of a bottom-line profit or loss focus in a particular decision may well be deemed suspect in overall values and orientation. Given these circumstances, it is interesting to note that highly sophisticated single-loop learning systems may actually serve to keep the organization on the wrong course, since people are unable or not prepared to challenge underlying assumptions. The existence of single-loop learning systems, especially when used as controls over employees, may thus prevent double-loop learning from occurring.

A second major barrier to double-loop learning is often associated with the principle of bureaucratic accountability. To the extent that employees are held responsible for their performance within a system that rewards success and punishes failure, they have an incentive to engage in various forms of deception to protect themselves. Thus employees often tend to find ways of obscuring issues and problems that will place them in a bad light. They find ways of deflecting attention and of covering up, as well as of engaging in forms of impression management that make the situations for which they are responsible look better than they actually are. In addition, there is often a temptation to tell managers exactly what one thinks they want to hear.

When systems of accountability foster this kind of defensiveness an organization is rarely able to tolerate high levels of uncertainty. Managers and their employees also have a tendency to want to 'tie things down' and be 'on top of the facts'. This frequently leads them to create oversimplified interpretations of the situations with which they are dealing. They tend to be interested in problems only if there are solutions at hand. Complex issues that are difficult to address are thus often discussed or downplayed in importance to create time for solutions to emerge, or in the hope that problems they pose will disappear. Bearers of bad news are rarely made welcome and are often fired. Under such circumstances, operating assumptions are rarely challenged in an effective way.

A third major barrier to double-loop learning stems from the fact that there is often a gap between what people say and what they do. Chris Argyris of Harvard and Donald Schon of MIT have referred to this as a distinction between 'espoused theory' and 'theory in use'. Many managers and employees attempt to meet problems with rhetoric or rationalizations that convey the impression that they know what they are doing. This may not be just to impress others, but also to convince themselves that all is well and that they have the ability to cope. They also often engage in diversionary behavior, consciously or unconsciously, as when threats to a basic mode of practice lead an individual to deflect blame elsewhere and to tighten up on that practice, intensifying rather than questioning its nature and effects. In such circumstances it becomes increasingly difficult for the manager to confront and deal with the realities of a situation. Developments here may be reinforced by social processes such as 'groupthink': group mind-sets developed on the basis of social reinforcement, which are often very difficult to break. Individuals, groups, and departments may thus develop espoused theories that effectively prevent them from understanding and dealing with their problems. Double-loop learning requires that we bridge this gulf between theory and reality so that it becomes possible to challenge the values and norms embedded in the theories in use, as well as those that are espoused.

These examples of how organizations often inhibit double-loop learning also indicate how it can be facilitated. In essence, a new philosophy of management is required, to root the process of organizing in a process of open-ended inquiry. As has been shown, the whole process of learning to learn hinges on an ability to remain open to changes occurring in the environment, and on an ability to challenge operating assumptions in a most fundamental way. The following four guidelines summarize how this learning-oriented approach to organization and management can be developed.

First, encourage and value an openness and reflectivity that accepts error and uncertainty as an inevitable feature of life in complex and changing environments. This principle is fundamental for allowing members of an organization to deal with uncertainty in a constructive way. This is particularly important in turbulent environments where the problems that organizations face are frequently large, complex, and unique, and hence difficult to analyze and address. Rather than create conditions which lead employees to hide or deny error and to avoid asking problematic questions, as often happens under bureaucratic systems of accountability, it is necessary to encourage them to understand and accept the problematic nature of the situations with which they are dealing. A philosophy that 'it is admissible to write off legitimate error against experience', and that 'negative events and discoveries can serve as a source of knowledge and wisdom of great practical value', is an example of the kind of stance required. Note here that we are talking about legitimate error, which is distinct from mistakes that could and should have been avoided. Legitimate error stems from the uncertainty in a situation, as when unique or unexpected circumstances arise for reasons that cannot be predicted or controlled, and does not necessarily reflect badly on those involved. Legitimate error under this philosophy provides a potential lesson rather than an occasion to allocate blame.

Second, encourage an approach to the analysis and solution of complex problems that recognizes the importance of exploring different viewpoints. This principle helps to define a means of framing and reframing issues and problems so that they can be approached in an open-ended way. Given that many of the issues faced by organizations in turbulent environments are unclear and multidimensional, one of the major problems is usually that of defining the nature of the problems with which one is faced. This is best facilitated by managerial philosophies that recognize the importance of probing the various dimensions of a situation, and allow constructive conflict and debate between advocates of competing perspectives. In this way issues can be fully explored, and perhaps redefined so that they can be approached and resolved in new ways. This kind of inquiry helps an organization absorb and deal with the uncertainty of its environment rather than trying to avoid or eliminate it. As an example here we can take those situations where competing action strategies lead to a consideration of the organization's mission, and perhaps a reformulation of that mission. For example, business firms confronted by competing opportunities are often forced to reflect on the question 'What business are we in?' The process of learning to learn requires that organizations keep themselves open to such deep and challenging questions, rather than trying to develop fixed foundations for action.

Third, avoid imposing structures of action upon organized settings. This principle relates to the importance of inquiry-driven action. In contrast with traditional approaches to planning, which tend to *impose* goals, objectives, and targets, it is important to devise means where intelligence and direction can emerge from ongoing organizational processes. When goals and objectives have a predetermined character they tend to provide a framework for single-loop learning but discourage double-loop learning. In such cases there is a danger that the organization will fail to keep abreast of the requirements of changing environments. More double-loop learning can be generated by encouraging a 'bottom-up' or participative approach to the planning process. But cybernetics also emphasizes the central role played by norms and standards in the learning process, and stresses that double-loop learning develops as we question the relevance and desirability of these norms and standards as guidelines for action. Cybernetics shows us that these guidelines are of significance as limits to be placed on system behavior, rather than as specific targets to be achieved. Double-loop learning is thus best understood as a process which, in essence, questions the limits that are to be placed on action.

We find here a radically new means of approaching the planning process. Whereas the traditional philosophy is to produce a master plan with clear-cut targets, cybernetics suggests that it may be systemically wiser to focus on defining and challenging constraints. Intelligent strategy making thus involves a choice of limits (the negative-feedback 'noxiants' one wishes to avoid) rather than just a choice of ends. Instead of just specifying profit objectives or desired market shares, an organization should also plan what it wishes to avoid, e.g. excessive dependence on one product or market segment, excessive reliance on a particular source of supplies, inflexibility of production systems, or employee layoffs. The effect of this approach to strategy is to define an evolving space of possible actions that satisfy critical limits. This leaves room for specific action plans to be generated on an ongoing basis and tested against these constraints for viability.

Interestingly, aspects of this approach to strategic management are found in many aspects of Japanese management practice, such as the ritual of *ringi*, a collective decision-making process in which a policy document passes from manager to manager for approval. The effect of this process is to explore the premises and values underlying the decision proposal. If a manager disagrees with what is being proposed he is typically free to amend the decision proposal and to allow the document to circulate again. In this way the decision process explores the decision domain until a proposal satisfies all critical parameters. This can be extremely time-consuming, since in important decisions a very large number of managers may be involved. But when the decision is made, one can be fairly certain that most errors will have been detected and corrected, and that the decision will carry the commitment of those involved.

The *ringi* is as much a process for exploring and reaffirming values as it is for setting a direction. Cybernetics shows us that coherent direction can emerge from a domain defined in terms of values, and the *ringi* provides an illustration in practice. By contrast, the emphasis placed in Western management on the achievement of specific objectives or ends forces the role of values as standards or guidelines for action into the background. This is one reason why Western management is a lot more mechanistic in orientation than Japanese management, which reveals a good intuitive grasp of cybernetic principles. [. . .]

In the American view objectives should be hard and fast and clearly stated for all to see. In the Japanese view they emerge from a more fundamental process of exploring and understanding the values through which a firm is or should be operating. A knowledge of these values, the limits that are to guide action, defines a set of possible actions. An action chosen from this set may not be the very best, but it will satisfy parameters deemed crucial for success.

In the Japanese *ringi* we thus find the basis of a cybernetic approach to organization. In the Japanese context, the process is often used to affirm standards rather than to question them, but the basic principle remains the same. By encouraging an approach to management that explores and defines appropriate limits or values, we have a means of promoting continued double-loop learning whereby actions are always evaluated in relation to relevant standards. Action emerges as a result of the learning process: it is not imposed.

The fourth principle facilitating the development of learning to learn relates to the need to make interventions and create organizational structures and processes that help implement the above principles. This brings us to the topic of our next section: the holographic approach to organization. As we will see, this provides many interesting and practical insights into the qualities that organizations must possess if they are to have the flexible self-organizing capacities of a brain.

BRAINS AND ORGANIZATIONS AS HOLOGRAPHIC SYSTEMS

To compare the brain with a hologram may seem to be stretching reason beyond the limits. However, the way a holographic plate enfolds all the information necessary to produce a complete image in each of its parts has much in common with the functioning of a brain. And it is possible to extend this image to create a vision of organization where capacities required in the whole are enfolded in the parts, allowing the system to learn and self-organize, and to maintain a complete system of functioning even when specific parts malfunction or are removed. Some highly innovative organizations have already begun organizing in this way. But the principles on which they build are usually intuitive rather than explicit. It is thus fruitful to look to some of the ideas emerging from modern brain research to help clarify how holographic systems work, so that these ideas can have a greater impact on how we design organizations of the future. Recognizing that a somewhat speculative and futuristic stance is required for dealing with this issue, let us explore.

The holographic character of the brain is most clearly reflected in the patterns of connectivity through which each neuron (nerve cell) is connected with hundreds of thousands of others, allowing a system of functioning that is both generalized *and* specialized. Different regions of the brain seem to specialize in different activities, but the control and execution of specific behaviors is by no means as localized as was once thought. Thus, while we can distinguish between the functions performed by the cortex (the captain or master planner which controls all nonroutine activity, and perhaps memory), the cerebellum (the computer or automatic pilot taking care of routine activity), and the mid-brain (the center of feelings, smell, and emotion), we are obliged to recognize that they are all closely interdependent and capable of acting on behalf of each other when necessary. [. . .] We also know that right and left brains combine to produce patterns of thought, and that the distinction between the functions of these hemispheres as the domains of creative and analytic capacities is accompanied by more general patterns of connectivity. For example, the creative or analogical right brain is richly joined to the limbic system and the emotions. The principle of connectivity and generalized function is also reflected in the way neurons serve both as communication channels and as a locus of specific activity or memory recall. It is believed that each neuron may be as complex as a small computer and capable of storing vast amounts of information. The pattern of rich connectivity between neurons allows simultaneous processing of information in different parts of the brain, a receptivity to different kinds of information at one and the same time, and an amazing capacity to be aware of what is going on elsewhere.

The secret of the brain's capacities seems to depend more on this connectivity, which is the basis of holographic diffusion, than on differentiation of structure. The brain is composed of repetitive units of the same kind (there may only be three basic types of brain cell), so that we find different functions being sustained by very similar structures. The importance of connectivity in accounting for complexity of functioning is also reinforced by comparisons between human and animal brains. For example, elephants have much larger brains than humans, but they are by no means so richly joined.

An interesting aspect of this connectivity rests in the fact it creates a much greater degree of cross-connection and exchange than may be needed at any given time. However, this redundancy is crucial for creating holographic potential and for ensuring flexibility in operation. The redundancy allows the brain to operate in a probabilistic rather than a deterministic manner, allows considerable room to accommodate random error, and creates an excess capacity that allows new activities and functions to develop. In other words, it facilitates the process of self-organization whereby internal structure and functioning can evolve along with changing circumstances.

This self-organizing capacity has been demonstrated in numerous ways. For example, when brain damage occurs it is not uncommon for different areas of the brain to take on the functions which have been impaired . . . Similar self-organizing capacities are also evident in the way activity can be modified to take account of new situations. This capacity was demonstrated dramatically by psychologist G. W. Stratton, who tried wearing spectacles that turned the world upside down. After just a few days vision was adjusted by restoring familiar images to their usual position. What is most surprising, however, is that when the spectacles were eventually removed, everything turned upside down again until Stratton's senses reorganized themselves to cope with life as usual.

The brain has this amazing capacity to organize and reorganize itself to deal with the contingencies it faces. Experiments have shown that the more we engage in a specific activity, e.g., playing tennis, typing, or reading, the more the brain adjusts itself to facilitate the kind of functioning required. The simple idea that 'practice makes perfect' is underwritten by a complex capacity for self-organization whereby the brain forges or revises patterns of neuronic activity. For example, experiments where monkeys were trained to use a finger to press a lever thousands of times a day showed that the area of the brain controlling that finger increased in size and changed in organization. Our awareness leads us to see the brain as a system which, in no small measure, has played an important role in designing itself in the course of evolution.

Now to our basic problem: how can we use these insights about the holographic character of the brain to create organizations that are able to learn and self-organize in the manner of a brain?

Our discussion provides many clues. For example, it suggests that by building patterns of rich connectivity between similar parts we can create systems that are both specialized and generalized, and that are capable of reorganizing internal structure and function as they learn to meet the challenges posed by new demands. The holographic principle has a great deal running in its favor. For the capacities of the brain are already distributed throughout modern organizations. All the employees have brains, and computers are in essence simulated brains. In this sense, important aspects of the whole are already embodied in the parts. The development of more holographic, brainlike forms of organization thus rests in the realization of a potential that already exists.

Facilitating self-organization: principles of holographic design

- Get the whole into the parts.
- Create connectivity and redundancy.
- Create simultaneous specialization and generalization.
- Create a capacity to self-organize.

These are the things that have to be done to create holographic organization.

Our task now is to examine the means. Much can be learned from the way the brain is organized, and much can be learned from cybernetic principles. I find it helpful to think in terms of the four interacting principles identified in Figure 18.1. The principle of *redundant functions* shows a means of building wholes into parts by creating redundancy, connectivity, and simultaneous specialization and generalization. The principle of *requisite variety* helps to provide practical guidelines for the design of part–whole relations by showing exactly how much of the whole needs to be built into a given part. And the principles of *learning to learn* and *minimum critical specification* show how we can enhance capacities for self-organization.

Any system with an ability to self-organize must have an element of redundancy: a form of excess capacity which, appropriately designed and used, creates room for maneuver. Without such redundancy, a system has no real capacity to reflect on and question how it is operating, and hence to change its mode of functioning in constructive ways. In other words, it has

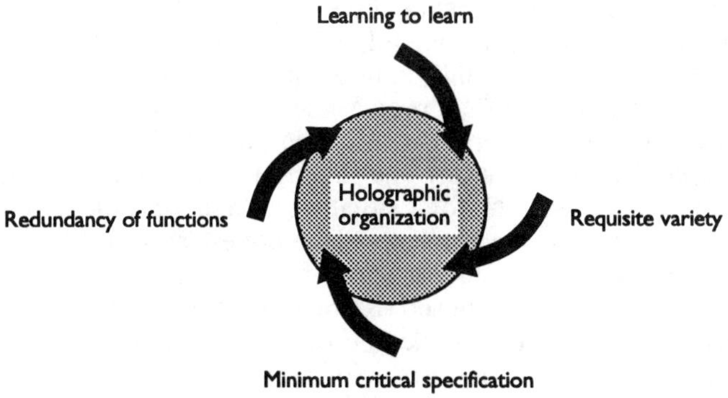

Figure 18.1 Principles of holographic design

no capacity for intelligence in the sense of being able to adjust action to take account of changes in the nature of relations within which the action is set.

Australian systems theorist Fred Emery has suggested that there are two methods for designing redundancy into a system. The first involves *redundancy of parts*, where each part is precisely designed to perform a specific function, special parts being added to the system for the purpose of control and to back up or replace operating parts whenever they fail. This design principle is mechanistic, and the result is typically a hierarchical structure where one part is responsible for controlling another.

If we look around the organizational world it is easy to see evidence of this kind of redundancy: the supervisor who spends his or her time ensuring that others are working; the maintenance team that 'stands by' waiting for problems to arise; the employee idly passing time because there's no work to do; employee X passing a request to colleague Y 'because that's his job not mine'; the quality controller searching for defects which, under a different system, could much more easily be rectified by those who produced them. Under this design principle the capacity for redesign and change of the system rests with the parts assigned this function; for example, production engineers, planning teams, and systems designers. Such systems are organized and can be reorganized, but they have little capacity to self-organize.

The second design method incorporates a *redundancy of functions*. Instead of spare parts being added to a system, extra functions are added to each of the operating parts, so that each part is able to engage in a range of functions rather than just perform a single specialized activity. An example of this design principle is found in organizations employing autonomous work groups, where members acquire multiple skills so that they are able to perform each other's jobs and substitute for each other as the need arises. At any one time, each member possesses skills that are redundant in the sense that they are not being used for the job at hand. However, this organizational design possesses flexibility and a capacity for reorganization within each and every part of the system.

Systems based on redundant functions are holographic in that capacities relevant for the functioning of the whole are built into the parts. This creates a completely new relationship between part and whole. In a design based on redundant parts, e.g., an assembly line where production workers, supervisors, efficiency experts, and quality controllers have fixed roles to perform, the whole is the sum of predesigned parts. In the holographic design, on the other hand, the parts reflect the nature of the whole, since they take their specific shape at any one time in relation to the contingencies and problems arising in the total situation. When a problem arises on an assembly line it is typically viewed as 'someone else's problem', since those operating the line often do not know, care about, or have the authority to deal with the problems posed. Remedial action has to be initiated and controlled from elsewhere. A degree of passivity and neglect is thus built into the system. This contrasts with systems based on redundant functions, where the nature of one's job is set by the changing pattern of demands with which one is dealing. Needless to say, the two design principles create qualitatively different relationships between people and their work. Under a system of redundant parts involvement is partial and instrumental, and under the principle of redundant functions more holistic and all-absorbing.

In implementing this kind of organizational design one inevitably runs into the question, how much redundancy should be built into any given part? While the holographic principle suggests that we should try and build everything into everything else, in many human systems this is an impossible ideal. For example, in many modern organizations the range of knowledge and skills required is such that it is impossible for everybody to become skilled in everything. So what do we do?

It is here that the idea of *requisite variety* becomes important. This is the principle, originally formulated by the English cybernetician W. Ross Ashby, that suggests that the internal diversity of any self-regulating system must match the variety and complexity of its environment if it is to deal with the challenges posed by that environment. Or to put the matter slightly differently, any control system must be as varied and complex as the environment being controlled. In the context of holographic design, this means that all elements of an organization should embody critical dimensions of the environment with which they have to deal, so that they can self-organize to cope with the demands they are likely to face.

The principle of requisite variety thus gives clear guidelines as to how the principle of redundant functions should be applied. It suggests that redundancy (variety) should always be built into a system where it is *directly* needed, rather than at a distance. This means that close attention must be paid to the boundary relations between organizational units and their environments, to ensure that requisite variety always falls within the unit in question. What is the nature of the environment being faced? Can all the skills for dealing with this environment be possessed by every individual? If so, then build around multifunctioned people, as in the model of the autonomous work group discussed earlier. If not, then build around multifunctioned teams that collectively possess the requisite skills and abilities and where each individual member is as generalized as possible, creating a pattern of overlapping skills and knowledge bases in the team overall. It is here that we find a means of coping with the problem that everybody can't be skilled in everything. Organization can be developed in a cellular manner around self-organizing, multidisciplined groups that have the requisite skills and abilities to deal with the environment in a holistic and integrated way.

The principle of requisite variety has important implications for the design of almost every aspect of organization. Whether we are talking about the creation of a corporate planning group, a research department, or a work group in a factory, it argues in favor of a proactive embracing of the environment in all its diversity. Very often managers do the reverse, reducing variety in order to achieve greater internal consensus. For example, corporate planning teams are often built around people who think along the same lines, rather than around a diverse set of stakeholders who can actually represent the complexity of the problems with which the team ultimately has to deal.

The principles of redundant functions and requisite variety create systems that have a capacity of self-organization. For this capacity to be realized and to assume coherent direction, however, two further organizing principles also have to be kept in mind: the principles of *minimum critical specification* and of *learning to learn*.

The first of these principles reverses the bureaucratic principle that organizational arrangements need to be defined as clearly and as precisely as possible. For in attempting to organize in this way one eliminates the capacity for self-organization. The principle of minimum critical specification suggests that managers and organizational designers should primarily adopt a facilitating or orchestrating role, creating 'enabling conditions' that allow a system to find its own form. It thus has close links with the idea of 'inquiry-driven action', discussed earlier. One of the advantages of the principle of redundant functions is that it creates a great deal of internal flexibility. The more one attempts to specify or predesign what should occur, the more one erodes this flexibility. The principle of minimum critical specification attempts to preserve flexibility by suggesting that, in general, one should specify no more than is absolutely necessary for a particular activity to occur.

For example, in running a meeting it may be necessary to have someone to chair the meeting and to take notes, but it is not necessary to institutionalize the process and have a chairperson and secretary. Roles can be allowed to change and evolve according to circumstances. In a group or project bureaucratic patterns of fixed hierarchical leadership can be replaced by a heterarchical pattern, where the dominant element at any given time depends on the total situation. Different people can take the initiative on different occasions according to the contribution they are able to make. Instead of making roles clear and separate, roles can be left deliberately ambiguous and overlapping, so that they can be clarified through practice and inquiry. The basic idea is to create a situation where inquiry rather than predesign provides the main driving force. This helps to keep organization flexible and diversified, while capable of evolving structure sufficient and appropriate to deal with the problems that arise.

The principle of minimum critical specification thus helps preserve the capacities for self-organization that bureaucratic principles usually erode. The danger of such flexibility, however, is that it has the potential to become chaotic. This is why the principle of *learning to learn* must be developed as a fourth element of holographic design.

. . . A system's capacity for coherent self-regulation and control depends on its ability to engage in processes of single- and double-loop learning. These allow a system to guide itself with reference to a set of coherent values or norms, while questioning whether these norms provide an appropriate basis for guiding behavior. For a holographic system to acquire integration and coherence and to evolve in response to changing demands, these learning capacities must be actively encouraged. In an autonomous work group, for example, members must both value the activities in which they are engaged and the products that they produce, and remain open to the kinds of learning that allow them to question, challenge, and change the design of these activities and products. Given that there are so few predetermined rules for guiding behavior, direction and coherence must come from the group members themselves as they set and honor the shared values and norms that evolve along with changing circumstances.

One of the most important functions of those responsible for designing and managing the kind of 'enabling conditions' referred to earlier is that of helping to create a context that fosters this kind of shared identity and learning orientation.

Herbert Simon has suggested that hierarchy is the adaptive form for finite intelligence to assume in the face of complexity. He illustrates this principle with a tale of two watchmakers. Both make good watches, but one is far more successful because instead of assembling the watches piece by piece as if he were building a mosaic, he constructs his watches by forming subassemblies of about ten parts each, which can then be joined with other subassemblies to create subsystems of a higher order. These can then be assembled to form the complete watch. In other words, the successful watchmaker has discovered the principle of hierarchy. By organizing in this way the watchmaker can exercise great control over the process of assembly and tolerate frequent interruptions and setbacks. He can thus achieve a much greater rate of productivity than his competitor, who, when interrupted, has to start all over again. It can be shown mathematically that if the watch comprises a thousand parts, and the assembly process is interrupted an average of once in every hundred assembling operations, the mosaic method will take four thousand times longer than the systems approach to assemble a single watch. Simon uses the parable to illustrate the importance of hierarchy in complex systems, and to argue that systems will evolve much more rapidly if there are stable intermediate forms. Cybernetician W. Ross Ashby has made the similar point that no complex adaptive system can succeed in achieving a steady state in a reasonable period of time unless the process can occur subsystem by subsystem, each subsystem being relatively independent of the others.

The same is true of self-organizing systems. If their organization is completely random they will take an almost infinite amount of time to complete any complex task. If, however, they use their autonomy to learn how to find appropriate patterns of connectivity, they can develop a remarkable ability to find novel and increasingly progressive solutions to complex problems. Such systems typically find and adopt a pattern graded in a hierarchical manner, in that sets of subsystems link to higher-order systems, but the pattern is emergent rather than imposed.

The principles of holographic organization attempt to create the conditions through which such patterns of order can emerge.

Holographic organization in practice

Is holographic organization just a pipe dream? Clearly not. Mention has already been made of the holographic characteristics found in many autonomous work groups. And some highly innovative organizations have begun to extend this principle to restructure major sections of their operations.

Consider, for example, a well-known computer firm that has reorganized many of its factories along lines that reflect the principles of holographic design. For example, in one plant employing almost 200 people the organization has been broken down into teams of 14 to 18 people. These operating teams have complete responsibility for production, from the arrival of supplies in the plant to the shipment of finished products. Every employee becomes certified in the twenty or so operating tasks needed to produce the whole product. The teams meet daily to make decisions about production, to divide work, and to attend to special issues such as improvements in work design, problems in supplies or shipping, or the hiring of new members. Members of the team are responsible for setting their own hours of work and production schedules, and conduct their own quality control. They even administer skills-certification tests to their colleagues. Each operating team has a leader or manager who acts as a resource, coach, and facilitator, and who has special concern for the team's identity.

In addition to the operating teams there are also administrative and technical teams who provide support systems, services, and materials. The technical staff also play an important function in helping the operating teams integrate new products, processes, and equipment into daily operations, so that the plant can remain at the front of the technological developments.

The whole ethos of plant operations is characterized by holographic integration. The work design was stimulated by a desire to create a holistic relationship between people and their work, so that employees would acquire a sense of identity with the firm and its products. Each and every worker knows almost everything about the products and processes with which the plant is concerned, and becomes involved with the productive process in the fullest sense. Employees are bound together in their common endeavor through extensive training and orientation programs that help them to develop common values and a sense of shared purpose, and are rewarded for their achievements in terms of skill levels. The results have been spectacularly successful, improving productivity, quality, innovation, and work life in almost every aspect.

Examples of piecemeal moves toward holographic organization are found in numerous other firms as well. In many of the highly innovative firms studied by Thomas Peters and Robert Waterman in their 'search for excellence', the rigorous predesign and close control of work give way to more experimental, learning-through-action processes that have much in common with holographic self-management. The emphasis that Peters and Waterman place on the ability of these organizations to develop a shared sense of identity, mission, and 'corporate culture' also resonates with the holographic model. For it is by building this shared sense of the corporate whole into each and every employee that holographic organization achieves its coherence. Though not usually discussed in this way, the role of corporate culture is important in modern organizations because of its holographic potential.

Strong holographic tendencies are also being created in modern organizations through the introduction of microprocessing technologies that diffuse information, communications, and control. Microprocessing creates a capacity for networks of information exchange and interlocking controls that make many aspects of hierarchy unnecessary. Under its influence many areas of middle management are thus becoming redundant and replaced by more integrated work systems like those of the computer firm discussed above.

However, despite the emergence of these holographic characteristics and potentials, it would be an exaggeration to suggest that the holographic image accurately describes many organizations at the present time.

BIBLIOGRAPHY

Argyris, C. and Schon, D. A. *Organizational Learning: A Theory of Action Perspective.* Reading, MA: Addison Wesley, 1978.

Ashby, W. R. *Design for a Brain.* New York: John Wiley, 1952.

Ashby, W. R. *An Introduction to Cybernetics.* London: Chapman & Hall, 1960.

Emery, F. E. *Systems Thinking.* Harmondsworth: Penguin, 1969.

Peters, T. J. and Waterman, R. H. *In Search of Excellence.* New York: Harper & Row, 1982.

Simon, H. A. 'The architecture of complexity' *Proceedings of the American Philosophical Society*, 106: 467–482, 1962.

CHAPTER 19

Organizational culture

Organizational culture is the set of, often unconsciously held, beliefs, ideas, knowledge and values which shape the way things happen and makes some courses of action unthinkable. An organization's culture thus determines, to a large extent, its capacity for solving problems. Bate describes six characteristic dimensions of culture likely to have a negative effect on problem-solving capacity which he observed in his studies of three UK companies. This piece, describing these observations, has been heavily edited to capture the essence of his findings.

The impact of organizational culture on approaches to organizational problem-solving

PAUL BATE

[. . .]

One general conclusion reached repeatedly . . . was that organizational change was substantially different in practice from the theory of change – and more difficult. One strand of this theory states that change will take place if and when the following 'preconditions' are present: a problem or problems and a desire or felt need to resolve them; an awareness of the existence and basic nature of the problem; and available information which allows the parties to the problem to define it and make appropriate choices between alternative courses of action (Lippitt et al., 1958; Schein, 1969). In practice it was discovered – initially in the footwear company and later in the others – that change did not always occur even when all of these conditions were in evidence. Something – whatever it may be – was enmeshing people in their problems in a persistent and repetitive way.

Increasingly attention became focused on the question: why were situations allowed to persist when they were accepted by the parties themselves as problematical and undesirable? Gradually a fascinating notion began to emerge that the parties were actively *colluding* in a process which effectively removed all possibility of a resolution to their problems. Closer investigation suggested that at the heart of this collusion process lay the organizational culture. The thesis that resulted from this line of inquiry provides the basis of this chapter. It can be summarized as follows: people in organizations evolve in their daily interactions with one another a system of shared perspectives of 'collectively held and sanctioned definitions of the situation' which make up the culture of these organizations. The culture, once established, prescribes for its creators and inheritors certain ways of believing, thinking and acting which in some circumstances can prevent meaningful interaction and induce a condition of 'learned helplessness' – that is a psychological state in which people are unable to conceptualize their problems in such a way as to be able to resolve them. In short, attempts at problem-solving may become culture-bound.

This chapter looks at that 'something' about organizational culture that has the power to lock people in with their own problems.

WHAT IS ORGANIZATIONAL CULTURE?

The layman's terms for organizational culture are, in their way, just as meaningful as those of the behavioural scientist. They may be found in the everyday conversations of managers and shop-floor personnel. Reference is made, for example, to the company way of doing things, or more generally to its style, philosophy, spirit, character, or even religion. Most people could (and do) paint a portrait of 'Mr Company' – the organization man who is the perfect embodiment of the company's ethos or culture – and his opposite, the square peg in a round hole whose face for some reason or other doesn't seem to fit. In my view these are everyday expressions about organizational culture in the sense that they spring from a set of generalized assumptions and beliefs about those characteristics of the organization that distinguish it from other organizations. Nevertheless, while providing the essence of the organizational culture phenomenon such expressions are limited in precision and do require further elaboration.

The first important point is that culture is predominantly *implicit* in people's mind; it is not something that is 'out there' with a separate existence of its own; neither is it directly observable. The components of organizational culture are really internalized social constructs – socially produced definitions of the situation that are part of and inseparable from a person's definition of him or herself. These constructs form the basis of that person's 'commonsense' view of her organizational world, something that is notable for its unconscious and unreflecting character. As Silverman (1970: 133) observes in this context, this world is 'a taken-for-granted world governed by what we understand as the laws of nature'.

The deeply embedded nature of culture partly explains why people have difficulty describing it in precise and critical terms. But this is not the only reason: culture forms the very foundation stone of our social existence; it gives meaning in a very literal sense to our social and organizational lives by providing us with a relatively self-contained 'order' or rationale – what Kluckhohn and Kelly (1945) call a design for living. To have this questioned can be both threatening and upsetting, and it is because of this that we defend ourselves by hiding alien values behind stereotypes, restricting our information to selective sources (reading only our 'colour' of newspaper), and limiting our interactions to those with other people of roughly similar outlooks (Hofstede, 1978, 1981).

Another key feature of culture is that it is *shared* – it refers to the ideas, meanings and values people hold in common and to which they subscribe collectively. Durkheim's concept of the 'collective consciousness' would be appropriate here were it not for the fact that a good deal of culture is unconscious and unremarked. While not denying the existence of differences – sometimes numerous and fundamental – in people's outlooks, motivation and interests, the cutlure concept tends to focus on the commonalities which give a work organization, for example, a recognizable personality and unity – shared perspectives which constitute what Baker (1980: 8) calls 'the social glue holding the company together'. Jaques (1952: 251) places similar emphasis when he defines the culture of the factory as follows:

> [It] is its customary and traditional way of thinking and doing things, which is shared to a greater or lesser degree by all [the factory's] members, and which new members must learn and at least partially accept, in order to be accepted into service in the firm.

The latter part of this quotation identifies a third important characteristic of organizational culture, namely that it is *transmitted* by a process of socialization. People are required to acknowledge and, to a degree at least, conform to patterns of thinking and acting that might stretch far back into an organization's history. This is an issue taken up by Berger (1963) in his portrayal of society as both a prison and a puppet theatre: he points out that people's lives can be dominated by those of men who have been dead for generations and that each situation in which they find themselves is not only defined by their contemporaries but predefined by their predecessors – all of which could apply equally well to organizations. It is organizational culture which acts as the vehicle for transmitting and giving continuity to the past – the 'living history' as Malinowski (1945) graphically describes it. [. . .]

Thus the term 'culture' can be defined as the meanings or aspects of the conceptual structures which people hold in common and which define the social or organizational 'reality'. McNeill (1979: 76) expresses similar sentiments:

> [It] consists of patterns for organizational behavior that are learned, transmitted, and symbolically derived. These patterns for behavior constitute a group's characteristic way of perceiving its organizational environment – a group's shared orientations to organizational stimuli. Organizational culture is neither an organizational attribute nor an individual attribute; rather, it is a system of shared orientations to organizational attributes, a 'consensus of perceptions' regarding organizational stimuli.

Superimposed upon these shared orientations are the idiosyncrasies of various individuals' conceptions of the organization. While their existence is recognized they are not the central concern of organizational culture research. [. . .]

SUMMARY OF FINDINGS

My main concern was to identify those aspects of each culture that had a strong impact on organizational problem-solving, and it gradually became clear that certain characteristics were present, to a greater or lesser extent and in different forms, in all three organizations. They have been labelled as follows:

Unemotionality
Depersonalization
Subordination
Conservatism
Isolationism
Antipathy

Unemotionality: 'Avoid showing or sharing feelings or emotions'

In two of the companies studied – the footwear manufacturer and the chemicals multinational – and to a lesser degree in the third, there appeared to be a hidden dictate that displays of feeling and emotion were not permitted or were somehow 'bad' for the individual and bad for the organization. This was well captured in the phrase 'civil service mentality' used by one junior manager, who then went on to define it:

> Everything is handled in a formal, stiff-upper-lip way. Problems are sterilized and laundered in the company washing machine, and come out whiter than white. One never need get one's hands wet or dirty. Our meetings are all the same – brisk, businesslike and to the point.

Unemotionality was also reflected in the apparent superficiality of work relationships. 'Work' and 'personal' relationships were separately defined: 'There are none of them personal friends. The word personal is watered down at work. One's judgement is a bit bland because one is talking about a work rather than total relationship' (senior manager). And, 'I don't think it's part of one's work to form likes or dislikes. I don't find many people sympathetic, nor do I want them to be' (middle manager). And, 'I would rather not have close, socially intimate relationships with people either on whom I depend or who conceivably depend on me as part of their job. I would find that quite difficult' (director).

Such a definition of the work relationship did appear to affect people's ways of dealing with each other:

> I suppose on those occasions when I have tried to get close to someone and actually speak my mind, I've sort of sensed the barriers coming down. You know, sort of seen a blank look coming over their face. You see this as a warning signal against getting too close, and begin to back off. (operator)

The reasons given for playing down feelings and emotions were that it was somehow impolite, embarrassing, or just 'plain useless' to do otherwise: 'Nobody wants to hear about my feelings and problems. And it's not for me to burden others with them' (foreman). And another, 'When somebody blows off steam, everyone else is made to feel uncomfortable. It doesn't really get anyone anywhere at all' (operator). When a female worker was asked why she had not brought her long-standing complaints to the attention of her supervisor, she replied: 'It would cause more trouble than it would solve – a bit like being sick over the floor: first it would upset me, second it would upset him, and third it might lead to me getting a black eye!'

In the case of managers, showing feelings and emotions was construed as a sign of unprofessionalism – a sign of weakness or inefficiency: 'If I blow my top, people will start to brand me an "hysterical woman" and suggest maybe I was working too hard' (female personnel officer). [. . .]

The evidence suggests that, as a result of this orientation, differences between people tended to be repressed (and allowed to smoulder on) or dealt with unsatisfactorily at a 'distance'. There was a fear of bringing true feelings about a problem into the open in case tempers would fray and the situation would become 'unmanageable' (a likely enough outcome in view of people's inexperience of confrontation and openness). Instead, people would tend to 'chew' on their problem for as long as they possibly could, even though this obviously produced a lot of tension and frustration. When the problem could no longer be ducked, the next stage was to approach it in a way that deterred people from opening it up too far. [. . .]

It is not difficult to understand why, in such an environment, joint attempts to deal effectively and creatively with problems often failed miserably. The culture, while having a rationale of sorts, made people inflexible and overcautious. Attempts at exploring issues and using others to collaborate in this would have been regarded – in sensitive areas – as highly dangerous, a case of (to use people's actual words) 'turning over stones and finding the worms' or of 'poking your nose into something that you would do better to keep out of'. People's concern, therefore, was to cope with the situation – *not* to change it – by avoidance and repression strategies, all of which added up to a failure to get to grips with the problems. [. . .]

Depersonalization of issues: 'Never point the finger at anyone in particular'

In all three organizations I found a tendency for people at all levels to be publicly vague about the source of their problems or grievances, even when they clearly had in mind a 'blacklist' of culprits and privately discussed this with one or two close colleagues. Confronting or 'naming' individuals was regarded (if regarded is the best word for an unreflecting and natural way of seeing things) as completely out of the question – ungentlemanly, unkind, unnecessary, and often dangerous. The corollary of this was that few people appeared to accept personal responsibility for things that were going wrong: collective responsibility on the lines of a government cabinet was considered to be the order of organizational life. [. . .] Employees in the footwear company frequently picked on the 'family' owners as the cause of their difficulties:

> It's one thing they all seem to bring with them – a sort of insincerity and lack of positive support . . . no, no one in particular; you've got to remember that they have all come out of the same mould. (manager)

[. . .] If it was not 'head office' or the 'family' then it was 'the workers', 'the unions', or 'the managers' who were to blame, depending on your standpoint. Even more widely it was often 'the government', 'the recession', or 'the strength of the pound' which were the cause of the problem – but rarely any one individual.

To try to explain this attitude, one must begin with the moral aspects. Widespread in the three organizations was a strong professed belief that to name names was wrong; that there was something uncouth about confronting or even talking about an individual in public. It was, however, a rather odd morality in that it was acceptable to engage in gossip or even smear campaigns behind someone's back. [. . .]

Several other factors contributed to this attitude: fear, for example – not many people would dare to go to their boss and blame him for any difficulties being experienced; then the view that 'speaking up for yourself' was 'forgetting your place'; it was also regarded as unprofessional to question or criticize individuals (or for individuals to break the party line and take a personal stand on things), and such a course of action was unquestioningly seen to be destructive rather than constructive.

As a result, attempts to resolve problems frequently dissolved into vague discussions which skirted the real issues, or hurried attempts to move on to easier, less contentious ones. [. . .] There was a conspiracy of silence in a literal and very powerful sense.

The evidence suggests that both unemotionality and depersonalization reflected and perpetuated a situation where people were incapable of directness in diagnosing and dealing with their problems. The requirement for diagnostic activities, 'valid information about the status quo, current problems and opportunities, and effects of actions as they relate to goal achievement' (French and Bell, 1973), was not met. 'Valid' information was neither gathered nor discussed; such information as existed was never really evaluated or put to the test – people were allowed to go around with semi-private opinions which might or might not have stood up to public scrutiny. The system also worked in such a way that no one needed to own up to a problem and no one needed to accept responsibility for doing anything about it.

Subordination: 'Never challenge those in authority and always wait for them to take the initiative in resolving your *problems'*

A member of staff in the footwear company pointed out how totally dependent his colleagues had become upon their bosses at the head office: 'All my colleagues now rely on "Mecca" speaking – so if nobody speaks from there nothing happens.' Some of these colleagues to whom he referred also had something to say on this issue: 'X is my boss in the Centre. He should be coming along and saying what needs to be done, and we should be listening to that.'

Leadership was defined – by many leaders and subordinates – as providing the initial impetus for change and problem resolution. The legitimacy of a subordinate doing this was questionable, since 'subordinate' connoted 'following', 'responding', 'carrying out instructions', and similar things. Subordination also symbolized not taking responsibility for solving problems – even if they were your own problems. When resolution was not forthcoming people would tend to suffer in silence or grumble quietly amongst themselves, oblivious to the fact that one of the reasons for the persistence of their problems was their own definition of their role. [. . .]

As with other aspects of culture this subordination was reinforced by sanctions of various kinds applied to deviants. If, for example, someone did challenge authority or take it upon himself to seek a resolution of his own problems, pressures would be applied to make him 'back off'. Such pressures – as evidenced by the following extract from a conversation with some of the workers in the chemicals company – can be very great indeed:

> *First worker*: 'It's all very well and good you telling us to speak up for ourselves at the meeting, but it wouldn't really be worth our while. Our life wouldn't be worth living.'
> *Researcher*: 'What do you mean?'
> *First worker*: 'You would know what I mean if you worked here.'
> *Second worker*: 'Take the people in the warehouse. They have a reputation for sticking up for themselves. And look what happens. If they see you've got views – are a bit bolshie – they pick on you. You get all the bad jobs.'
> *First worker*: 'And black eyes into the bargain.'
> *Second worker*: 'People need protection.'
> *First worker*: 'It pays to keep your mouth shut.'

[. . .] This had the effect of . . . producing a situation where decisions were made without consultation and explanation, and only minimal input was made by workers themselves concerning their problems and anxieties. Consequently, managers were often blissfully unaware that these problems existed and therefore did nothing to search for a solution.

Conservatism: 'Better the devil you know'

Managers and workers alike often had an ingrained conservatism about organizational life that partly stemmed from an underlying scepticism either that 'things will never change', or that if they did the situation might actually become worse than it currently was. The result was that problem-solving was often approached in a half-hearted way, and tended to be superficial or marginal in content. 'What it boils down to is a question of personalities. You'll never change these. What is the point in trying?' (factory manager). And, 'What's the use? Participation is a load of rubbish. If we were to put anything forward it would be squashed – a case of you can't have it, goodbye. There's no point is there?' (operator).

The following example from a recent experience (Bate and Mangham, 1981: 119) shows that such a frame of mind can completely deactivate a change effort. A colleague and I were meeting a group of workers in the chemicals company for the first time to ascertain their views on 'more' participation:

> The operators on the whole were fairly indifferent and off-hand about the whole thing – yes, that would be nice, yes, it sounds a good idea, but well, you know, nothing much will come of it . . . etc. 'What's the supervision like round here?' we asked, trying to stir them into some kind of action. 'Oh, not bad', they replied with a yawn. And taking another tack, 'Do you find things you raise get blocked?' 'Yes', came the reply – followed by another yawn. 'Well, would you like to enlarge on that?' 'Yes, things do get blocked.' 'Oh, thank you. Are there any issues you could raise at the new meeting?' (Yawning) 'Yes, hundreds, but there's not much point, is there?' 'Why not?' 'Well, things get blocked, don't they?'

Similar pockets of secpticism were encountered in the other two organizations, with broadly similar consequences for the change programme.

Isolationism: 'Do your own thing and avoid treading on other people's toes'

In all three companies there was a widely shared belief that one should be able to stake out a personal territory in the organization in which one could 'do one's own thing'. In return one was expected to let others do likewise. This belief had found institutional expression through a highly differentiated organizational structure: each of the three companies was divisionalized, each division was strongly departmentalized, and each department sectionalized. Horizontal and vertical links between people in these areas tended to be weak, and there was little evidence of people working in teams that actually came to decisions. Any approach to problem-solving was highly individualistic: only when a person failed to make progress would he approach his superior for guidance and support, usually on a one-to-one basis. When meetings were held, those who had not been involved would be *informed* of the one-to-one deal that had been struck, but would be discouraged from influencing the matter further. Other people, on the whole, tended to be regarded as more of a hindrance than a help, an obstruction rather than a resource to be tapped, a problem to be 'managed' or avoided. They were also a threat, in so far as they were seen to be competing to take away some of your territory.

[. . .] The evidence suggests that the problematical consequences of extreme isolationism are numerous. Information may be withheld, leaving others to piece together a picture of what is happening or to invest considerable energy in 'teasing out' information by various means. Rumour systems may be working overtime to plug the gaps in direct information. Decisions may be made which reflect only one view of a problem and fail to take into account different perceptions of that problem. Available expertise may not be fully utilized. Perhaps more important, long-standing differences between people remain a running sore so long as isolationism is used as a way of avoiding conflicts. [. . .]

Antipathy: 'On most things people will be opponents rather than allies'

In view of what has already been said about the superficiality of relationships, low trust, and isolationism, it is not surprising that all three companies – though, in fairness, some factories less than others – were characterized by a particular brand of extreme pluralism. [. . .] Relationships between [groups] were belligerent, distant and untrusting. Meanings attached to intergroup relations were firmly rooted in a 'them' and 'us' tradition. Antipathy was the order of the day.

[. . .] It was assumed by the parties involved – notably (but not exclusively) managers and shop stewards – that all or most of the important issues were of a win–lose nature. Any gains would have to be at the expense of the other party. It was further assumed that there were conflicts of interest over most of the major issues. Even when this was clearly not the case, the parties – ritually and almost instinctively – took up their opposing positions and flatly refused to budge from them. Problems were 'solved' by brinkmanship and confrontation. [. . .]

What the parties did have in common was the belief that pluralism of this kind was inevitable – a fact of industrial life:

> The fact is that you can't trust the management an inch. If you turn your back for a moment they'll get you. (shop steward)
>
> [. . .]
>
> It's called 'playing the Italian defence' – you hack down the opposition before they get too near your goal, or run them out at the corner. (director)

What was not said, but was nonetheless patently obvious, was that this 'way of going about things' actually suited the interests of the parties concerned. A point made by Barbash (1979: 456) is relevant in this regard:

> Management prefers the adversary relationship, because it fears that union collaboration will dilute management authority and thereby impair efficiency. The union prefers it that way, because the adversary relationship is most consistent with the maintenance of the union as a bargaining organization, and bargaining is what the union is all about.

However, while pluralist conceptions have developed chiefly to preserve the survival interests of the parties this is a very different issue from – and one which may well work against – the need to develop effective problem-solving processes.

DISCUSSION

[. . .]

[We] can see that culture has a social consequence, in shaping relationships and interactions. It therefore directly affects the *activity* of joint problem-solving. But this is not the entire picture: my research findings suggest that certain cultural orientations have an important psychological impact, producing a sense of futility and pessimism in people long before they enter the problem-solving arena. The culture induces a condition similar to Seligman's 'learned helplessness' (1975) – a psychological state which results when a person perceives that he can no longer control his own destiny. If this perception finds confirmation in experience – if one learns from trying that one is indeed helpless – 'this saps the motivation to initiate responses' (Seligman, 1975: 74). In other words one simply gives up trying; the energy and will to resolve problems and attain goals drains away.

There is a good deal of data in this chapter to support Seligman's theory: the quotations offer many variations on the theme 'there is no point in trying; there is nothing I can do to change the situation', and in practice there were few if any actual attempts to do so. There is, however, an important difference: whereas Seligman stated that helplessness resulted when a person tried and failed, my findings suggest that an organizational culture can transmit to its members, a priori, the assumption that they are powerless – without them actually having to experience this at all. A state of *socialized* helplessness results, and this becomes an internalized, unquestioned 'fact'. Its reality is never tested and the resulting lack of change reinforces the initial cultural assumption. The culture is confirmed, and the circuit between no action and no motivation is closed. The one predicts the other.

An example of this was mentioned earlier, in the section on subordination where two workers were explaining why they did not air their long-standing problems at meetings. They believed that, as a result, they would end up with all the bad jobs, 'and black eyes into the bargain'. Perhaps this was a realistic assumption but more to the point is that they had never really put it to the test. Helplessness had been socialized, by peers and managers,and had come to be taken for granted. When we challenged them, they confirmed our suspicions:

> *Self*: 'Can I ask you, Maggie, whether in fact anyone has been given a black eye?'
> *Maggie*: 'I can't recall any specific instances – I suppose it's this fear of getting one that prevents it happening.'

[. . .] The evidence from this and other studies suggests that [there are] a limited number of basic problems that are endemic to the process of organization, and for which people have to find solutions. [. . .] Table 19.1 gives my rating of the degree of variation that was observed in the six cultural orientations in the three organizations.

TABLE 19.1
Comparative ratings of each company by cultural orientation

ORIENTATION	CHEMICALS COMPANY	FOOTWEAR COMPANY	DAIRY PRODUCTS COMPANY
Unemotionality	High	High	Medium
Depersonalization	Medium	High	Medium
Subordination	High	High	Low
Conservatism	Medium	Medium	Medium
Isolationism	Low	High	Medium
Antipathy	Medium	High	Low

Although it is not possible to show the qualitative differences between the organizations, and while the table is based on a highly subjective assessment, nevertheless it can be seen that the overall profile for each organization is different. Thus, while organizational cultures may hold certain categories of meaning and values in common, they may be unique in the way these are elaborated and given expression. [. . .]

In Table 19.2 I have suggested six basic organizational issues, in the form of questions, to which my six cultural orientations are the seemingly imperfect solutions.

TABLE 19.2

BASIC ORGANIZATION ISSUES		CULTURAL RESPONSES
1	How emotionally bound up do people become with others in the work setting? (Affective orientation)	Unemotionality
2	How far do people attribute responsibility for personal problems to others, or to the system? (Animate–inanimate orientation to causility)	Depersonalization
3	How do people respond to differences in position, role, power and responsibility? (Hierarchical orientation)	Subordination
4	How far are people willing to embark with others on new ventures? (Change orientation)	Conservatism
5	How far do people choose to work alone or with and through others? (Individualist–collectivist orientation)	Isolationism
6	How do people in different interest groups relate to each other? (Unitary–Pluralistic orientation)	Antipathy

My argument now is that these six basic issues represent an unavoidable and important range of choices facing people in organizations everywhere: every organization has to find *some* cultural 'solution' to each of the problems. Thus, *some degree* of unemotionality, depersonalization, and so on will be present in every organization. [The] choices facing organizations are universal, [but] the solutions are infinitely variable. What exactly do these choices involve, and what are the consequences? Lack of space prevents a detailed discussion here, but some examples will suffice: the first of the basic issues requires evaluations about how emotionally bound up people will become with each other – the degree of intimacy, disclosure of 'self' and feelings. The preferred decision, once made, will influence specific norms such as whether a person is addressed formally or by their Christian name (and by whom), whether one shows feelings in a meeting, whether one should handle a sensitive issue personally or by memorandum, and so on. The sixth item (Unitary-Pluralistic orientation) represents some of the most important issues facing organizations today. These have also tended to be the most contentious and vituperative. The choice, for example, for employers and trade unions is whether to continue to engage in jungle warfare (where, as Cole [1963: 15] has it, the relationship is entered into in a 'spirit of futility and belligerence') or to begin putting into practice 'visions of more constructive, integrative, cooperative problem-solving and trusting relationships' (Barbash, 1979: 455).

[. . .] The data show that the six cultural orientations discussed appear to be linked with the following range of problematical predispositions: a low commitment to and involvement in the change process; a disowning of problems and an abdication of responsibility for the search for solutions; a lack of openness in confronting and dealing jointly with issues; avoidance of data-gathering on the causes of problems; overcaution and a lack of decisiveness and creativity in problem-solving; erection of barriers to change; and a taking of adversary positions on all issues regardless of whether any potential measure of agreement between the parties exists.

Clearly the degree to which some or all of the six cultural orientations is present will greatly affect issues such as problem-solving and an organization's willingness or resistance to change. Argyris (1965: 11) has noted that some relational orientations are more conducive than others to 'interpersonal competence in problem-solving', and suggests that the latter will be low in organizations where the degree of subordination is high and the culture is highly cognitively rational. Arguably we can now include depersonalization, conservatism, isolationism and antipathy in this list. Can change agents therefore be optimistic if they find an organization that is 'low' on some or all of these? Generally speaking, from the results of our studies I feel this to be the case. I have written elsewhere about the many resistances to change encountered in the footwear and chemicals companies (Bate, 1978; Bate and Mangham, 1981); reference to Table 19.1 shows these rank higher overall in the problem traits than the dairy products company, where on the whole the 'dynamic conservatism' (Schon, 1971: 32) that plagued attempts at innovation elsewhere has been less prevalent, and there had been more rapid progress in implementing new forms of joint problem-solving process. Not that each trait carries equal weight: my impression is that unemotionality, depersonalization and subordination had the greatest impact, since they directly affected the conduct of meetings. Conservatism became less of a problem once a change programme was under way, and isolationism only hinders *joint* attempts at problem-solving. The impact of antipathy will depend on the locus and distribution of power in an organization, and will be greatest when power is distributed equally between the various interest groups.

Nevertheless, despite these qualifications, the evidence remains that the three companies studied showed a leaning towards the same cultural 'solutions' to each of the basic organizational issues, that is a preference for the adversary brand of pluralism, individualism rather than collectivism, and so on. Perhaps, then, there are cultural approaches as yet largely untried which might provide more effective solutions to the problems described above. Perhaps the 'alternative organization' – the commune, the cooperative, and copartnership – has already begun to experiment with alternative cultural solutions (emotionality, personalization, power equalization, and so on). The scope for alternatives is unquestionably great, but whether the existing cultural preferences will allow this scope to be explored is quite another matter.

REFERENCES

Argyris, C. (1965) *Organization and innovation.* Homewood, Ill.: Irwin.

Baker, E. L. (1980) 'Managing organizational culture', *Management Review*, 69(7): 8–13.

Barbash, J. (1979) 'The American ideology of industrial relations', *Proceedings of Industrial Relations Research Association Spring Meeting*, 30(8): 453–7.

Bate, S. P. (1978) 'Cultural analysis, confrontation, and counter-culture as strategies for organization development'. Paper read at XIXth International Congress of Applied Psychology, Munich.

Bate, S. P., and Mangham, I. (1981) *Exploring participation.* Chichester: Wiley.

Berger, P. L. (1963) *Invitation to sociology: humanistic perspective.* Harmondsworth: Penguin.

Cole, D. L. (1963) *The quest for industrial peace.* New York: McGraw-Hill.

French, W. L., and Bell, C. H. (1973) *Organization development.* Englewood Cliffs, NJ: Prentice-Hall.

Hofstede, G. (1978) 'National cultures and work values'. Paper read at XIXth International Congress of Applied Psychology, Munich.

Hofstede, G. (1980) *Culture's consequences: international differences in work-related values.* London: Sage.

Jaques, E. (1952) *The changing culture of a factory.* London: Tavistock.

Kluckhohn, C., and Kelly, W. H. (1945) 'The concept of culture', in *The science of man in world crisis*, ed. R. Linton. New York: Columbia University Press.

Lippitt, R., Watson, J. and Westley, B. (1958) *The planning of change.* New York: Harcourt Brace.

Malinowski, B. (1945) *The dynamics of culture change.* New Haven, Conn.: Yale University Press.

McNeill, J. D., Jr (1979) 'Organization culture: an exploratory taxonomic investigation'. PhD thesis, University of Kentucky.

Schein, E. H. (1969) *Process consultation: its role in organization development.* Reading, Mass.: Addison-Wesley.

Schon, D. A. (1971) *Beyond the stable state.* London: Smith.

Seligman, M. E. P. (1975) *Helplessness: on depression, development, and death.* San Francisco: Freeman.

Silverman, D. (1970) *The theory of organisations.* London: Heinemann.

CHAPTER 20

Interorganizational Relations

The traditional view is that organizations operate as unitary entities controlled by hierarchies. They compete in markets where rational pursuit of advantage is limited only by market regulation. This piece charts the erosion of that view and challenges the idea that markets and hierarchies are the end-points of a continuum. Instead it proposes a more complex model of relationships between organizations.

Neither market nor hierarchy: network forms of organization

WALTER W. POWELL

In recent years, there has been a considerable amount of research on organizational practices and arrangements that are network-like in form. This diverse literature shares a common focus on lateral or horizontal patterns of exchange, interdependent flows of resources, and reciprocal lines of communication.

[. . .]

I begin by discussing why the familiar market-hierarchy continuum does not do justice to the notion of the network forms of organization. I then contrast three modes of organization – market, hierarchy, and network – and stress the salient features of each.

[. . .]

MARKETS AND FIRMS

In his classic article on the nature of the firm, the economist Ronald Coase (1937) conceived of the firm as a governance structure, breaking with orthodox accounts of the firm as a 'black box' production function. Coase's key insight was that firms and markets were alternative means for organizing similar kinds of transaction. This provocative paper, however, lay fallow, so to speak, for nearly four decades, until it was picked up by Williamson and other proponents of transaction cost economics in the 1970s. This work took seriously the notion that organizational form matters a great deal, and in so doing moved the economics of organization much closer to the fields of law, organization theory, and business history.

The core of Williamson's (1975, 1985) argument is that transactions that involve uncertainty about their outcome, that recur frequently and require substantial 'transaction-specific investments' – of money, time, or energy that cannot be easily transferred – are more likely to take place within hierarchically organized firms. Exchanges that are straightforward, nonrepetitive and require no transaction-specific investments will take place across a market interface. Hence, transactions are moved out of markets into hierarchies as knowledge specific to the transaction (asset specificity) builds up. When this occurs, the inefficiencies of bureaucratic organization will be preferred to the relatively greater costs of market transactions. There are two reasons for this: (1) bounded rationality – the inability of economic actors to write contracts that cover all possible contingencies; when transactions are internalized, there is little need to anticipate such contingencies since they can be handled within the firm's 'governance structure'; and (2) 'opportunism' – the rational pursuit by economic actors of their own advantage, with every means at their disposal, including guile and deceit; opportunism is mitigated by authority relations and by the stronger identification that parties presumably have when they are joined under a common roof.

This dichotomous view of markets and hierarchies (Williamson, 1975) sees firms as separate from markets or more broadly, the larger societal context. Outside boundaries of firms are competitors, while inside managers exercise authority and curb opportunistic behavior. This notion of sharp firm boundaries was not just an academic view. A good deal of management practice as well as antitrust law shared the belief that, in Richardson's (1972) colorful language, firms are 'islands of planned coordination in a sea of market relations'.

But just as many economists have come to view firms as governance structures, and are providing new insights into the organization of the employment relationship and the multi-divisional firm (to cite only two examples), firms appear to be changing in significant ways and forms of relational contracting appear to have assumed much greater importance. Firms are blurring their established boundaries and engaging in forms of collaboration that resemble neither the familiar alternative of arm's length market contracting nor the formal ideal of vertical integration.

Some scholars respond to these changes by arguing that economic changes can be arrayed in a continuum-like fashion with discrete market transactions located at one end and the higher centralized firm at the other. In between these poles, we find various intermediate or hybrid forms of organization.[1] Moving from the market pole, where prices capture all the relevant information necessary for exchange, we find putting-out systems, various kinds of repeated trading, quasi-firms, and subcontracting arrangements; toward the hierarchy pole, franchising, joint ventures, decentralized profit centers, and matrix management are located.

Is this continuum view satisfactory? Can transaction costs logic meet the task of explaining this rich array of alternative forms? [. . .]

The view that transactions are distributed at points along a continuum implies that markets are the starting point, the elemental form of exchange out of which other methods evolve. Such a view is, obviously, a distortion of historical and anthropological evidence. As Moses Finley (1973) tells us so well, there was no market in the modern sense of the term in the classical world, only money in the nature of free booty and treasure trove. Nor did markets spring full blown with the Industrial Revolution. Economic units emerged from the dense webs of political, religious, and social affiliations that had enveloped economic activity for centuries. Agnew (1986) documents that the word market first enters the English language during the twelfth century to refer to specific locations where provisions and livestock were sold. The markets of medieval England had a highly personal, symbolic and hierarchical flavor. E. P. Thompson (1971) used the term 'the moral economy' to characterize the intricate pattern of symbolic and statutory expectations that surrounded the eighteenth-century marketplace. It was not until the latter part of the eighteenth century that among the British educated classes the term market became separated from a physical and social space and came to imply a boundless and timeless phenomenon of buying and selling (Agnew, 1986).[2]

By the same token, hierarchies do not represent an evolutionary endpoint of economic development. A long view of business history would suggest that firms with strictly defined boundaries and highly centralized operations are quite atypical.[3] The history of modern commerce, whether told by Braudel, Polanyi, Pollard, or Wallerstein, is a story of family businesses, guilds, cartels, and extended trading companies – all enterprises with loose and highly permeable boundaries.

Recent work on the growth of small firms also casts doubt on the utility of a continuum view of economic exchange. Larson (1988) and Lorenzoni and Ornati (1988) draw similar portraits from very different settings – high-tech start-ups in the United States and craft-based firms in Northern Italy – which do not follow the standard model of small firms developing internally through an incremental and linear process. Instead, they suggest an entirely different model of externally driven growth in which pre-existing networks of relationships enable small firms to gain an established foothold almost overnight. These networks serve as conduits to provide small firms with the capacity to meet resource and functional needs.[4]

The idea that economic exchanges can be usefully arrayed along a continuum is thus too quiescent and mechanical. It fails to capture the complex realities of exchange.[5] The continuum view also misconstrues patterns of economic development and blinds us to the role played by reciprocity and collaboration as alternative governance mechanisms. By sticking to the twin pillars of markets and hierarchies, our attention is deflected from a diversity of organizational designs that are neither fish nor fowl, nor some mongrel hybrid, but a distinctly different form.

To be sure, there are a number of social scientists who question whether the distinction between market and hierarchy is particularly useful in the first place.[6] They contend that no sharp demarcation exists and that the argument is more a matter of academic pigeon-holing than of substantive operational differences. These analysts are united, however, more by their dislike of stylized models of economic exchange than by any shared alternative perspective.

One group of critics emphasizes the embeddedness of economics in social and cultural forces. Markets, in this view, are structured by a complex of local, ethnic, and trading cultures, and by varying regimes of state regulation (Gordon, 1985). [. . .] Others maintain that markets cannot be insulated from social structure because differential social access results in information asymmetries, as well as bottlenecks, thus providing some parties with considerable benefits and leaving others disadvantaged (Granovetter, 1985; White, 1981).

Another chorus of skeptics point to the intermingling of various forms of exchange. (See Bradach and Eccles, 1989, for a good review of this literature.) Stinchcombe (1985) shows that there are strong elements of hierarchy and domination in written contracts. Goldberg (1980: 338) notes that many market exchanges have been replaced by interorganizational collaborations. He contends that much economic activity 'takes place within long-term, complex, multiparty contractual (or contract-like) relationships; behavior is in various degrees sheltered from market forces'. Similarly, much of the observed behavior in hierarchical firms seems unrelated to either top management directives or the logic of vertical integration. For example, a firm's relationship with its law, consulting, accounting, and banking firms may be much more enduring and personal than its employment relationship with even its most senior employees.[7] The introduction of market processes into the firm also appears to be widespread. Eccles (1985) observes that large firms commonly rely on such market-like methods as transfer pricing and performance-based compensation schemes, while Eccles and Crane (1987) report that dual reporting relationships, internal competition, and compensation based on services provided to clients are the current norm in investment banking.

MARKETS, HIERARCHIES, AND NETWORKS

I have a good deal of sympathy regarding the view that economic exchange is embedded in a particular social structural context. Yet it is also the case that certain forms of exchange are more social – that is, more dependent on relationships, mutual interests, and reputations – as well as less guided by a formal structure of authority. My aim is to identify a coherent set of factors that make it meaningful to talk about networks as a distinctive form of coordinating economic activity. We can then employ these ideas to generate arguments about the frequency, durability, and limitations of networks.

When the items exchanged between buyers and sellers possess qualities that are not easily measured, and the relations are so long-term and recurrent that it is difficult to speak of the parties as separate entities, can we still regard this as a market exchange? When the entangling of obligation and reputation reaches a point that the actions of the parties are interdependent, but there is no common ownership or legal framework, do we not need a new conceptual tool kit to describe and analyse this relationship? Surely this patterned exchange looks more like a marriage than a one-night stand, but there is no marriage license, no common household, no pooling of assets. In the language I employ below, such an arrangement is neither a market transaction nor a hierarchical governance structure, but a separate, different mode of exchange, one with its own logic, a network.

Many firms are no longer structured like medieval kingdoms, walled off and protected from hostile forces. Instead, we find companies involved in an intricate latticework of collaborative ventures with other firms, most of whom are ostensibly competitors. The dense ties that bind the auto and biotechnology industries cannot be easily explained by saying that these firms are engaged in market transactions for some factors of production, or by suggesting that the biotechnology business is embedded in the international community of science. At that point is it more accurate to characterize these alliances as networks rather than as joint ventures among hierarchical firms?

We need fresh insights into these kinds of arrangement. Whether they are new forms of exchange that have recently emerged or aged-old practices that have gained new prominence they are not satisfactorily explained by existing approaches. Markets, hierarchies, and networks are pieces of a larger puzzle that is the economy. The properties of the parts of this system are defined by the kinds of interaction that take place among them. The behavior and interests of individual actors are shaped by these patterns of interaction. Stylized models of markets, hierarchies, and networks are not perfectly descriptive of economic reality, but they enable us to make progress in understanding the extraordinary diversity of economic arrangements found in the industrial world today.

Table 20.1 represents a first cut at summarizing some of the key differences between markets, hierarchies, and networks. In market transactions the benefits to be exchanged are clearly specified, no trust is required, and agreements are bolstered by the power of legal sanction. Network forms of exchange, however, entail indefinite, sequential transactions within the context of a general pattern of interaction. Sanctions are typically normative rather than legal. The value of the goods to be exchanged in markets is much more important than the relationship itself; when relations do matter, they are frequently defined as if they were commodities. In hierarchies, communication occurs in the context of the employment contract. Relationships matter and previous interactions shape current ones, but the patterns and context of intra-organizational exchange are most strongly shaped by one's position within the formal hierarchical structure of authority.

The philosophy that undergirds exchange also contrasts sharply across forms. In markets the standard strategy is to drive the hardest possible bargain in the immediate exchange. In networks, the preferred option is often one of creating indebtedness and reliance over the long haul. Each approach thus devalues the other: prosperous market traders would be viewed as petty and untrustworthy shysters in networks, while successful participants in networks who carried those practices into competitive markets would be viewed as naive and foolish. Within hierarchies, communication and exchange is shaped by concerns with career mobility – in this sense, exchange is bound up with considerations of personal advancement. At the same time, intra-organizational communication takes place among parties who generally know one another, have a history of previous interactions, and possess a good deal of firm-specific knowledge, so there is

TABLE 20.1
Stylized comparison of forms of economic organization

	FORMS		
KEY FEATURES	MARKET	HIERARCHY	NETWORK
Normative basis	Contract – property rights	Employment relationship	Complementary strengths
Means of communication	Prices	Routines	Relational
Methods of conflict resolution	Haggling – resort to courts for enforcement	Administrative fiat – supervision	Norm of reciprocity – reputational concerns
Degree of flexibility	High	Low	Medium
Amount of commitment among the parties	Low	Medium to high	Medium to high
Tone or climate	Precision and/or suspicion	Formal, bureaucratic	Open-ended, mutual benefits
Actor preferences or choices	Independent	Dependent	Interdependent
Mixing of forms	Repeat transactions (Geertz, 1978)	Informal organization (Dalton, 1957)	Status hierarchies
	Contracts as hierarchical documents (Stinchcombe, 1985)	Market-like features: profit centers, transfer pricing (Eccles, 1985)	Multiple partners
			Formal rules

considerable interdependence among the parties. In a market context it is clear to everyone concerned when a debt has been discharged, but such matters are not nearly as obvious in networks or hierarchies.

Markets, as described by economic theory, are a spontaneous coordination mechanism that imparts rationality and consistency to the self-interested actions of individuals and firms. [. . .]

The market is open to all comers, but while it brings people together, it does not establish strong bonds of altruistic attachments. The participants in a market transaction are free of any future commitments. The stereotypical competitive market is the paradigm of individually self-interested, non-cooperative, unconstrained social interaction. As such, markets have powerful incentive effects for they are the arena in which each party can fulfill its own internally defined needs and goals.

Markets offer choice, flexibility, and opportunity. They are a remarkable device for fast, simple communication. No one need rely on someone else for direction, prices alone determine production and exchange. Because individual behavior is not dictated by a supervising agent, no organ of systemwide governance or control is necessary. Markets are a form of noncoercive organization, they have coordinating but not integrative effects. As Hayek (1945) suggested, market coordination is the result of human actions but not of human design.

Prices are a simplifying mechanism, consequently they are unsuccessful at capturing the intricacies of idiosyncratic, complex, and dynamic exchange. As a result, markets are a poor device for learning and the transfer of technological know-how. In a stylized perfect market, information is freely available, alternative buyers or sellers are easy to come by, and there are no carry-over effects from one transaction to another. But as exchanges become more frequent and complex, the costs of conducting and monitoring them increase, giving rise to the need for other methods of structuring exchange.

Organization, or hierarchy, arises when the boundaries of a firm expand to internalize transactions and resource flows that were previously conducted in the marketplace. The visible hand of management supplants the invisible hand of the market in coordinating supply and demand. Within a hierarchy, individual employees operate under a regime of administrative procedures and work roles defined by higher-level supervisors. Management divides up tasks and positions and establishes an authoritative system of order. Because tasks are often quite specialized, work activities are highly interdependent. The large vertically integrated firm is thus an eminently social institution, with its own routines, expectations, and detailed knowledge.

A hierarchical structure – clear departmental boundaries, clean lines of authority, detailed reporting mechanisms, and formal decision-making procedures – is particularly well-suited for mass production and distribution. The requirements of high volume, high-speed operations demand the constant attention of a managerial team. The strength of hierarchical organization, then, is its reliability – its capacity for producing large numbers of goods or services of a given quality repeatedly – and its accountability – its ability to document how resources have been used (DiMaggio and Powell, 1983; Hannan and Freeman, 1984). But when hierarchical forms are confronted by sharp fluctuations in demand and unanticipated changes, their liabilities are exposed.

Networks are 'lighter on their feet' than hierarchies. In networks modes of resource allocation, transactions occur neither through discrete exchanges nor by administrative fiat, but through networks of individuals engaged in reciprocal, preferential, mutually supportive actions. Networks can be complex: they involve neither the explicit criteria of the market, nor the familiar paternalism of the hierarchy. A basic assumption of network relationships is that one party is dependent on resources controlled by another, and that there are gains to be had by the pooling of resources.[8] In essence, the parties to a network agree to forgo the right to pursue their own interests at the expense of others.

In network forms of resource allocation, individuals units exist not by themselves, but in relation to other units. These relationships take considerable effort to establish and sustain, thus they constrain both partners' ability to adapt to changing circumstances. As networks evolve, it becomes more economically sensible to exercise voice rather than exit. Benefits and burdens come to be shared. Expectations are not frozen, but change as circumstances dictate. A mutual orientation – knowledge which the parties assume each has about the other and upon which they draw in communication and problem solving – is established. In short, complementarity and accommodation are the cornerstones of successful production networks. As Macneil (1985) has suggested, the 'entangling strings' of reputation, friendship, interdependence, and altruism become integral parts of the relationship.

Networks are particularly apt for circumstances in which there is need for efficient, reliable information. The most useful information is rarely that which flows down the formal chain of command in an organization, or that which can be inferred from shifting price signals. Rather, it is that which is obtained from someone whom you have dealt with in the past and found to be reliable. You trust best information that comes from someone you know well. Kaneko and Imai (1987) suggest that information passed through networks is 'thicker' than information obtained in the market, and 'freer' than that communicated in a hierarchy. Networks, then, are especially useful for the exchange of commodities whose value is not easily measured. Such qualitative matters as know-how, technological capability, a particular approach or style of production, a spirit of innovation or experimentation, or a philosophy of zero defects are very hard to place a price tag on. They are not easily traded in markets nor communicated through a corporate hierarchy. The open-ended, relational features of networks, with their relative absence of explicit *quid pro quo* behavior, greatly enhance the ability to transmit and learn new knowledge and skills.

Reciprocity is central to discussions of network forms of organization. Unfortunately it is a rather ambiguous concept, used in different ways by various social science disciplines. One key point of contention concerns whether reciprocity entails exchanges of roughly equivalent value in a strictly delimited sequence or whether it involves a much less precise definition of equivalence, one that emphasizes indebtedness and obligation. Game theoretic treatments of reciprocity by scholars in political science and economics tend to emphasize equivalence. Axelrod (1984) stresses that reciprocal action implies returning ill for ill as well as good for good. As Keohane (1986) notes, the literature in international relations 'emphatically' associates reciprocity with equivalence of benefits.[9] As a result, these scholars take a view of reciprocity that is entirely consistent with the pursuit of self-interest.

Sociological and anthropological analyses of reciprocity are commonly couched in the language of indebtedness. In this view, a measure of imbalance sustains the partnership, compelling another meeting (Sahlins, 1972). Obligation is a means through which parties remain connected to one another. Calling attention to the need for equivalence might well undermine and devalue the relationship.[10] To be sure, sociologists have long emphasized that reciprocity implies conditional action (Gouldner, 1960). The question is whether there is a relatively immediate assessment or whether 'the books are kept open', in the interests of continuing satisfactory results. This perspective also takes a different tack on the issue of self-interest. In his classic work *The Gift*, Marcel Mauss (1967), attempted to show that the obligations to give, to receive, and to return were not to be understood simply with respect to rational calculations, but fundamentally in terms of underlying cultural tenets that provide objects with their meaning significance, and provide a basis for understanding the implications of their passage from one person to another. Anthropological and sociological approaches, then, tend to focus more on the normative standards that sustain exchange; game theoretic treatments emphasize how individual interests are enhanced through cooperation.

Social scientists do agree, however, that reciprocity is enhanced by taking a long-term perspective. Security and stability encourage the search for new ways of accomplishing tasks, promote learning and the exchange of information, and engender trust. Axelrod's (1984) notion of 'the shadow of the future' – the more the immediate payoff facing players is shaped by future expectations – points to a broadened conception of self-interest. Cooperation thus emerges out of mutual interests and behavior based on standards that no one individual can determine alone. Trust is thereby generated. Trust is, as Arrow (1974) has noted, a remarkably efficient lubricant to economic exchange. In trusting another party, one treats as certain those aspects of life which modernity rendered uncertain (Luhmann, 1979). Trust reduces complex realities far more quickly and economically than prediction, authority, or bargaining.

It is inaccurate, however, to characterize networks solely in terms of collaboration and concord. Each point of contact in a network can be a source of conflict as well as harmony. Recall that the term alliance comes from the literature of international relations where it describes relations among nation states in an anarchic world. Keohane (1986) has stressed that processes of reciprocity or cooperation in no way 'insulate practitioners from considerations of power'. Networks also commonly involve aspects of dependency and particularism.[11] By establishing enduring patterns of repeat trading, networks restrict access. Opportunities are thus foreclosed to newcomers, either intentionally or more subtly through such barriers as unwritten rules or informal codes of conduct. In practice, subcontracting networks and research partnerships influence who competes with whom, thereby dictating the adoption of a particular technology and making it much harder for unaffiliated parties to join the fray. As a result of these inherent complications, most potential partners approach the idea of participating in a network with trepidation. All of the parties to network forms of exchange have lost some of their ability to dictate their own future and are increasingly dependent on the activities of others.

NOTES

1. See Koenig and Thietart (1988) on intermediate forms in the aerospace industry, Thorelli (1986) on industrial marketing networks, Eccles and White (1986) on transfer pricing, and Powell (1987) on hybrid forms in craft and high technology industries.

2. This does not mean that market forces were of little consequence before the eighteenth century. Braudel (1982) argues that economic history is the story of slowly evolving mixtures of institutional forms. He suggests that we can speak of a market economy when the prices in a given area appear to fluctuate in unison, a phenomenon that has occurred since ancient times. But this does not imply that transactions between individuals were of a discrete, impersonal nature.
3. I owe this observation to comments made by Jim Robins.
4. What is remarkable about the firms in these two studies is how explicitly the entrepreneurs follow a 'network' strategy, intentionally eschewing internalization for such crucial and recurrent activities as manufacturing, sales, and research and development.
5. On this point, Macneil (1985: 496) suggests that 'the transaction costs approach is far too unrelational a starting point in analyzing' relational forms of exchange. Richardson (1972: 884) provides an apt example of these densely connected forms of exchange: 'Firm A . . . is a joint subsidiary of firms B and C, has technical agreements with D and E, subcontracts work to F, is in marketing association with G – and so on. So complex and ramified are these arrangements, indeed, that the skills of a genealogist rather than an economist might often seem appropriate for their disentanglement.'
6. Bob Eccles and Mark Granovetter have repeatedly made this point to me in personal communications, insisting that all forms of exchange contain elements of networks, markets, and hierarchies. Since they are smarter than I, I should listen to them. Nevertheless, I hope to show that there is merit in thinking of networks as an empirically identifiable governance structure.
7. Some economists (Alchian and Demsetz, 1972; Klein, 1983) go so far as to regard the firm as merely a set of explicit and implicit contracts among owners of different factors of production.
8. Many other scholars have their own definitions. Jarillo (1988: 32) defines strategic networks as 'long-term, purposeful arrangements among distinct but related for-profit organizations that allow those firms in them to gain or sustain competitive advantage vis-à-vis their competitors outside the network'. Kaneko and Imai (1987) conceive of networks as a particular form of multi-faceted, interorganizational relationships through which new information is generated. Johanson and Mattsson (1987) regard networks as a method of dividing labor such that firms are highly dependent upon one another. Coordination is not achieved through hierarchy or markets, but through the interaction and mutual obligation of the firms in the network. Gerlach (1990) suggests that alliances among Japanese firms are an important institutional alternative that links Japanese firms to one another in ways that are fundamentally different from US business practices. Alliances, in his view, are coherent networks of rule-ordered exchange, based on the mutual return of obligations among parties bound in durable relationships.

   I find these various definitions very helpful, but also limited. They all describe networks as a form of dense interorganizational relationships. But networks can also evolve out of personal ties, or market relationships among various parties. Many of the arrangements discussed below, commonly found in the publishing, fashion, computer software, construction, and entertainment businesses are among individuals, independent production teams, or very small business units. Thus, my conception of networks is closer to Macneil's (1978, 1985) ideas about relational contracts than to the above views.
9. In an illuminating essay, Keohane (1986: 8) defines reciprocity as exchanges of roughly equivalent values in which the actions of each party are contingent on

the prior actions of the others in such a way that good is returned for good, and bad for bad.

10. For example, successful reciprocal ties in scholarly book publishing – between authors and editors or between editors in competing houses – were highly implicit, of long-standing duration, and not strictly balanced (Powell, 1985). It was widely believed that the open-ended quality of the relationship meant that the goods being exchanged – advice, recommendations, or manuscripts – were more valuable and reliable.
11. Parties are, of course, free to exit from a network. But the difficulty of abandoning a relationship around which a unit or a company has structured its operations and expectations can keep a party locked into a relationship that it experiences as unsatisfactory. This problem of domination in networks obviously lends itself to transaction costs discussions of credible commitments.

REFERENCES

Agnew, J. (1986) *Worlds Apart: The Market and the Theater in Anglo-American Thought, 1550–1750*. New York: Cambridge University Press.

Alchian, A. and Demsetz, H. (1972) 'Production, information costs, and economic organization', *American Economic Review*, 62(5): 777–95.

Arrow, K. (1974) *The Limits of Organization*. New York: Norton.

Axelrod, R. (1984) *The Evolution of Cooperation*. New York: Basic Books.

Bradach, J. L. and Eccles, R. G. (1989) 'Markets versus hierarchies: from ideal types to plural forms', *Annual Review of Sociology*, 15: 97–118.

Braudel, F. (1982) *The Wheels of Commerce*. New York: Harper & Row.

Coase, R. (1937) 'The nature of the firm', *Economica*, 4: 386–405.

Dalton, M. (1957) *Men Who Manage*. New York: Wiley.

DiMaggio, P. and Powell, W. W. (1983) 'The iron cage revisited: institutional isomorphism and collective rationality in organizational fields', *American Sociological Review*, 48: 147–60.

Eccles, R. (1985) *The Transfer Pricing Problem: A Theory for Practice*. Lexington, MA: Lexington Books.

Eccles, R. G. and Crane, D. (1987) 'Managing through networks in investment banking', *California Management Review*, 30 (1): 176–95.

Eccles, Robert G. and White, Harrison, C. (1986) 'Firm and market interfaces of profit center control', pp. 203–20 in *Approaches in Social Theory*, ed. S. Lindenberg, J. S. Coleman and S. Novak. New York: Russell Sage.

Finley, M. (1973) *The Ancient Economy*. Berkeley: University of California Press.

Geertz, C. (1978) 'The bazaar economy: information and search in peasant marketing', *American Economic Review*, 68 (2): 28–32.

Gerlach, M. L. (1990) *Alliances and the Social Organization of Japanese Business*. Berkeley: University of California Press.

Goldberg, V. P. (1980) 'Relational exchange: economics and complex contracts', *American Behavioral Scientist*, 23 (3): 337–52.

Gordon, R. W. (1985) 'Macaulay, Macneil, and the discovery of solidarity and power in contract law', *Wisconsin Law Review*, 3: 565–80.

Gouldner, A. (1960) 'The norm of reciprocity: a preliminary statement', *American Sociological Review*, 25: 161–78.

Graham, M. (1985) 'Corporate research and development: the latest transformation', *Technology in Society*, 7 (2/3): 179–96.

Granovetter, M. (1985) 'Economic action and social structure: a theory of embeddedness', *American Journal of Sociology*, 91 (3): 481–510.

Hannan, M. and Freeman, J. H. (1984) 'Structural inertia and organizational change', *American Sociological Review*, 49: 149–64.
Hayek, F. (1945) 'The use of knowledge in society', *American Economic Review*, 35: 519–30.
Jarillo, J.–C. (1988) 'On strategic networks', *Strategic Management Journal*, 9: 31–41.
Johanson, J. and Mattsson, L.–G. (1987) 'Interorganizational relations in industrial systems: a network approach compared with the transactions-cost approach', *International Studies of Management and Organization*, 18 (1): 34–48.
Kaneko, I. and Imai, K. (1987) 'A network view of the firm'. Paper presented at 1st Hitotsubashi-Stanford conference.
Keohane, R. (1986) 'Reciprocity in international relations', *International Organization*, 40 (1): 1–27.
Klein, B. (1983) 'Contracting costs and residual claims: the separation of ownership and control', *Journal of Law and Economics*, 26: 367–74.
Koenig, C. and Thietart, R. A. (1988) 'Manager, engineers and government', *Technology in Society*, 10: 45–69.
Larson, A. (1988) 'Cooperative alliances: a study of entrepreneurship'. PhD. dissertation, Harvard Business School.
Lorenzoni, G. and Ornati, O. (1988) 'Constellations of firms and new ventures', *Journal of Business Venturing*, 3: 41–57.
Loveman, G., Piore, M. and Sengenberger, W. (1987) 'The evolving role of small business in industrial economies'. Paper presented at conference on New Developments in Labor Market and Human Resource Policies, Sloan School, MIT.
Luhmann, N. (1979) *Trust and Power.* New York: Wiley.
Macneil, I. (1978) 'Contracts: adjustment of long-term economic relations under classical, neoclassical, and relational contract law', *Northwestern University Law Review*, 72 (6): 854–905.
Macneil, I. (1985) 'Relational contract: what we do and do not know', *Wisconsin Law Review*, 3: 483–526.
Mauss, M. (1967) *The Gift.* New York: Norton (first published 1925).
Powell, W. W. (1985) *Getting into Print: The Decision Making Process in Scholarly Publishing*, Chicago: University of Chicago Press.
Powell, W. W. (1987) 'Hybrid organizational arrangements: new form of transitional development?' *California Management Review*, 30 (1): 67–87.
Richardson, G. B. (1972) 'The organization of industry', *Economic Journal*, 82: 883–96.
Sahlins, M. (1972) *Stone Age Economics.* Chicago: Aldine.
Stinchcombe, A. (1985) 'Contracts as hierarchical documents', pp. 121–71 in A. Stinchombe and C. Heimer, *Organization Theory and Project Management.* Oslo: Norwegian University Press.
Thompson, E. P. (1971) 'The moral economy of the English crowd in the eighteenth century', *Past and Present*, 50: 78–98.
Thorelli, H. B. (1986) 'Networks: between markets and hierarchies', *Strategic Management Journal*, 7: 37–51.
White, H. C. (1981) 'Where do markets come from?', *American Journal of Sociology*, 87: 517–47.
Williamson, O. E. (1975) *Markets and Hierarchies: Analysis and Antitrust Implications.* New York: Free Press.
Williamson, O. E. (1985) *The Economic Institutions of Capitalism.* New York: Free Press.

Index